Practices	
1. Read closely. You can assume that everything i̶... carefully calculated to contribute to the work's unity—figures of speech, point of view, diction, recurrent ideas or events, etc. 2. Find oppositions, tensions, ambiguities, and ironies in the work. 3. Indicate how all these various elements are unified—what idea holds them together?	...elements does this work have? (Structure, imagery, diction, etc.) 2. How can these formal elements be arranged in opposing pairs or groups? 3. What unifying idea holds these opposing elements together? (Think in terms of an "Although X, Y" thesis sentence.)
1. Move through the text in slow motion, describing the responses of an ideal reader— what is anticipated, what is experienced. 2. Or, move through the text describing your own personal response. 3. Focus on how particular details shape readers' expectations and responses.	1. What is your response to the text? 2. If the text were changed in some specific way (a word, a phrase, a sentence, etc.), how would your response change? 3. Is your response personal and idiosyncratic, or is it shaped by the text and shared norms of interpretation?
1. Identify the oppositions in the text, and determine which items are favored. 2. Identify what appears to be central to the text, and what appears to be marginal and excluded. 3. Reverse the text's hierarchy (the system of favoring), opening up another (or an other) reading; and/or argue that what appears to be marginal is actually central.	1. What does the text most obviously seem to say? 2. How can the text be turned against itself, making it say also the opposite of what it most obviously seems to say? 3. How can something apparently marginal or trivial in the text be brought to the center of attention?
1. Research the author's life and relate that information, cautiously, to the work. 2. Research the author's time (the political history, economic history, intellectual history, etc.) and relate that information, cautiously, to the work. 3. Research how people reasoned during the author's lifetime, the patterns and limits involved in making sense. Relate those logical strategies to the work.	1. How can you connect the author's life to his or her writing? Are there common issues, events, concerns? 2. How can you connect the literary work to its historical context, including its literary context? 3. Is the author part of a dominant culture, or a colonial culture, or a postcolonial culture, and how does that status affect the work?
1. Apply a developmental concept to the work— for example, the Oedipal complex, anal retentiveness, castration anxiety, gender confusion. 2. Relate the work to psychologically significant events in the author's life. 3. Consider how repressed material may be expressed in the work's pattern of imagery or symbols.	1. What appears to be motivating the author, or character, or even reader? 2. What other motivations, repressed or disguised, might be at work? 3. What developmental concepts might help to explain this behavior?
1. Identify the qualities of gender, class, race sexual preference, religion, etc. of the author and/or characters: that is, say how individuals are portrayed as members of some group. 2. Consider whether the text promotes or undermines stereotypes. 3. Imagine how the text might be read by a certain type of reader; or how a text might have been neglected by a certain type of reader.	1. How does this work advance or question a particular political agenda? 2. How would readers of different political stances read this work differently? 3. How are the individuals in this work portrayed as part of a group or class?

TEXTS AND CONTEXTS

Writing About Literature with Critical Theory

Fifth Edition

STEVEN LYNN

University of South Carolina

PEARSON
Longman

New York San Francisco Boston
London Toronto Sydney Tokyo Singapore Madrid
Mexico City Munich Paris Capetown Hong Kong Montreal

For Annette and Anna

Acquisitions Editor: Matthew Wright
Senior Development Editor: Michael Greer
Senior Supplements Editor: Donna Campion
Executive Marketing Manager: Joyce Nilsen
Production Manager: Eric Jorgensen
Project Coordination, Text Design,
    and Electronic Page Makeup: Electronic Publishing Services, Inc., NYC
Cover Design Manager: John Callahan
Cover Photo: Shutterstock. Photographer James R. Hearn
Visual Researcher: Rona Tuccillo
Manufacturing Manager: Mary Fischer
Printer and Binder: RR Donnelley & Sons Company
Cover Printer: Phoenix Color Corporation

For permission to use copyrighted material, grateful acknowledgment is made to the
copyright holders on pp. 301–302 which are hereby made part of this copyright page.

Library of Congress Cataloging-in-Publication Data

Lynn, Steven, 1952
  Texts and contexts : writing about literature with critical theory /
Steven Lynn. — 5th ed.
      p. cm.
  Includes bibliographical references and indexes.
  ISBN 978-0-321-44907-8
  1. English language—Rhetoric. 2. Literature—History and criticism—Theory, etc.
3. Criticism—Authorship. 4. Academic writing. 5. College readers. I. Title.
  PE1479.C7L96 2007
  808'.0668—dc22

                                2007034906

Please visit us at www.ablongman.com

ISBN-13: 978-0-321-44907-8
ISBN-10:   0-321-44907-X

12345678910—DOH—10 09 08 07

Contents

4   Creating the Text: Reader-Response Criticism   67

5   Opening Up the Text: Structuralism and Deconstruction   107

6   Connecting the Text: Historical, Postcolonial, and Cultural Studies   145

7 Minding the Work: Psychological Criticism 199

8 Gendering the Text: Feminist Criticism, Post-Feminism, and Queer Theory   227

Preface

As teachers, we need to
remember what the world looked
like before we learned our
discipline's way of seeing it. We
need to show our students the
patient and painstaking processes
by which we achieved expertise.
Only by making our footsteps
visible can we expect students to
follow in them.

—Sam Wineburg, Professor,
Stanford University

*The Chronicle of Higher
Education* (4/11/03), B20

This book aims to show students as clearly as possible how to think of interesting and insightful things to say about literary texts, and how to organize these insights and observations into effective arguments and responses. Like the previous four editions, this book aspires to invigorate literary study by "making our footsteps visible," as Sam Wineburg puts it above, conveying at an introductory level the assumptions, strategies, and questions available in the practice of critical analysis. This edition continues to update some of the exciting and influential ways that literary study continues to evolve.

Critical theories are the invention strategies that drive the process of writing about texts. By explaining critical theories, this book aims to take the mystery and frustration out of writing about literature. Critical theory isn't too difficult for students who are just learning how to write and think about challenging literary texts; writing about literature is in fact unnecessarily difficult and frustrating *without a clear understanding of theory.* And since every discipline depends on various assumptions about language, meaning, and knowledge; and every discipline involves reading and writing, interpreting data, and constructing arguments, then critical theory and literary study are vitally important. Every educated person can and should understand the fundamentals involved.

ORGANIZATION

The first two chapters prepare students for the in-depth tour of the world of critical theory in Chapters 3 through 8. The first chapter addresses some fundamental questions: "Is there one correct interpretation of a literary work?" "Are all opinions equally valid?" "Does theory distract from literary study?" "Is theory too difficult for an introductory-level course?" The answers to these deceptively simple questions underscore both the necessity and the feasibility of working with theory in introductory courses. The second chapter then offers a survey of the theories covered here, illustrating a variety of approaches by explaining how each one might be applied to the same text.

Each particular theoretical orientation is in a sense like a different place, a different culture that inhabits its own set of values and practices. The maps at the beginnings of these chapters are intended as playful reminders of this insight: each theory involves a different way of seeing, from a different perspective. The first section in each chapter is an orientation: the basic principles of a particular theoretical orientation are elicited out of the analysis of a poem. In "The Purpose of New Criticism," for instance, which is the first part of Chapter 3, an analysis of an Archibald MacLeish poem reveals the assumptions of what is called New Criticism. The second section of each theory chapter explains the process of applying these assumptions. In Chapter 3 the section entitled "How to Do New Criticism" takes students step by step through the process of "doing" a New Critical reading.

The third section of these chapters illustrates the construction of an essay, from start to finish, using that chapter's theory. The sample essay in Chapter 3, for instance, traces the evolution of an essay on Gwendolyn Brooks's masterful poem, "The Mother." The fourth and final section provides some literary works to practice upon—works that will resonate in some way with the other works in the chapters. In "Practicing New Criticism," three poems about fatherhood are offered, balancing in several senses Brooks's "The Mother." The tour of each theory ends with a list of the "Works Cited" in the chapter, and recommendations for "Further Reading."

After this theoretical tour, a final chapter discusses writing a research paper in a digital age—how to locate and evaluate library and Internet sources, and how to use literary texts and databases. The chapter reviews the theories covered by working through a research paper about the application of various theories to a W. B. Yeats poem.

WHAT'S NEW IN THIS EDITION?

There are many changes in this edition, both subtle and obvious. I wasn't able to include a GPS to help students find their classrooms, as one student suggested, but I have benefited from many other suggestions by students and teachers. Like any human endeavor, literary criticism is dynamic, and so the additions, deletions, and alterations are also an attempt to reflect the evolution of the field. In particular:

- **Structuralism** gets more attention in this edition because some readers and reviewers persuasively argued that deconstruction would be more richly understood with an expanded treatment of its precursor, and also because structuralism is an important approach in its own right.

- **Postcolonialism, queer theory, African-American criticism, gender studies, and cultural studies** continue to be increasingly important and interesting movements, transforming the study of literature. These approaches receive updated and expanded coverage in this edition.

- **The recommended reading** lists have again been updated and expanded, reflecting the most current trends and offering more guidance on where to go for additional treatment.

- **Websites** are included as part of the recommended sources, but I have again tried to be careful to include only those sites that are authored or controlled by reliable entities. The sites recommended are likely to exist when you try to check them out, and they are also likely to provide good materials. Alan Liu's Voice of the Shuttle website or Jack Lynch's bibliographical site, for instance, offers information that can be used with confidence. A high school student's class project on "post-modernism" is equally accessible on the Internet, but it is not likely to be equally authoritative.

- **The research paper** coverage includes consideration of electronic sources and the ethics of research—topics that are especially important given the easy availability of misleading information and ready-made essays.

- The electronic **Instructor's Manual** has been updated to reflect the additions to this edition. The manual can be requested from your local Longman representative.

ACKNOWLEDGMENTS

To those people who have adopted a previous edition, I am very grateful. Many people have made helpful suggestions, sometimes when I was walking across campus or losing golf balls, and their names may not appear in the long list below. In that case, I'm sorry. I do appreciate your help. I'm especially indebted to Bill Rivers, Ed Madden, and Lee Bauknight, my fellow teacher-trainers, and to all the graduate students who have taken English 701B with me, and who have helped to establish that this pedagogy works.

I also want to thank the following reviewers, some of whom assessed the need for a fifth edition and made extremely useful suggestions, and others who evaluated previous editions:

Patricia Angley, University of Central Florida; M. Bracher, Kent State University; Suzanne Bunkers, Minnesota State University; Bryon Lee Grigsby, Centenary College; Catherine Lewis, Louisiana State University; Judith K. Moore, University of Alaska; Warren Moore, Ball State University; B. Orton, Truman State University; Sally Bishop Shigley, Weber State University; Jack Fisher Solomon, California State University Northridge; Don Ulin, University of Pittsburgh at Bradford.

I much appreciate Michael Greer's astute analysis of these reviews, and Erika Berg's guidance through all the previous editions has been inspiring. Matthew Wright's development has been congenial, patient, and effective. I celebrate the existence of Lisa Saxon, my superb former assistant and departmental budget manager, and Latasha Middleton, my superb current assistant. Pang Li, my research assistant, is a wonderful person and an amazing helper. My brothers and sisters, congenital and acquired, have provided comfort, counsel, and comic relief at various opportune moments. Gregory Jay and David Miller got me interested in critical theory, and I appreciate their patient inspiration so long ago. Karl Beason, Todd Stebbins, and Ken Autry helped me develop these ideas as we worked with Advanced Placement high school teachers.

I gratefully acknowledge the support of the University of South Carolina.

I'm most thankful for my parents, Ben and Leora Lynn; for my parents-in-law, Chester and Dorothy Williams; and for my wife and daughter, Annette and Anna, to whom this book is dedicated.

STEVEN LYNN

TEXTS AND CONTEXTS

An Introduction, Theoretically

*We should study literary criticism
and the theories of literature for
the same reasons we read
literature—to forever alter our
perspectives, to escape our own
vanities, and to extend the
horizons of our limitations.*

—Lynn Jordan Stidon
(from her Final Exam
in English 102)

TEXTUAL TOURS

Why should we read literature? For some of the same reasons we ought to travel—to have fun, to learn things, and to be able to talk about it later.

Literary works are, in a way, like places we can visit. Some are foreign, mysterious, puzzling; others make us feel right at home. Some call us back again and again; others we feel obliged to experience, knowing they'll do us good even though we never quite enjoy them. Inhabiting a literary work, we can see how other people live; we can see, to a certain extent, through other people's eyes. We can momentarily transcend the boundaries of our lives.

But why should we write about literature? For some of the same reasons that we like to write and think about where we've been. Indeed, we send postcards and letters back home, we make pictures and even movies (for sometimes captive audiences), in part because we want to share our experiences with others, but also because we want to reconsider and ponder and make sense of our travels for ourselves. Life is the journey, it's often said, but reflecting on where you've been can be the most meaningful part of travel. Our understanding and appreciation of a literary work are likewise often enhanced by our efforts to say something about it. Sometimes the insights are huge; sometimes they seem insignificant; sometimes they move from one category to the other.

Although wandering around is always an option, travelers who know what they're looking for and have a plan for getting there are often more likely to have satisfying, interesting visits. Literary criticism aims to bring such order and organization to our experience of literary works, focusing our attention on this, disregarding that, putting various parts together, helping us make sense of what we see. When you write about literature, you serve as a kind of tour guide, leading your reader (and yourself) through the work. Readers usually can see what's in front of them, but they don't necessarily know what to make of it without some persuasive commentary. Plus, different readers have different interests, different backgrounds, and they necessarily bring different insights and desires to a work. Some travelers, with lots of experience, keen eyes, and fertile imaginations may tend to provide especially wonderful guides and reports, but even inexperienced travelers may come upon marvels and notice things that no one else has seen in quite the same way. Even if you are an unseasoned traveler in the literary world, you just can't substitute someone else's experience for your own: Don't believe that anyone's "Notes," whether by Clifford or Sparkie or your best friend, will expand your horizons or deepen your awareness in the same way as a firsthand encounter. This is not to say that we all cannot benefit from the advice and guidance of genuine experts, of scholars who publish in academic journals and with university presses. Your teachers and reference librarians and the last chapter of this book can help you locate this kind of reliable and helpful commentary. But you have to see for yourself first and foremost.

Critical theories are like the different travel agencies through which the various tour guides generally work. Different agencies feature different kinds of tours, just as different theories generate different kinds of readings: one specializes in cultural immersion, another in artistic appreciation, another in historical recollection, still another in personal indulgence. The agencies provide the frameworks, the general guidelines for the performances of the tour guides. "The Museums of London," "Shakespeare's London," and "The Pubs of London" are all tours of the same city, but they start from very different assumptions about what the travelers are there for. A theory is set of assumptions, a context for assigning value, making meaning, and guiding behavior. If you are familiar with a variety of theories, then you're able to draw upon a wider range of assumptions and strategies as a reader; you're better able to see how other readers are motivated. If an assignment asks you to focus on the formal features of a literary work, you're less likely, given some familiarity with various critical theories, to concentrate on how the work affects you personally, or on how it reflects its author's psychological state, or its racial and ethnic implications.

Just as no one who is living in any significant sense can avoid having a personality, it is impossible to read (meaningfully) without some theoretical orientation. Even the belief that one should just experience a text without saying anything about it, without any self-consciousness, without considering one's own purposes or suppositions, without exploring other ways of reading—even this effort to evade a theoretical stance is itself theoretical. It stands to reason, then, that some understanding of the kinds of tours available, and how they might be combined or adapted, will be valuable and reassuring. The goal of this book is to give you a working understanding of a variety of critical theories and practices. You won't find every theory covered here, and I freely affirm that many complexities, controversies, and ambiguities have been overlooked here. This is after all an introduction, a starting point, for people who have some familiarity with required literary study, but who aren't familiar with different strategies for talking and writing about literature. If you've ever read a literary work, a writing assignment in a literature class, and wondered "now what?"—then this is the book for you.

CHECKING SOME BAGGAGE

Before we begin, let's consider some basic questions often asked by embarking students, and then address a bit more directly the purpose and plan of this book.

"Is There One Correct Interpretation of a Literary Work?"

Perhaps there are English teachers somewhere like the one in John Cheever's "Expelled," who tells students that her interpretation of *Hamlet* is the only one they need to know—it's "the one accepted on college-board papers," she says. But most teachers (and certainly your own if this book has been assigned) cherish variety and difference in literary criticism, encouraging students to think for themselves when they write about literature. Just as there is no one best place to view the Blue Ridge Mountains, so there is no one best reading of *Hamlet* or any work (although it might be fun to argue about such things). Shift your vantage point a little, change your interests, or just let some time pass; and you'll see something new.

"So Are All Opinions About Literature Equally Valid?"

Still, surely some opinions seem more convincing or satisfying than others. Endorsing variety doesn't necessarily mean that all opinions are equal, that any piece of literary criticism is just as good as any other. Just because we appreciate various views of the mountains, we need not also agree that all vantage points are equally satisfying to all people. If you construct a reading of *Hamlet* this week and a different interpretation next week, it's unlikely that you or your readers will value both of them equally or even that everyone will agree on which one is superior. Some readings are arguably better than others, but to make such a determination, we need first to ask: better for what? Better for whom? This book aims to address such questions, attempting not only to explain clearly and explicitly how to use various critical approaches but also to assess what purposes different approaches are likely to serve (better for what), as well as what sort of audience is likely to be influenced and even created by different critical strategies (better for whom).

Consider, for instance, this photograph:

What does it mean?

- Are these men standing so close together because they're close friends? Are they from some other culture, in which men stand this close? Are they in fact standing unusually close, or am I revealing something about myself in asking this question?
- Are they father and son, perhaps—genetically disposed to superior beards? Is that the wife/mother in between and behind them? What is the expression on her face?
- Are they trying to kiss, and laughing because their caps are getting in the way? The younger man's attire does have sort of a Village People look. Is it possible these men are gay?
- Are they perhaps actors or politicians? Don't they seem a little too jovial? Is this scene staged or real?

- Is it possible these men never actually met? Perhaps the picture has an air of unreality about it because it is a computer-generated fake? Perhaps these are wax models?

Some of these suggestions no doubt seem to you less plausible than others, but it would be very difficult to exclude totally even the wackiest of readings on the basis of the picture alone, wouldn't it?

If the meaning here is limited only by the creativity of the interpreter (and perhaps by the receptivity of anyone the interpreter wants to persuade), then what happens when we bring a context to the work—when we put the picture in a frame, in a sense? This famous photograph, taken in 1960, captures Ernest Hemingway, the legendary American writer (on the left), talking with Fidel Castro, Cuba's equally legendary dictator. Now that we have a historical context, do we know any more about what the picture means? Perhaps. But in terms of Hemingway's life, the photo still might mean any number of things. Since Hemingway took his own life in 1961, reportedly in despair after extended illness, the "meaning" of the picture for some viewers might be what it suggests about Hemingway's health in 1960. Do we see hints that Hemingway is not well? (I don't; he appears virile and vigorous, although there is other evidence that his physical and mental health was failing at this time.) For Castro's biography, the photo would have quite different meanings. And in a history of Cuban-American relations, the photo would likely have other meanings.

In fact, although this picture has appeared in many contexts, one of the more interesting surely occurred in *Newsweek* in September 1994, illustrating an article on the Clinton Administration's Cuban policies. What, one might wonder, does the great American writer meeting with the notorious Cuban leader in 1960 have to do with foreign policy in the 1990s? The picture is captioned "Tangled up in Myths: Hemingway with the Cuban leader in 1960" (26), and Michael Elliott's accompanying article argues that U.S. attitudes toward Cuba are clouded by fantasies and misperceptions. To understand the picture in the context of Elliott's essay, one must not only have some familiarity with Hemingway and Castro, but also realize that Hemingway lived in Cuba a substantial part of his life, fishing, drinking, entertaining buddies. When we think of Cuba, Elliott writes, we think of "romance, casinos, and marlin" (27). "From Teddy Roosevelt to Jimmy Buffett, with contributions from Ernest Hemingway . . . and the U.S. officers who first mixed rum and Coke to form a *cuba libre*," Elliott says, Americans have formed an unrealistic vision of Cuba, thinking of it as a country that naturally ought to be an extension of the United States—our playground, a tropical resort.

Thus, the picture's meaning within the context of Elliott's essay would seem to be pretty clear: it's an allusion to "Hemingway's Cuba," as we have imagined it, versus the real Cuba, as Castro has controlled and strangled it. But there is always more that can be said if we look again, more closely, if we reconsider the context, thinking from a different perspective. The picture might be seen in larger symbolic terms, for instance: why not think of Hemingway as standing, in a sense, for America, and Castro, in the same way, for Cuba? In this sense, Hemingway the brilliant writer, able to express his dreams and desires, embodies the openness, creativity, and accomplishment of the United States. His casual shirt and comfortable cap contrast sharply with Castro's rigid hat and stiffly starched shirt—just as the freedom and comfort of America contrast sharply with the oppressive, impoverished regime of communist Cuba. Castro's military-style costume lacks decoration or insignia, as if he wants to promote the misleading notion that he is an ordinary man, one of the common people. The truly common people in Castro's Cuba are represented by the woman in the background, frowning as she is being squeezed out of the picture, ignored by her communist dictator. Even the background of the picture reinforces this reading, with lush vegetation and windows behind Hemingway, and a blankness behind Castro.

However "correct" (or "incorrect") this interpretation might seem, it does not exhaust the photograph's potential meaning. In fact, from the point of view of a Cuban revolutionary, loyal to Castro, a contrasting reading emerges. Employing that context, one might see Hemingway as a symbol of America's moral and social bankruptcy. Despite the appearance of health, America, like Hemingway, is headed toward its inevitable self-annihilation. Years of self-indulgence will take their toll. Compare the vigor and strength of Castro. Rather than a rumpled shirt, not even entirely buttoned, Castro is wearing a crisp shirt, a smart hat, reflecting the discipline of his people. And our imaginary Castro communist might smugly look back and reflect that just as Castro has outlasted Hemingway by many years, so will Cuba be thriving long after the United States has destroyed itself. The point I'm emphasizing here is that our understanding of a "text" is shaped by the context in which we see it. If this insight isn't surprising to you, its implications are nonetheless profound—and often overlooked. Although a picture sometimes might, as we say, be worth a thousand words, even a picture can be read in many different ways, including opposing ways. When we think about how to take, or create, the meaning of anything—a poem, a story, a photograph, a life—we cannot avoid this interplay of texts and contexts. This territory, in which we think explicitly about how meaning is made, is called "critical theory."

The modifier "critical" in this context doesn't mean theory that is "inclined to find fault or judge severely"—just as "literary criticism" is not devoted to making harsh or negative judgments. "Critical" also means "involving skillful judgment" and "of essential importance" (Webster's definitions). Critical theory is thus concerned with those ideas that are essential to the process of making skillful judgments about literature.

Anything to Declare?

Theory Enables Practice

The focus in this text on the assumptions, strategies, and purposes shaping literary criticism—on critical theories in other words—is not a step away from literature or writing about literature; rather, such assumptions, strategies, and purposes make a deeply rewarding engagement with literature possible. Even the simplest acts of literary response, such as "This is boring," depend on a certain theoretical stance: in this case, the stance includes the assumption that the purpose of literature includes entertaining the reader and that the critic's job includes identifying works that fail this test.

You Already Have a Theoretical Stance

Even if you're unaware of them, some kind of principles guide you in determining what you expect a literary work to do, how you evaluate its performance, what you decide to say about it. (Even the absence of principles constitutes a theoretical position, as does the presence of contradictory principles.) The "elements" of literature, such as plot, character, and point of view, are easy to understand, and most students have been through these terms and concepts many times, often without noticing much help from them in interpreting literature. What is harder, and where more guidance is needed, is in knowing what to say about such elements—how to approach them and how to use them. In the following explanations and illustrations of the various critical approaches, you'll get to see the "elements" in action. You'll see, for instance, how New Criticism, psychological criticism, and deconstruction provide very different views of "character," or "plot," or "theme," giving you a wider range of purposes and strategies in writing about literature.

To begin enhancing your awareness of literary criticism, take an inventory of what you already assume, asking yourself the following questions:

- What do I suppose is the function of literature? What do I look for in a literary work?
- What do I think is the function of writing about literature? What should literary criticism do?
- How do I believe the task of criticism is carried out? What strategies, routines, procedures, and activities do literary critics engage in?

As you try out the various approaches discussed here, you'll be able to compare your own starting assumptions with some of the various options available. At the least, you'll have a better understanding of the critical possibilities, allowing you to understand published criticism more readily; more likely, you'll find yourself incorporating new strategies or stances into your writing about literature, enriching and deepening your insights.

This Is an Introduction

Such theoretical work is challenging at times, but it isn't beyond your abilities. There are, to be sure, many controversies, variations, complexities, exceptions, and qualifications that are not treated here. Critical theory can be astonishingly difficult (and often just astonishing). After working through this book, you may find the work of Jacques Derrida or Annette Kolodny more accessible, but they certainly won't be easy to understand—just as an introduction to physics wouldn't make the scientific papers of Stephen Hawking or John Wheeler a breeze to comprehend. But there's no reason you shouldn't be told about black holes or deconstruction simply because the theories, in all their specifics and intricacies, are difficult. Few people, if pressed, could read Isaac Newton's monumental works with complete understanding, but just about anyone can understand in a useful way how momentum and gravity work.

This text offers a basic, working understanding of critical theory and practice, freely acknowledging that a more advanced understanding is possible. I have tried hard to clarify without distorting, but some matters have no doubt been represented to be simpler than they are.

Here's the Plan

Unfortunately, there's no way a reasonably sized textbook (one without wheels and a handle) can cover adequately all the different kinds of criticism that can be identified today—even if I understood them all. Nor can any one particular theory in all its mutations, combinations, and complexities be presented here. What I can do is provide a practical introduction to some of the most influential theories, leaving aside for now, and with considerable regret, some of the most interesting and exciting. My goal is to put you in a position to develop and refine your understanding, to move into other critical arenas, to evolve your own readings and even theories.

The plan is simple. The second chapter briefly visits all the approaches discussed here by applying them to a single passage. Then each of the next six chapters inhabits a theory or a cluster of related theories in some detail, again applying the theory or theories to various passages and evolving essays step by step from each of the various critical stances. The ninth chapter deals with research. At the end of each chapter, you'll find a very select list of suggested further readings. I've annotated these items to give you a better sense of what's out there and where you might want to go from here.

Recommended Further Reading: Introductions and Overviews

Adler, Mortimer, and Charles Van Doren. *How to Read a Book*. Revised and updated. New York: Simon and Schuster, 1972. Originally published in 1940, this book still offers valuable advice—on "How to Be a Demanding Reader," "How to Use a Dictionary," and much else. Chapter 15 deals with "Suggestions for Reading Stories, Plays, and Poems."

Bressler, Charles. *Literary Criticism: An Introduction to Theory and Practices*. 4th ed. Upper Saddle River, NJ: Prentice-Hall, 2006. A thorough overview including a valuable historical survey.

Culler, Jonathan. *Literary Theory: A Very Short Introduction*. Oxford: Oxford UP., 2000. Sophisticated yet extremely lucid.

Denby, David. *Great Books: My Adventures with Homer, Rousseau, Woolf, and Other Indestructible Writers of the Western World.* New York: Simon and Schuster, 1996. An inspiring book for anyone embarking on serious literary studies: Denby, a movie critic, tells the story of his decision at age 48 to return to Columbia University and read great literature.

Harmon, William, and C. Hugh Holman. *A Handbook to Literature.* 8th ed. Upper Saddle River, NJ: Prentice-Hall, 1999. If you want to know what the "Spasmodic School" was, or what a Spoonerism is, or the meaning of just about any other word related to literature, here's a handy place to look. There are many good handbooks, but this one is especially lucid and thorough.

Lentricchia, Frank, and Thomas McLaughlin. *Critical Terms for Literary Study.* 2nd ed. Chicago: U. of Chicago P, 1995. Somewhat challenging but richly rewarding essays by leading scholars on various topics: "Representation," "Structure," "Writing," "Narrative," and so forth.

Lynn, Steven. *Literature: Reading and Writing with Critical Strategies.* New York: Pearson Longman, 2004. An intro-to-lit anthology (poetry, fiction, drama; 1213 pages) based on the same principles as *Texts and Contexts.* Includes discussions of the elements of literature (e.g., plot, character, theme) as well as critical theories (as invention strategies).

Scholes, Robert. *The Rise and Fall of English: Reconstructing English as a Discipline.* New Haven: Yale University Press, 1998. An entertaining and enlightening history of English departments and literary study.

Trimble, John. *Writing with Style: Conversations on the Art of Writing.* 2nd ed. Upper Saddle River, NJ: Prentice-Hall, 2000. The best little book on writing I know. Many times I've assigned the first chapter to first-year English students, and they show up for the next class having read the whole book. If you're at all weak as a writer, or if you just want to get stronger, get this book. It's lively, fun, and useful, and the examples are mostly drawn from writing about literature.

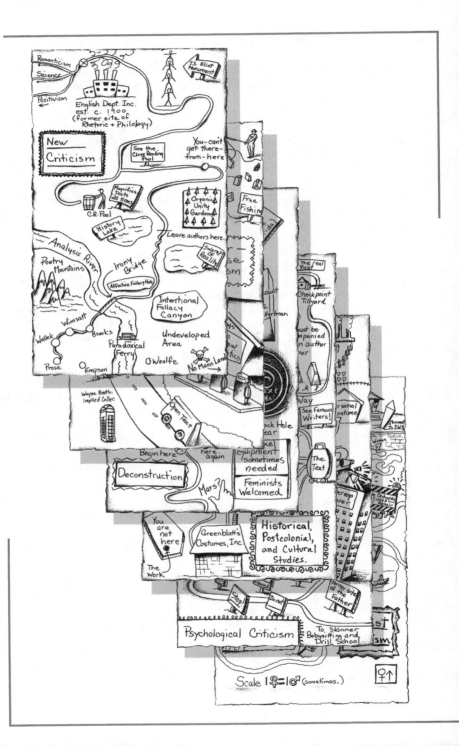

CHAPTER 2

Critical Worlds

A Selective Tour

> "The question is," said Alice,
> "whether you can make words
> mean so many things."
>
> "The question is," said Humpty
> Dumpty, "which is to be master—
> that's all."
>
> —Lewis Carroll

This chapter begins to show you how critical theories work—how bringing different contexts to a text will lead you to different insights. Each theory introduced here is presented and illustrated in more detail in a subsequent chapter. But why so many different strategies? Why not just show you the best way to write about literature? Because there isn't any way that everyone would agree is best for writing about any given work for any given purpose. As we noted in the first chapter, there is no single "correct" reading of a particular text. Some interpretations are no doubt more sophisticated, insightful, stimulating, or useful than others. But for different readers at different times and places, what is best will be a matter of opinion.

When you finish reading this chapter, you should have a pretty good idea of the basic assumptions and strategies of the various approaches treated in the rest of this book. There are many advanced books on theory and history, and you'll find some recommendations for further reading at the end of this chapter. But the emphasis throughout this book will be on what is practical—on how to use critical theories.

It's entirely possible that you are encountering some or all of these critical strategies for the first time, and your prior experience with literature also may be limited; don't be dismayed if some of the terms and ideas are unfamiliar and a bit challenging. In subsequent chapters, each approach and its use in the process of writing about literature will be explained in more detail. The brief excursions in this chapter are a preview. You may want to use this chapter as a review also, returning to it after you've read the other chapters. As you may have noticed, there are brief summaries of these theories inside the front cover for handy reference.

To allow you to compare and contrast different theories, I illustrate how each one might be applied to the same passage, an excerpt from Brendan Gill's *Here at "The New Yorker."* It's a wonderful passage, and since it will be used for all the theories presented here, you'll want to read it carefully:

> When I started at *The New Yorker*, I felt an unshakable confidence in my talent and intelligence. I revelled in them openly, like a dolphin diving skyward out of the sea. After almost forty years, my assurance is less than it was; the revellings, such as they are, take place in becoming seclusion. This steady progress downward in the amount of one's confidence is a commonplace at the magazine—one might almost call it a tradition. Again and again, some writer who has made a name for himself in the world will begin to write for us and will discover as if for the first time how difficult writing is. The machinery of benign skepticism that surrounds and besets him in the form of editors, copy editors, and checkers, to say nothing of fellow-writers, digs a yawning pit an inch or so beyond his desk. He hears it repeated as gospel that there are not three people in all America who can set down a simple declarative sentence correctly; what are the odds against his being one of this tiny elect?
>
> In some cases, the pressure of all those doubting eyes upon his copy is more than the writer can bear. When the galleys of a piece are placed in front of him, covered with scores, perhaps hundreds, of pencilled hen-tracks of inquiry, suggestion, and correction, he may sense not the glory of creation but the threat of being stung to death by an army of gnats. Upon which he may think of nothing better to do than lower his head onto his blotter and burst into tears. Thanks to the hen-tracks and their consequences, the piece will be much improved, but the

author of it will be pitched into a state of graver self-doubt than ever. Poor devil, he will type out his name on a sheet of paper and stare at it long and long, with dumb uncertainty. It looks—oh, Christ!—his name looks as if it could stand some working on.

As I was writing the above, Gardner Botsford, the editor who, among other duties, handles the copy for "Theatre," came into my office with the galleys of my latest play review in his hand. Wearing an expression of solemnity, he said, "I am obliged to inform you that Miss Gould has found a buried dangling modifier in one of your sentences." Miss Gould is our head copy editor and unquestionably knows as much about English grammar as anyone alive. Gerunds, predicate nominatives, and passive periphrastic conjugations are mother's milk to her, as they are not to me. Nevertheless, I boldly challenged her allegation. My prose was surely correct in every way. Botsford placed the galleys before me and indicated the offending sentence, which ran, "I am told that in her ninth decade this beautiful woman's only complaint in respect to her role is that she doesn't have enough work to do."

I glared blankly at the galleys. Humiliating enough to have buried a dangling modifier unawares; still more humiliating not to be able to disinter it. Botsford came to my rescue. "Miss Gould points out that as the sentence is written, the meaning is that the complaint is in its ninth decade and has, moreover, suddenly and unaccountably assumed the female gender." I said that in my opinion the sentence could only be made worse by being corrected—it was plain that "The only complaint of this beautiful woman in her ninth decade..." would hang on the page as heavy as a sash-weight. "Quite so," said Botsford. "There are times when to be right is wrong, and this is one of them. The sentence stands." (7–8)

What can you say about this passage? How can an understanding of different critical strategies give you more options, more material to work with? Let's begin with New Criticism, the critical approach that transformed the study of literature in the modern age. It's no longer "new," but New Criticism is still a pervasively influential way of looking at literary texts.

NEW CRITICISM

New Criticism focuses attention on the work itself, not the reader or the author or anything else. New Critics are not allergic to talking about the responses of readers or the intentions of authors, but they believe that the work itself ultimately must stand on its own as an artistic object. This commitment to the work itself as an aesthetic object is what made the New Critics' strategies distinctive and "new." The purpose of giving attention to the work itself is, first, to expose the work's unity. In a unified work, every element works together toward a theme. Every element is essential. In addition, the "close reading" (a phrase popularized by New Critics) of a literary work reveals its complexity. Great literature, New Critics assume, contains oppositions, ambiguities, ironies, tensions; these are unified by the work—if it is successful by the standards of New Criticism.

So how does one do New Criticism? Begin by reading closely. Since everything should contribute to the work's unity—figures of speech, point of view, diction, imagery, recurrent ideas or events, and so forth—then careful analysis of any aspect of the work should be revealing. Look for oppositions, tensions, ambiguities. These add complexity to the work's unity. A mediocre work might be unified but have little complexity, or it might be complex but never really come together. The New Critic, ultimately, shows how the various elements of a great work unify it.

Let's see how New Criticism can be applied to our passage from *Here at "The New Yorker."*

My New Critical reading of this passage was developed by reading carefully, marking up the text, asking myself questions, drafting answers to the questions, brainstorming and freewriting, and then putting my ideas together. Although this reading didn't just pop out of my head, it wasn't a frustrating struggle because I knew what I was trying to do, and I was confident that my assumptions and strategies would eventually produce something interesting. Specifically, I knew that a New Critical reading would identify some tension (or irony, or opposition) in the text, and I immediately saw that some tensions in the story are pretty clear:

> editor vs. writer
>
> the world vs. *The New Yorker*
>
> grammar vs. style
>
> confidence vs. doubt
>
> right vs. wrong

I also knew that such tensions must somehow be resolved if the text succeeds (by New Critical standards). Therefore, how the text ends is especially important from a New Critical perspective.

New Critics might have some trouble with the idea of an "ending" in this case, because the "work" I've chosen is not really a work, but rather an excerpt from a work. But for the purposes of demonstration, let's imagine this passage stands alone, entitled "Writing a Wrong." This title, as is often the case, points toward the unifying idea that I am finding in the work. Endings are crucial, especially for New Critics, and this reading focuses on the reconciliation at the end, when Botsford pronounces "right is wrong." As a New Critic, I had to consider, "How does this idea—'right is wrong'—unify or resolve the work in a complex or ambiguous way?" In other words, what conflicting ideas are at work in the passage that are brought into balance and harmony by this theme? So, New Criticism invites you to do three things: focus on the text's details and read closely; look for oppositions, ironies, tensions; and show how the work's complexity is artistically unified.

You'll benefit most, I think, if you try to sketch out your own New Critical reading before (and perhaps after) you read mine.

The Paradoxical Unity of "Writing a Wrong"

In Brendan Gill's story of a dangling modifier, "Writing a Wrong," the editor Botsford solves the conflict between Miss Gould's rules and Gill's taste. He does so by offering a paradox that unifies Gill's story: sometimes "right is wrong," Botsford says. It turns out that Miss Gould was right to spot the error, but Gill was right to have written the sentence as he did. The irony of this solution is reinforced by various paradoxical images in the story.

For example, the dolphin in the second sentence is "diving skyward." This action simultaneously suggests a downward movement ("diving") and an upward motion ("skyward"). The description thus embodies the same sort of logic as a wrong rightness. Likewise, the "progress downward" of the writer and even his "becoming seclusion" ("becoming"—attractive and appealing to others; "seclusion"— unknown to others) convey the same kind of image. In larger terms, the writer's "unshakable confidence" quickly becomes a "dumb uncertainty"—which again suggests the kind of reversal that resolves the story.

In such an upside-down world we would expect to find imagery of struggle and violence, and we do encounter a "yawning pit" and an "army of gnats." Such tension is harmonized by Gill's brilliant conclusion: in writing, conducted properly, the demands of correctness and style are unified by the writer's poetic instincts. Similarly, the story itself is resolved by the notion of a correct error.

READER-RESPONSE CRITICISM

Reader-response criticism starts from the idea that the critic's interest ultimately ought to be focused on the reader rather than the text itself or the author. Without readers, it seems safe to say, there would be little reason to talk about literature; it is the reader who brings the text to life, who gives it meaning. Otherwise, it's just black marks on a white page.

The reader-response critic focuses on the reader's activity in one of two ways: by describing how readers *should* respond to the text or by giving the critic's own personal response. That is, the reader-response critic either is claiming to be describing what is "normal," or conventional, or ideal, or implied by the text; or the critic is expressing that which is personal, subjective, perhaps even eccentric. One could argue that reader-response critics are always engaging in subjective response, even when they think they're objectively describing "the" response. In any event, reader-response critics tend to deal with works eliciting responses that are somehow noteworthy.

How does one do reader-response criticism? If the goal is to offer a personal, subjective response, one simply reads the text and responds. As you can imagine, such a strategy has been especially popular because it really liberates the reader. It's difficult to see how any response could be wrong: who could say, "No, that isn't your response"? Some responses may seem richer than others; some responses may seem to deal more fully with the text; some responses may seem more authentic and honest than others. But any particular response may well help another reader to a more interesting or satisfying experience of the work.

If the idea is to describe how a reader *ought* to respond, which might better be called "reader-reception" criticism, then you'll need to try to suppress whatever is personal in your response and offer instead an "ideal" response, one that is (or rather ought to be) shared by all attentive and intelligent readers. Describing in careful detail the slow-motion progress of a hypothetical reader through the text, such "objective" or receptive reader-response criticism may consider these kinds of questions: What expectations does the text create? What happens to those expectations? (Are they met, undermined, exploited, transformed, denied?) What literary conventions does the text employ to affect the reader? How, in other words, does the text shape the reader's response?

Although I'm presenting these two versions of reader-response criticism as oppositions, flip sides of a single coin, it may be more accurate and helpful to see them in terms of a progression. Reader-response critics unavoidably must use their own personal responses as a starting point for talking about how the ideal, or implied, or common reader responds; but the close examination of such "ideal" responses would seem inevitably to reveal some personal and subjective features. (No one, I would suggest, not even the author, can be *the* ideal reader.)

At this point, before we get any deeper into the question of whether reader-response criticism is unavoidably subjective, let's see how the theory applies to our passage.

The following essay tries to present a record of my movement through this passage. It was fairly easy and fun to write because I simply read through the passage slowly and asked myself, "Okay, how am I responding now? What does this make me think? What am I expecting next?" Although I decided that the passage was continually surprising me, I would not argue that surprise is the only or the correct response: I might have focused on the passage's humor, on a pervading sense of doom, or something else. That's the beauty of reader-response criticism: different responses. As a piece of reader-response criticism, this essay strives to be neither rabidly subjective nor dogmatically objective. I focus on my personal response, but I also try to play the reader's role that I believe Gill has imagined. I quote the text repeatedly, trying to show my reader exactly what I'm responding to.

The Reader's Surprise in an Excerpt from *Here at "The New Yorker"*

Beginning with its first sentence, the story of the buried dangling modifier in Brendan Gill's *Here at "The New Yorker"* is continually surprising, setting up expectations and then knocking them down. Gill begins the first sentence with "When I started at *The New Yorker*," and I naturally expect him to talk about how nervous and insecure he was starting off at one of the largest and most famous magazines in the world. Instead, Gill refers to his "unshakable confidence." The third sentence begins with

"After almost forty years," leading me to expect some explanation of how his joy at the magazine has grown. But forty years of experience, it turns out, have not developed Gill's confidence and happiness. Instead, his "assurance is less than it was." How, I must wonder, has he managed to work there for forty years and yet grow less confident?

Expecting Gill to explain the oddity of his deteriorating confidence, I find, surprisingly, that such an effect "is a commonplace at the magazine," a "tradition" even. Since the loss of confidence occurs for everyone, we might then expect that *The New Yorker* staff sticks together, sharing insecurities and supporting each other. Such is hardly the case, as Gill continues to surprise me by tracing one imaginary writer's loss of confidence to the point of what appears to be a nervous breakdown. The writer, who is said to have "made a name for himself in the world," is reduced to weeping on his blotter and trying to revise his name. Such is not what I expect from a famous writer.

Given this tradition of disaster, it seems clear to me that Gardner Botsford is appearing in the third paragraph to star in the story of Gill's own downfall. Botsford points to a major error Gill has made, and Gill's assertion that he "boldly challenged" the allegation seems to set him up for a major humiliation. "Unshakable" confidence and bold challenges certainly seem unwarranted in the atmosphere of *The New Yorker*. But, once more, Gill crosses me up and provides a story of triumph. Rather than undermining his confidence, which is what everything in the story suggests will happen, Botsford becomes Gill's champion. "The sentence stands," he says, as the last reversal provides a happy ending.

STRUCTURALIST AND DECONSTRUCTIVE CRITICISM

Language makes meaning by oppositions: we know what "good" means because it is the opposite of "bad"; "tired" means something to us because it is the opposite of "rested." So words make sense because of their relationship *to other words*, not because of any "natural" grounding in reality. Although we may like to think "bad" and "rested" refer to something solid and real, they don't. "Bad" has come to mean "good" in certain contexts. It could come to mean "blue," or "hungry," or anything. "Rested" with regard to a fighter pilot during combat may mean "having had three hours' sleep in the last twenty-four." Meaning is relative and relational, based on language's structure. So a structuralist reading of a text exposes the system of meaning that is at work in that text.

Structuralism is thus a bit like New Criticism, except that structuralists are interested in an individual text not as an artistic object, but rather as an example of a system of meaning.

Deconstructive criticism, in a sense, takes the insights of structuralism (meaning is made by a binary structure) or New Criticism (literary works unify oppositions) and reverses or inverts or explodes them. Whereas New Criticism aims to reveal the coherence and unity of the work, deconstruction aims to expose the gaps, the incoherences, the contradictions of the text. Whereas a structuralist reading of a text reveals its underlying system of meaning, a deconstructive reading shows how the system falls apart. Deconstructive critics assume that gaps are present in texts because of what they assume about the arbitrary and unstable nature of language. By taking texts apart—undoing them until we see how a text inevitably contradicts itself, containing traces of its opposite or "other"—deconstructive critics are able to call into question many of our settled and comfortable assumptions. Depending on how you feel about these assumptions (truths or prejudices?), deconstruction will seem scandalously offensive or delightfully inventive.

One of the many ironies of deconstruction, it appears, is that any effort to explain deconstruction is doomed according to the theory itself. Any effort to say *anything*, in fact, must go astray. Such an assumption could be dismaying, but many deconstructive critics have chosen to adopt a comic and even shocking stance, practicing a critical strategy that by its own definition cannot be defined. Although deconstructive criticism can be very difficult to read (perhaps as an illustration of how language eventually fails?), it can also be very amusing and engaging—and a lot of fun to try.

Thus, deconstructing a text calls for careful reading and a bit of creativity. One way to think of your goal as a deconstructive critic is that you're trying to turn the text against itself. For instance, Botsford's concluding decision, "The sentence stands," may appear to be reassuring. Here is a case where a writer makes a mistake, but the mistake turns out to be okay. If we were to press this reading, however, asking if the text might say something other than what it appears to say, we may begin to move into the realm of deconstruction. If you are a student in a writing-about-literature class, I suspect that Gill's passage is only superficially comforting. If a writer at *The New Yorker* can't always tell whether a sentence is right or wrong—if in fact the rules of writing are so complex that not even three people in America "can set down a simple declarative sentence correctly"—then how is a college student to feel? If a grown man and an established writer is weeping onto his desk blotter and considering revising his name, then how can the ordinary student hope to write an error-free paper—especially when the rules seem to apply in one case and not in another, and the rules for determining such exceptions don't seem to exist but are instead invented and applied by those who happen to be in charge? Writing becomes a nightmare.

In fact, one might observe that Botsford's "reassuring" vindication is deceptive, for he does not actually say that sometimes right is wrong and wrong is right. He only says that sometimes "right is wrong." But Botsford's apparent reversal of the dismantling of authors at *The New Yorker* is finally ambiguous, since we never know if the writer is ever correct, no matter what he does: "The sentence stands" indeed, but it stands with its error intact, a monument to Gill's inability to correct it and to the inevitable errors of writing—a monument to the way language masters us.

Although deconstructive critics may well deal with obviously major features of a text, like its ending, they may also choose some marginal element of the text and vigorously explore its oppositions, reversals, and ambiguities. In fact, for some critics, deconstruction is simply a name for "close reading" of an especially rigorous kind. The deconstructive critic, for example, might well decide to concentrate on the assertion that because of the editors' merciless correction, "the piece will be much improved." A New Critic, I think, would not be very likely to consider this assertion central, the key to the passage. But a deconstructive critic might. Here is what happened when I turned around the idea that "the piece will be much improved" and questioned it.

"The Sentence Stands" Triumphant: A Deconstructive Reading

In *Here at "The New Yorker"* (see pages 7–8), Brendan Gill offers an anecdote that clearly sets the world's writers against the editors, and the latter control the game. Gill has written an essay, but the editors and their accomplices, the checkers and copy editors, get to say what is wrong with it. They get to dig the "yawning pit" in front of the helpless writer's desk; they determine the "tiny elect" who can write correctly; they make the scores and hundreds of "hen-tracks" on the writer's manuscript, which serve as testimony to the incompetence of writers, the near-impossibility of writing, and the arbitrary power of the editor.

To be sure, it is acknowledged that these editorial assaults upon the writer serve their purpose, for "thanks to the hen-tracks and their consequences, the piece will be much improved." But the cost is terrible. Not only is the writer unable to write his own name with any confidence; he has also become a "poor devil," outside "the elect." In delivering his writing over to the editors, conceding their dominance, the writer inevitably places his own identity, perhaps even his very soul, in jeopardy. Thus, the cry, "oh, Christ!" comes to be an invocation to the only power who can save the writer from the devil and the editor's destructive forces.

But this story of the hopelessness of writers also reveals that the kingdom of editors is based upon a lie: it simply is not true, despite the beleaguered writer's admission under torture, that "the piece will be much improved" by editorial intervention. In this instance, Miss Gould's enormous grammatical lore does not in fact improve the piece at all; her effort nearly made it "worse." And Botsford's contribution as editor involves simply leaving the piece as it was written—a strange method of improvement! So who is in charge—writers or editors?

In the end, Gill can never again become like the gill-less dolphin of the first paragraph, confidently "diving skyward," because the dangling modifier defiantly remains: it is a part of the sea of language the author cannot leave. In the end, both writer and editor are defeated by their inability to control their language. The status of the writer at *The New Yorker* becomes a paradigm for the alarming status of writing itself: deceptive, mute, and intractable, "the sentence stands," neither improved nor made worse, standing really for nothing that is under the writer's or editor's rule.

HISTORICAL, POSTCOLONIAL, AND CULTURAL STUDIES

One way to think about literature is to consider the people who wrote it. Not the text itself (New Criticism), not the reader's reactions (reader response), not the system of language at work in the text (structuralism), not how the text falls apart (deconstruction), but rather the life and times of the author. It is a fascinating approach, appealing to our natural curiosity: Inquiring minds want to know how great works of art came into being, and whether great writers are ordinary people, or eccentrics, or something else. Writers must live and write in particular places and particular times, and so biographical research is intertwined with historical research. "History" includes the history of literature, so the effort to enrich our understanding of a work by examining the conditions of its production can usefully include studying the literary tradition.

In theory, this approach to criticism is simple: just find out the biographical and historical facts and see how they illuminate the literature. If you are reading a novel set in the Vietnam War, wouldn't you like to know if the author perhaps fought in that war, or protested against it, or both? Are there letters from that period of the author's life? Wouldn't it also be helpful to know the history of the Vietnam War? And be familiar with other novels written about this war? And even literary works about other wars?

Of course we cannot know everything, and we don't always know what we don't know, as Yogi Berra might have said. And so the discovery of new historical or biographical facts may substantially or entirely alter our perception. What if a work that we thought was written by a combat veteran turns out actually to be written by a journalist who never saw a battle? Or by a soldier's mother, who never even visited Vietnam? One reasonable response to these questions would be that such information doesn't matter at all. The text of the work isn't altered by this information. If one accepts this response, then the value of historical criticism is certainly diminished. It may be interesting to learn about the author's biography and the relevant history, but if the text is all we need, then this information is extraneous to the work, nonessential.

The validity and importance of biographical and historical criticism can, however, be defended. For starters, some readers have larger purposes than simply appreciating a literary work. If readers want to understand the insights and expressions of a brilliant mind, or of an age, then the work itself is just the visible part of a much larger picture. Further, a writer's audience inevitably has knowledge and assumptions that are not immediately available to a later audience, removed in time and space. In other words, even if the reader's interest is limited to the literary work, biographical and historical research are still valuable, arguably crucial, to an understanding of the work itself. It would be, however, a naïve mistake to equate writers with their work: If we learn that a writer protested against the Vietnam War, we should not therefore assume that his novel is a political statement against the war. It might be, but he might also have changed his mind, or grown tired of that issue and is working on some other problem in the novel. Biographical and historical research can highlight certain aspects of a work for us, calling our attention to one thing or another, suggesting ways of reading, but the work itself must still somehow support the argument.

In the last half-century or so, even more fundamental problems have been raised regarding our traditional views of history and biography. New ways of thinking about language and meaning, coming out of structuralism and post-structuralism, have led to a movement called "New Historicism" (often called "cultural materialism" in Great Britain), which emphasizes that it is no longer possible to assume that there are stable "facts" objectively out there, waiting to be discovered; instead, all we really have access to is an indeterminate number of texts waiting on a process of interpretation. Hence, New Historicists shift their attention away from trying to determine what "really" happened, and toward exploring how different versions of history are made. Since history is unavoidably motivated by the interests and values of the historian, it cannot be objective. Literature, biography, and history from this perspective all participate in creating a "discourse," which embodies a set of values and assumptions. As a result, literary critics who embrace New Historicism end up reading all sorts of texts—literary works, newspapers, advertisements, graffiti, anything that can be used to expose the discourse that is at work.

But how is this "new"? Or for that matter, "historical"? Haven't good historians always doubted the objectivity of their "facts," and haven't they always looked for coherent systems for making meaning? Perhaps the key distinction of New Historicism is that history itself becomes textual. The point is not that New Historicists deny Shakespeare's existence, for instance; it is rather that "Shakespeare" for us is meaningful only as a text—or rather as a whole range of texts that construct the meaning of that name, which is constantly evolving. In a sense, Shakespeare's existence *is not a fact*, but "Shakespeare" is rather a name that marks the site of a struggle—the struggle to create Shakespeare. New Historicism encourages readers to connect all sorts of texts, extending beyond literary texts to build an understanding of the web of culture at a particular time. New Historicism gives up the quest to find singular causes for historical events, and attempts instead to identify an ideology—or ideologies—at work in a particular time and place. Rather than moving through time, to put this another way, from an origin which leads to an effect, which leads to another event, New Historicists move in a sense through space, reading poems, advertisements, music, novels, law textbooks, medical texts, children's stories, graffiti, anything—as if they were intellectual archaeologists revealing what drives disparate aspects of a culture.

Postcolonial criticism is in some ways similar to New Historicism: postcolonial criticism examines the shaping ideas and values in a particular kind of culture. That kind of culture is one that has been colonized—subjected to the rule of another, or an "other." Literature is often an important part of the way a ruling power thinks about and influences its subjects, and also an important feature of the way the "native" people both absorb and resist the colonizing power. Like New Historicism, postcolonial criticism is not restricted to the analysis of literary texts, but rather seeks to connect any grouping of texts that may help us to understand the complex relationships of a dominant to a dominated culture. The goal here is to intervene: to expose the way that one culture represents and therefore controls another, and thereby to undermine that power. Thus, the excluded, repressed, "savage," "primitive" culture can be rewritten in other terms.

The idea of writing about culture as a way of intervening in culture is also at the heart of cultural studies. Cultural studies, like New Historicism and postcolonial criticism, assumes that meaning is constructed. That means, for instance, that we cannot assume European culture, with its technological and industrial achievements, is superior to some other culture; we cannot assume that *Seinfeld* is inferior to *Hamlet*. The popularity of cultural studies derives in part from this dizzyingly liberating erasure of our assumptions, which may be no more than our prejudices. Cultural values are invented, and cultural studies seeks to expose the systems of meaning-making that create the worlds of culture that human beings inhabit. Cultural studies is indeed so open in terms of what it studies and the methods that are employed that even its adherents are not entirely clear or united regarding what cultural studies is. But people who say they are "doing" cultural studies do appear to share, it seems, a commitment to a radical or alternative political stance. That is, they seem to be exposing how culture works from an antagonistic or at least questioning perspective. This stance is not surprising, given cultural studies' roots in poststructuralism (emphasizing the arbitrariness of meaning) and Marxism (emphasizing the shaping power of economics and class).

Because new historical, postcolonial, and cultural studies require readers not only to control a literary text, but also to assemble diverse historical materials into coherent systems of meaning, these strategies are likely to seem more appropriate for advanced students. Biography and history, however, are fascinating (as the success of *People* magazine and *The History Channel* perhaps suggest), and students at almost any level will benefit from efforts to link the work to its world. The following passage illustrates briefly how a little biographical and historical research can be applied to a text, drawing on both traditional and new historical strategies.

"To Take a Favorable View": Brendan Gill and the Writer's Depression

Brendan Gill began working at *The New Yorker* in 1936—"almost forty years ago," as he says in *Here at "The New Yorker,"* published in 1975. Thus, the "unshakable" confidence that Gill mentions in the first sentence of the excerpt quoted above is particularly remarkable for having arisen in the midst of the Great Depression, with failure and fear of failure presumably rampant all around him. It appears that the confidence is extraordinarily fragile, however, as the writer who is reveling in his talent and intelligence as the passage begins is bursting into tears, his head on his blotter, before many more sentences pass by. Does the skepticism and correction really account for this collapse? Did real writers typically experience emotional collapses at the magazine? Does Gill really believe that at any time between 1935 and 1975 fewer than three people "in all America" could "set down a simple declarative sentence correctly"?

Although Gill's book is presented as a memoir, an autobiography, the reality of his life begins to seem a bit elusive. Elsewhere in *Here at "The New Yorker,"* for instance, Gill writes, "I am always so ready to take a favorable view of my powers that even when I am caught out and made a fool of, I manage to twist this circumstance about until it becomes a proof of how exceptional I am" (62). Obviously this sentiment is not consistent with the weeping writer, his confidence shattered. In another passage, Gill writes, "I started out at the place where I wanted most to be and with much pleasure and very little labor have remained here since" (24). This comment also does not sound at all like the experience of the sobbing writer with "hundreds" of "hen-tracks of inquiry," endlessly revising even his name. In fact, the writer whose confidence has been broken, who cannot bear "all those doubting eyes upon his copy," is not, strictly speaking, Gill. It is "some writer who has made a name for himself in the world," the generic writer, not Gill personally, who is crushed into a state of "dumb uncertainty" by his service at *The New Yorker.* Gill says only that after "almost forty years, my assurance is less than it was." Why does Gill mention this typical writer, suggesting—despite contrary evidence elsewhere—that his own career follows this same structural path?

The structure of the passage, the story of the dangling modifier, involves three movements: first, the writer exudes mastery and confidence; then the writer falls into doubt and uncertainty; finally, the writer is vindicated, his confidence restored. It is this structure that shapes the autobiography Gill presents: "unshakable confidence," "progress downward," "rescue" and vindication. Thus, the anecdote becomes an example of his experience at the magazine, which is one instance of everyone's experience at the magazine. This structure is of course a pervasive one, easily relevant to both the mid-1930s (the passage's starting point) and the mid-1970s (where it ends). Both the mid-1930s and mid-1970s followed periods of exuberant assurance and represented times of doubt and crisis, as Americans struggled to rise above the Depression in 1935 and the Vietnam War in 1975. Like many narratives, Gill's life as he presents it here fits the national paradigm. This structure suggests a positive view of history: although writers lose their confidence, it can be restored, just as a depression or war can be surmounted. This plot structure is reassuring, giving shape to biography and history.

PSYCHOLOGICAL CRITICISM

Anyone whose writing is evaluated will be intrigued, I think, by what Gill's passage implies about the psychological effects of criticism. You too may have felt at some point the discomfort of "pencilled hentracks of inquiry, suggestion, and correction." The passage provides a good opportunity to consider how such feelings arise and what purpose, if any, they serve. You don't, in other words, have to be a psychologist in order to do psychological criticism. Common sense and an interest in human thinking and behavior are the only essentials.

Still, psychological concepts can be valuable and stimulating in writing about literature. Take, for instance, the idea put forward by Sigmund Freud that creative writing is like dreaming: both allow wishes or fears to be fulfilled that would otherwise be suppressed. A desire or a fear too powerful to be confronted directly can be disguised by the unconscious and expressed by the author or dreamer, Freud said. One possible task of the psychological critic, then, like the psychologist, would be to decode what is being disguised. The critic may make educated guesses about what has been repressed and transformed by the author, or by characters, or even by other readers.

Another useful psychological concept is the idea that there are basic patterns of human development, even though everyone's formative history is different in particulars. One of the most famous and controversial of these developmental concepts is Freud's idea of the Oedipus complex. In Greek myth, Oedipus was the man who unknowingly murdered his father and married his mother. For Freud, this myth depicted the infantile desire experienced by all little boys, who want to see the mother as the principal object of their affections and resent sharing her with the father. The Oedipus complex comes about when this sensual desire for the mother is not suppressed. And the vehicle for this suppression, Freud argued, is the young boy's recognition that the father is more powerful. Rather than lose his capability for pleasure, the boy pulls back from his focus on the mother and eventually turns his desires elsewhere. At its most instinctual level, Freud maintained, the threat to the boy's sexuality is perceived as a threat to that which determines his sex: It is ultimately a fear of castration that motivates the boy's withdrawal.

Although many of Freud's ideas, including the Oedipus complex, have been vigorously challenged or revised, especially by post-structuralist and feminist thinkers, his work has formed the basis for modern psychology. Many of his ideas are so well known that any educated person can be expected to be familiar with them. It would be difficult to go very far toward understanding psychology or psychological criticism today without some awareness of Freud, who relied heavily on literature in developing his ideas. By no means, however, should you infer that psychological criticism means Freudian criticism. Other approaches are welcome. But since an introduction to the field of psychology isn't practical here, I've elected to indicate simply how psychological concepts can be applied by using Freud, who is arguably the most important single figure. If you can apply Freud, you can apply Abraham Maslow or Luce Irigaray or whomever.

The following essay was developed primarily by applying Freud's central theory of the Oedipus complex to Gill's passage.

A Psychological Reading of Gill's Passage

Writers are brought into the world by editors, and Brendan Gill is thus in a sense the product of Miss Gould and Gardner Botsford's union. Gardner Botsford imposes the grammatical law in a fatherly enough way, but his counterpart, Miss Gould, functions only as a kind of uncreating anti-mother: she is a "Miss," and her notion of "mother's milk" is truly indigestible—"gerunds, predicate nominatives, and passive periphrastic conjugations." She nurtures neither writing nor writer.

But, at the same time, the well-being of the writers at *The New Yorker* depends on her approval because, like Gill, they have accepted the criterion of correctness as the law of the father. Miss Gould imposes that law to the letter, undermining the writer's self-esteem until finally his very identity is threatened, plunging him into such "self-doubt" that his name is called into question. He may then become an orphan; his work may be abandoned.

In fact, the source of the writer's neurotic breakdown seems to be the linking of self to writing. Although the many corrections are imprinted upon the paper, Gill shifts them to the writer and transforms them from "pencilled hen-tracks" into stings. It is not, as we might suppose, the particular work that may be attacked so much that it dies, but rather *the writer* who may be "stung to death by an army of gnats." Gnats do not, so far as I know anyway, have stingers; they bite. The displacement here, one might argue, is the result of the writer's sense of personal vulnerability, making the threat more plausible since being bitten to death by gnats sounds absurd, while being stung is more ominous.

The more serious threat to Gill's identity is posed by Botsford, his editor and symbolic father. Botsford enters the scene with Gill's review "in his hand." Part of the review has been illegally "buried" and may subsequently be removed. This threat to Gill's writing is a disguised fear of castration because the writer identifies with his writing. The writer's identity, his name, is crucial to his potency. His name is the key to his ability to reproduce and promulgate himself. Yet, his name "looks as if it could stand some working on."

Gill recognizes then that his editorial parent may correct and improve his "piece," but the cost may be terrible, for the piece may be taken over by the authorities who control the emissions of his pen. Gill's image for what he has lost, the dolphin, thus becomes a rather blatant phallic symbol, reemerging as the pen (the grammatical penis) that the "dumb" writer loses. In other words, the writer must give up his "piece" to be published, to survive as a writer, but he is no longer intact as the writer.

We now may see the psychological fittingness of the error Miss Gould finds: it is a structure that is "dangling." The writer may see his own fate in the sentence that sticks out, for it has suddenly "assumed the female gender." The writer's castration anxiety emerges here: He has desired to please Miss Gould, but focusing on grammar and correctness will render him impotent and emasculated. Thus, Gill's story works to resolve his Oedipus complex by pointing out the advantages of accepting the values of the father (Botsford) and shifting his desire from Miss Gould to a more appropriate object: the reader. Gill evades symbolic castration. "The sentence stands," the father says, saving the writer's pen(is).

POLITICAL CRITICISM

Political criticism starts from the idea that the study of literature is not part of some ivory tower of learning, withdrawn from the real world. Rather, literary criticism is inevitably involved in politics—in shaping our understanding of the culture we inhabit and the role that literature (including all sorts of texts) plays in altering or reinforcing values and beliefs. Even when literary critics argue that literary study should avoid political issues, focusing instead on the literature itself, they are taking a political position, as politically alert critics would say.

Political criticism can proceed from any number of positions—liberal, conservative, moderate; free-market capitalist, socialist, communist. The idea is simply that the reader brings a certain political stance to the text. Perhaps it can be argued that the text supports or opposes this political stance, or there is evidence that the author supported or opposed this stance, or the text somehow illuminates or obscures or otherwise influences our understanding of this political stance. Clearly, the most successful avowedly political criticism has been feminist criticism, which has transformed the study of literature in the modern era by bringing attention to how gender and sexuality are represented. Feminist criticism has led to masculine studies, queer theory, gay and lesbian criticism, and a striking number of influential studies. But Marxist criticism, African-American studies, Chicano studies, and Native American studies have also made significant contributions by foregrounding political concerns.

Any political orientation can drive a reading. Although the idea of left-handed criticism may seem silly, many cultures stigmatize left-handedness. "Right" means "correct" as well as the opposite of "left," while "left" in Latin is "sinister," which has come to mean "evil"; the Irish word *ciotag*, used for left-handed people, also means "a very strange person"; the Portuguese word for a left-handed person, *canhoto*, also referred to the devil at one time, and *canhestro* means "clumsy"; in Mandarin, the word for "left" also means "improper." In Norwegian, saying that something is left-handed work means that it was done poorly. Left-handed criticism, so far as I know, doesn't exist, but it could if readers were to identify representations of left-handedness, or other textual evidence that would illuminate how we see people who use the wrong hand (so to speak!).

In this text, I've elected to focus on feminist criticism to illustrate political approaches, while glancing at a few other political strategies. If you understand how to use feminist criticism, then you can easily make use of other political stances—if you understand the politics. If you don't know anything about Marxism or Native American issues, then of course you are unlikely to be able to make much use of these orientations.

Feminist criticism generally assumes, like reader-response criticism, that a literary work is shaped by our reading of it, and this reading is influenced by our own status, which includes significantly gender, or our attitude toward gender. But, as feminists point out, since the production and reception of literature have been controlled largely by men, the role of gender in reading and writing has been slighted. The interests and achievements of half the human race have been neglected—or appreciated largely from only one sex's point of view.

You don't have to consider yourself a feminist to benefit from feminist criticism. Simply taking gender into account, regardless of your social and political views, is likely to open your eyes to important works, authors, and issues you would have missed otherwise.

Although it is difficult to generalize, given the diversity and development of feminist criticism in recent decades, particularly as post-feminism and queer theory have challenged the very terms of gender and sexuality, there are still some basic strategies you can adopt. You'll want to consider the significance of the gender of the author and the characters. You'll want to observe how sexual stereotypes might be reinforced or undermined in the work. How does the work reflect or alter or complicate the place (or the construction) of women (and men) in society? Perhaps most powerful, imagine yourself reading the work as a woman. If you happen to be female, this last suggestion may seem easy enough; but feminist critics point out that women have long been taught to read like men or to ignore their own gender. And post-feminist critics have challenged the idea that there is some particular thing that "as a woman" refers to. So, reading as a woman, even if you are a woman, may be easier said than done.

I developed the following feminist reading of Gill's passage simply by noticing references to gender and paying attention to any potential stereotypes.

A Feminist Reading of the Gill Passage

We know not all the writers at *The New Yorker* were men, even during the period Brendan Gill discusses in this passage from *Here at "The New Yorker."* When he speaks of "some writer who has made a name for himself in the world," and about the editorial "machinery" that besets "him," Gill is of course referring to writers in the generic sense. One may still assert today, although with less assurance than in 1975, that "himself" and "him" in this passage include "herself" and "her."

Such a claim, that one sexual marker includes its opposite, may seem absurd—as if "white" included "black" or "communist" included "democratic." But the motivations for such a claim are suggested even in this brief passage, for Gill's story not only contains this obvious bias in pronouns, still accepted by some editors and writers; the story also conveys more subtle messages about sexuality and sexual roles.

For example, Miss Gould functions as a familiar stereotype: the finicky spinster, a Grammar Granny, who has devoted her life to "English grammar" and its enforcement. She is a copy editor, subservient to the male editor and writer, and her lack of imagination and taste, as Gill presents it, seem to testify to the wisdom of this power structure.

This division of labor—male/creative, female/menial—is subtly reinforced by the reference to the "hen-tracks" that cover the writer's galley. Petty correction is the realm of the hen, the feminine. But these "hen-tracks" (they could not be rooster tracks) are more than aggravating correction; they come to threaten the writer's very identity. In attempting to produce "his copy," the writer is in a sense attempting to reproduce himself. The "glory of creation" is his literary procreation, and thus Miss Gould's effort to remove a particular sentence is a symbolic threat to cut off some more essential part of the writer. It is, after all, a "dangling modifier" that she has located; and this dangling structure is in danger of being fed to the "yawning pit," symbolic of the feminine editing and its excising dangers. Thus, men should fear women, the passage suggests. Do not give women power.

Because Gill's initial image for the writer starting out at the magazine, the dolphin in the sea, derives some of its power from the well-established association of the ocean and the womb, the images of the "yawning" pit, not to mention the poisonous "mother's milk," become more telling. Even the error itself is subtly connected to the feminine, for the problem with the sentence is that part of it has "assumed the female gender." That part, in the context of nagging copy editors who chop up one's prose, can only be a "complaint."

The nonagenarian's complaint itself seems significant: in the mode of feminine busybodies like Miss Gould, she laments not having "enough work to do." Miss Gould, similarly overzealous, has herself done more work than is reasonable, and Botsford's pronouncement that "The sentence stands" returns her to her place, negating her feminine fussiness.

OTHER APPROACHES

The feminist reading above does include some interest in money, class, and power, but these features could conceivably be brought to the forefront. Criticism that focuses on the economic and class structures involved in literature is sometimes called "Marxist" criticism, even if the critic does not endorse Marxism. Historical criticism might also be particularly attuned to representations of class and power.

If I were to add another chapter to this book, it might for example deal with ethical and religious criticism. These interests are arguably not prominent at the moment in literary studies, or they are embedded in other approaches, and so I have resisted enlarging what is supposed to be a brief introduction. But a critic interested in religious issues might wonder if the reference to "this tiny elect" in Gill's passage signals the importance of religious values or their trivialization. Likewise, what does the reference to "oh, Christ!" tell us? Is Botsford a Christ figure, forgiving Gill for his sins? Indeed, is there a religious backdrop that makes this passage meaningful?

Certainly another chapter could be devoted to African-American criticism. Using that stance to think about this passage might start from the question of the role that race plays in it and indeed at *The New Yorker* of the time. At first glance, one might respond that race plays no discernible part in the passage. And that might be in fact quite to the point. Do any *New Yorker* advertisements from the 1970s feature African Americans? Do we assume that any of the characters in Gill's tale are or even might be black? What difference does our assumption make? In this respect, one might suggest, the passage reads *us,* perhaps showing us some of our racially motivated assumptions. If you were to do a reader-response criticism of the passage, would your racial or ethnic status play any part in your reading?

In an ideal world, an introduction to writing about literature would include every identifiable approach. The goal of this introduction is necessarily more limited: using a sampling of the most visible approaches, it aims to show you how theory shapes practice—how assumptions stimulate and guide the process of developing critical essays. This goal is still an ambitious one but well worth your effort, providing a powerful passport to the various ways meaning is made, preparing you for these and other kinds of literary excursions. For the goal here is not an understanding of the maps and the travel guides and the stories that other travelers have told. It is of course your own rich and stimulating engagement with literature.

Works Cited

Gill, Brendan. *Here at "The New Yorker."* New York: Random House, 1975.
————. *A New York Life.* New York: Poseidon, 1990.

Recommended Further Reading: Critical Worlds

Barry, Peter. *Beginning Theory: An Introduction to Literary and Cultural Theory.* 2nd ed. Manchester: Manchester UP, 2002. A lively and genuinely useful introduction, including good questions and exercises for students.

Bressler, Charles. *Literary Criticism: An Introduction to Theory and Practice.* 4th ed. Upper Saddle River, NJ: Prentice-Hall, 2006. An excellent advanced introduction, including a nice historical survey of criticism, a chapter on "Cultural Studies," information on websites, and sample essays and excerpts from students and professionals.

Carpenter, Scott. *Reading Lessons: An Introduction to Theory.* Upper Saddle River, NJ: Prentice-Hall, 2000. This is "not a how-to manual," Carpenter says, refusing to "present recipes for producing" different kinds of criticism. He does, however, provide an often entertaining overview that includes website resources and films.

Eagleton, Terry. *Literary Theory: An Introduction.* 2nd ed. Minneapolis: U of Minnesota, 1996. Witty and opinionated, the first introduction to theory. For advanced students.

Liu, Alan, ed. *Voice of the Shuttle Website on Literary Theory.* http://vos.uscb. edu/shuttle/english.html. This website contains pages introducing various topics—hypertext fiction, cyberculture, gender studies, deconstruction, etc. Also a good portal to other electronic resources.

Remnick, David. "Miss Gould." *New Yorker,* February 28, 2005. A lovely elegy for Miss Gould, who died the week before this issue at the age of 87. This essay can be accessed on the *New Yorker*'s website.

Selden, Raman, Peter Widdowson, and Peter Brocker. *A Reader's Guide to Contemporary Literary Theory.* 5th ed. New York: Prentice-Hall, 2005. Detailed and authoritative introductions to ten theories, including "Russian Formalism," "Marxist Theories," "Postcolonialist Theories," and "Gay, Lesbian and Queer Theories."

Sim, Stuart, and Borin Van Loon. *Introducing Critical Theory.* Cambridge: Totem, 2002. This advanced introduction is especially user-friendly, employing a comic-book style and an irreverent sense of humor.

Webster, Roger. *Studying Literary Theory: An Introduction.* 2nd ed. London: Arnold, 1998. An elegant and concise (138 pages) overview.

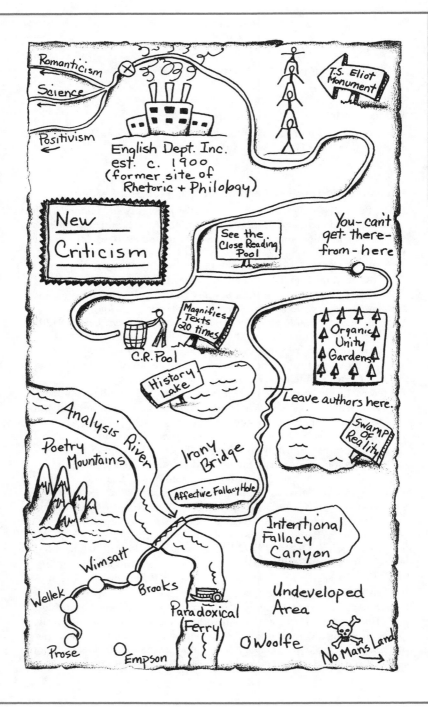

Unifying the Work

New Criticism

> The study of literature means the
> study of literature, not of
> biography nor of literary history
> (incidentally of vast importance),
> not of grammar, not of etymology,
> not of anything except the works
> themselves, viewed as their
> creators wrote them, viewed as
> art, as transcripts of humanity—
> not as logic, not as psychology,
> not as ethics.
>
> —Martin Wright Sampson

THE PURPOSE OF NEW CRITICISM

For much of the previous century, "traditional" criticism was in
large part synonymous with what has become known as "New
Criticism." This way of looking at literature began to emerge clearly
in the 1920s and dominated literary criticism from the late 1930s
into the 1960s. In 1941, John Crowe Ransom's *The New Criticism*
gave this movement its name (even though the point of Ransom's
book, ironically, is that *the* New Critic had not appeared). Its effects
continue even to the present day, when it might better be called
"the old New Criticism." Although those who have been called
"New Critics" have not agreed in every respect, and some have even

rejected the title, it is possible to identify a number of fundamental assumptions shared by an enormous number of critics and teachers and their students. The odds, in fact, are excellent that some of your English teachers were trained in the methods of New Criticism, even if they never heard the term; and in surprisingly many classrooms today, even in the midst of a cornucopia of critical options, New Criticism is often essentially the only approach on the menu, its principles so pervasive that they seem natural and obvious—and therefore remain, often enough, unarticulated.

Basic Principles Reflected

One way to get at these principles, and begin to see why they have remained so appealing, might be to look at a famous poem written about the time that New Criticism was emerging as a critical force. This poem is of particular interest because it is about poetry, attempting to define it, advising us how to view it. Thus it seeks to provide a kind of guide for criticism: "Here is what poetry ought to be," the poem says; "read it with these standards in mind." Widely anthologized in introduction-to-literature texts since its appearance, the poem not only reflects the ideas of a nascent New Criticism, but it also probably helped to promote those ideas over several generations. Read it through carefully a few times, noting any questions or confusions that arise. It will be discussed in detail below.

Ars Poetica
Archibald MacLeish

A poem should be palpable and mute
As a globed fruit,

Dumb
As old medallions to the thumb,

Silent as the sleeve-worn stone   5
Of casement ledges where the moss has grown—

A poem should be wordless
As the flight of birds.

A poem should be motionless in time
As the moon climbs,   10

Leaving, as the moon releases
Twig by twig the night-entangled trees,

Leaving, as the moon behind the winter leaves,
Memory by memory the mind—

A poem should be motionless in time   15
As the moon climbs.

A poem should be equal to:
Not true.
For all the history of grief
An empty doorway and a maple leaf.   20

For love
The leaning grasses and two lights above the sea—

A poem should not mean
But be.

                                                    (1926)

The poem is startling from its opening lines, asserting that a poem should be "palpable and mute." How can a poem possibly be "palpable," or "capable of being handled, touched, or felt" (*American Heritage Dictionary*)? Whether we think of a poem as an idea, or a group of ideas, or the writing on a piece of paper, or a group of spoken words, none of these seems to be the sort of thing we can handle. And how can a poem be "mute"? Isn't a poem made of words? Don't we at least imagine a voice speaking the words? Suggesting that a poem be mute seems a bit like suggesting that a movie be invisible, or a song be inaudible, or a sculpture be without shape.

But MacLeish reiterates these ideas in subsequent lines, saying explicitly that a poem should be "Dumb," "Silent," and (most amazingly) "wordless" (lines 3, 5, and 7). He uses comparisons that reinforce particularly the idea of being "palpable." In comparing the poem to a "fruit," for instance, MacLeish suggests that the poem should be a real thing, having substance. The idea that it should be "globed" (a "globed fruit") emphasizes the three-dimensionality that MacLeish desires: Like a globe, the poem should have more extension in time and space than a map or a picture. Not just a depiction of a fruit, it should *be* a *globed* fruit. Likewise, "old medallions to the thumb" and "the sleeve-worn stone / Of casement ledges where the moss has grown" are both not only "silent" or "dumb," but they also have an enduring solidity, a tangible reality. These images of fruit, old medallions, and worn ledges may also seem a bit mysterious, like "the flight of birds" (line 8), which in some "wordless," seemingly magical way is organized and orchestrated—as anyone knows who's ever seen a flock of birds rise together and move as one, silently.

From lines 1–8, then, we draw our first principle of New Criticism:

☞ 1. A poem should be seen as an object—an object of an extraordinary and somewhat mysterious kind, a silent object that is not equal to the words printed on a page.

Lines 9–16 articulate another idea: "A poem should be motionless in time." This idea seems easy enough to understand: MacLeish believes that poems shouldn't change. Aren't Shakespeare's sonnets the same today as they were when he wrote them? ("So long as men can breathe or eyes can see, / So long lives this, and this gives life to thee," as Sonnet 18 says.) But MacLeish's comparison, "As the moon climbs," is not so easy to grasp: how can the moon be "climbing" through the sky, yet be "motionless in time"? Perhaps the answer lies in the repeated idea that the moon, like the poem, should be "Leaving, as the moon releases / Twig by twig the night-entangled trees" (11–12); it should be "Leaving, as the moon behind the winter leaves / Memory by memory the mind" (13–14). Something that is "leaving" is neither fully here nor fully gone; it is caught in time and space, in an in-between contradictory timespace. We do not notice a memory deteriorating: it is there, unchanging; then it is only partly there; then it may be gone. The moon climbing in the sky does seem like this: it appears to sit there, motionless in time, yet it is leaving and will "release" the trees. MacLeish repeats lines 9–10 in lines 15–16, as if his own poem is motionless, continuing on but remaining in the same place it was.

This paradox adds to the mystery of the earlier lines and also suggests a second principle:

☞ 2. The poem as silent object is unchanging, existing somehow both within and outside of time, "leaving" yet "motionless."

Lines 17–18 offer a third surprising idea: "A poem should be equal to: / not true." It's difficult to believe that MacLeish is saying that poems should lie. But what is he saying? Lines 19–22 appear to explain his point, but these lines seem particularly difficult. What can these lines possibly mean—ignoring for the moment the concluding assertion of lines 23–24, which seems to be that poems ought not have meanings? The lines are obscure basically because the verbs are missing, so our task of making sense must include imagining what has been left out.

First MacLeish says, "For all the history of grief / An empty doorway and a maple leaf" (19–20). If we look closely at this state-ment, its form is familiar and clear enough: "For X, Y." Or, adding a verb, "For X, substitute Y." Thus, I take these lines to mean sim-ply that instead of recounting "all the history of grief," the poet should present instead "An empty doorway and a maple leaf." An empty doorway can speak to us of someone departed, conveying an emptiness and an absence that may be more compressed and intense than an entire history of grief. A maple leaf, perhaps lying on the ground, bursting with fall colors inevitably turning to brown and crumbling, may tell us something about loss more directly and powerfully and concisely than any history book.

The next two lines are similarly structured: "For love / The leaning grasses and two lights above the sea." That is, "For love," an abstraction, impossible to grasp, the poet should present some-thing concrete: "The leaning grasses and two lights above the sea." Although I can't say precisely how the grasses and lights here stand for love, somehow as images they do seem romantic, mysterious, moving. This principle of selecting something concrete to stand for an abstraction had already been advocated by T. S. Eliot in 1919 in what turned out to be an extremely influential opinion for the formation of New Criticism: "The only way of expressing emo-tion in the form of art," Eliot said, "is by finding an 'objective cor-relative'; in other words, a set of objects, a situation, a chain of events which shall be the formula of that *particular* emotion" (124–125). Not surprisingly, throughout its history New Criticism has been especially concerned with analyzing the imagery of particular works, noticing how a poem's "objective correlatives" structure its ideas.

It is not then that the poem should lie, but rather that it does not strive to tell the truth in any literal or historical or prosaic way. Poetry, MacLeish is saying, should speak metaphorically, substitut-ing evocative images for the description of emotions, or historical details, or vague ideas. Instead of telling us about an idea or emotion, literature confronts us with *something* that may spark emotions or ideas. A poem is an experience, not a discussion of an experience.

The final two lines summarize this point in a startling way: "A poem should not mean / But be." Ordinarily we assume that words are supposed to convey a meaning, transferring ideas from an author to a reader. But the images that MacLeish's poem has given us—the globed fruit, the old medallions, the casement ledges, the flight of birds, the moon climbing, the empty doorway and the maple leaf, the leaning grasses and the two lights—these do not "mean" anything in a literal, historical, scientific way. What is the meaning, for example, of a flight of birds? Of a casement ledge where some moss has grown? These things just *are*. They are suggestive and even moving, but their meaning is something we impose on them; they simply exist, and we experience their being more powerfully than any abstract idea. It would be a mistake to think an empty doorway is somehow a *translation* of all the history of grief.

In much the same way, poems (MacLeish is asserting) do not mean, but rather have an existence—which takes us to the third principle:

☞ 3. Poems as unchanging objects represent an organized entity, not a meaning. In this way, poems are therefore fundamentally different from prose: prose strives to convey meaning; but poems cannot be perfectly translated or summarized, for they offer a being, an existence, an experience perhaps—not a meaning.

Radicals in Tweed Jackets

What was the appeal of these principles? Why did New Criticism, a drastically new way of reading, become so popular on college campuses?

In the landmark study that did much to solidify the academic prestige of the New Criticism, Wellek and Warren's *Theory of Literature* (1949), René Wellek declares, "The work of art is an object of knowledge" (156). Because the literary work has an "objective" status, Wellek says, critical statements about a work are not merely opinions of taste. "It will always be possible," he maintains, "to determine which point of view grasps the subject most thoroughly and deeply." Thus, "all relativism is ultimately defeated" (156).

Although this assumption that the poem exists like an object, like fruit, like medallions, allows New Critics to think of literary criticism as a discipline just as rigorous and prestigious as a science, it is clear that for New Critics poems are, in an important way, also not like the objects studied by science. Poems, as MacLeish puts it, are "motionless in time"; they embody, as Marianne Moore says, "imaginary gardens with real toads in them." Thus, a poem is an entity somehow transcending time, existing in a realm different from that of science, the realm of the literary, of the imagination.

The implications of this second crucial assumption, that poems exist outside of time, can already be seen in the criticism of T. S. Eliot, whose ideas (as we just noted) influenced the New Critics. In "Tradition and the Individual Talent," Eliot's famous essay of 1919, poetry is said to be "not the expression of personality, but an escape from personality" (10). The New Critics are aware of course that poems have authors, and they will sometimes refer to biographical information, but it is not the focus of their attention. Close reading of the work itself should reveal what the reader needs to know. Historical and biographical information, to be sure, may sometimes be helpful, but it should not be essential.

This exclusion of authors and their contexts is taken to what might appear to be its logical extreme in Wimsatt and Beardsley's influential essay on "The Intentional Fallacy." Even when biographical and historical information is meticulously and voluminously gathered, as in the case of Lowe's work on Coleridge and "Kubla Khan," Wimsatt and Beardsley question its value for reading the work. Even Coleridge's own account of how the poem came to him (in a dream, supposedly), Wimsatt and Beardsley say, does not tell us anything about how to read the poem itself—even if we could be sure Coleridge is telling the truth. Only the poem can tell us how to read the poem.

By the same token, Wimsatt and Beardsley question the importance of the individual reader's response in "The Affective Fallacy." The groundwork for their position had already been worked out in the 1920s by I. A. Richards. Richards conducted a series of close-reading experiments with his students at Cambridge. He began with the assumption that students should be able to read poems richly by applying careful scrutiny to the works themselves. To focus students' attention on the work itself, Richards would often remove the distraction of authors' names, dates, even titles. In 1929, when he reported his results in *Practical Criticism,* two things appeared to be clear.

First, his students seemed not to be very good at reading texts carefully. Richards thought, and many people agreed, that students obviously needed much more training in "close reading." They needed to learn how to look carefully at a text, suppressing their own variable and subjective responses, as Wimsatt and Beardsley would later persuasively argue. How a work affects a particular reader, Wimsatt and Beardsley assert, is not critically significant. Whereas "the Intentional Fallacy," they say, "is a confusion between the poem and its origins," the "Affective Fallacy is a confusion between the poem and its *results*" (21). Biographers may want to speculate on the poet's intention, and psychologists may want to theorize about a poem's effects, but literary critics should study the poem itself.

The second thing made evident by Richards's "experiments" was that such close reading was not only possible but very rewarding, as Richards himself was able to read these isolated works in revealing and stimulating ways, exposing unsuspected complexities and subtleties in the works he examined. Even in the following description of the creative process of poets, taken from Cleanth Brooks and Robert Penn Warren's New Critical textbook, *Understanding Poetry* (1938), the author's intention is of little enduring interest:

> At the same time that he [the poet] is trying to envisage the poem as a whole, he is trying to relate the individual items to that whole. He cannot assemble them in a merely arbitrary fashion; they must bear some relation to each other. So he develops his sense of the whole, the anticipation of the finished poem, as he works with the parts, and moves from one part to another. Then as the sense of the whole develops, it modifies the process by which the poet selects and relates the parts, the words, images, rhythms, local ideas, events, etc. . . . It is an infinitely complicated process of establishing interrelations. (527)

Implicit in this description of how a poet works are the directions for what a critic should do: most obviously, the critic will want to recover the idea, or principle, or theme, that holds the poem's parts together and thereby reveal how the parts relate to each other and to the whole. (Such a careful unfolding of the poem's parts and their relationships is often called an "explication.") Although speculation about the poet's actual process of creating the poem may be entertaining, it is finally irrelevant, for the critic's real interest is in the finished poem, not how it was finished. We can tell what the poet was working toward, the poem as a whole, the "interrelations" of its parts, simply by looking carefully at the shape and structure of the poem—at its form, in other words.

This emphasis on a work's form has led some thinkers to link New Criticism to another movement, Russian formalism, which originated with the work of Viktor Shklovsky in 1917—about the same time that New Criticism's ideas first began to emerge in Western Europe and North America. The Russian formalists do seem to prefigure the New Criticism when they assume that a writer should be evaluated as a craftsman who fashions an artistic object. The writer should *not* be evaluated, New Critics and Russian formalists would agree, on the basis of the work's message. *Paradise Lost* is a great poem (or it isn't) because of Milton's artistic performance, not because of the validity of its theological or political message. Russian formalism (not too surprisingly) was rather short-lived, fading away by the late 1920s, discouraged by the Russian authorities, who no doubt noted that focusing on style and technique would tend to let all sorts of ideas float around.

Although New Criticism has been criticized at times for its lack of political commitment, one could argue (especially in light of Russian formalism's fate) that an attention to form (not message) is in fact a subtly powerful commitment to openness and freedom: you can say whatever you like, New Criticism implicitly suggests, as long as you say it well. Admittedly, in celebrating a certain kind of form (unified complexity), New Criticism has perhaps not been so entirely open in its actual practice, as feminist critics have persuasively argued, noticing the predominance of white males in the canon of works valued by New Critics. Is the relative absence of women in the traditional canon of New Criticism really a consequence of its principles? One could argue that women have tended to write in genres that may resist New Criticism's particular kind of close reading (in journals and letters, for instance), but certainly some women (Jane Austen, George Eliot, Emily Dickinson, Virginia Woolf) have produced works celebrated by New Critical readings.

It is clear enough that New Criticism's kind of formalism, which turns away from politics, must take place within some (unacknowledged, invisible) political context, but at the same time it does not seem clear to me that any particular political stance is inherently more or less suited to New Critical strategies. New Criticism discriminates against works that are "poorly made" by its definition—works that are simplistic, single-sided, shallow, inarticulate, lacking in irony and self-consciousness. New Criticism champions works that repay our careful and imaginative attention, works that seem to challenge us to look again, to look more deeply, to find a more complex unity. It might even be said that New Criticism makes it both possible and necessary for other kinds of approaches to arise. At the least, many critics would agree that New Criticism remains a kind of "norm" against which other approaches can be delineated. At its best, it remains an exciting and revealing strategy for unfolding literary works.

HOW TO DO NEW CRITICISM

You may already have a pretty good idea how to apply New Criticism, but to make sure the process is clear in your mind, let's think of it in three steps:

1. What complexities (or tensions, ironies, paradoxes, oppositions, ambiguities) can you find in the work?
2. What idea unifies the work, resolving these ambiguities?
3. What details or images support this resolution (that is, connect the parts to the whole)?

Let's examine each step.

1. The first step assumes that great works are complex, even when they appear to be simple. Literature does not imitate life in any literal way, according to the New Critics; instead, poems (and other works) create concrete realities of their own, transforming and ordering our experience. A poem, as Coleridge says in a quotation often cited by New Critics, is an act of the imagination, "that synthetic and magical power"—an act that "reveals itself in the balance or reconciliation of opposites or discordant qualities" (11). Poems have the power, Coleridge says, "of reducing multitude into unity of effect." And, for the New Critics, the richer and more compelling the "multitude" of ideas or "discordant qualities," the greater the poem's power. The sort of complexity that New Critics particularly value is captured in Keats's concept of

"negative capability," which is also often cited by New Critics: it is the capability "of being in uncertainties, mysteries, doubts, without any irritable reaching after fact and reason" (1:193).

When New Critics identify a poem's complexities (the first step here), they use a number of closely related terms, especially "irony," "ambiguity," "paradox," and "tension." Although these terms mean slightly different things, they all point to the idea of complexity—that the poem says one thing and means another, or says two things at once, or seems to say opposing things, or strains against its apparent meaning. For instance, in "The Language of Paradox," a celebrated essay from *The Well-Wrought Urn* (1947), Cleanth Brooks shows how Donne's famous poem "The Canonization" (included here in an Appendix) sets up a dilemma:

> Either: Donne does not take love seriously; here he is merely sharpening his wit as a sort of mechanical exercise. Or: Donne does not take sainthood seriously; here he is merely indulging in a cynical and bawdy parody. (11)

2. The second step assumes that great works do have a unifying idea, a theme. It's much more useful to think of this theme in terms of a complete thought or a sentence rather than a phrase. For instance, to say that the theme of Donne's "Canonization" is "love and religion" really doesn't tell us much about how Donne solves the dilemma of sainthood versus love. Here's what Brooks tells his readers:

> Neither account [that Donne doesn't take love seriously, or that he doesn't take religion seriously] is true; a reading of the poem will show that Donne takes both love and religion seriously; it will show, further, that the paradox is here his inevitable instrument. (11)

A cynical reader might observe (with some justification) that paradox is Donne's "inevitable" instrument because the New Critics inevitably find something like paradox in every great poem. But Brooks's point, of course, is that paradox is inevitable because Donne, with the imagination of a great poet, sets up the problem in such a way that only paradox will resolve it.

3. The third step unfolds or explicates the poem, indicating how the parts work together. This description of the poem is no substitute for the poem itself, but it should enrich our experience of it.

Oftentimes, as in the case of Brooks's essay on "The Canonization," the critic will move through the work carefully from beginning to end, dividing the work into parts, and then suggesting how every aspect of the parts relates to our sense of the whole. Following Aristotle's ancient ideas, New Critics have talked about the "organic unity" of works, as if the poem were a creature, a living being, with every part playing an essential role.

Here is a sample of Brooks's explication:

> In this last stanza, the theme receives a final complication. The lovers in rejecting life actually win the most intense life. This paradox has been hinted at earlier in the phoenix metaphor. Here it receives a powerful dramatization. (15)

In this passage, notice how Brooks identifies a paradox related to the theme and then connects that paradox to an earlier image. These are both characteristic moves for New Critics.

© Photofest, Inc.

Film and Other Genres

These steps won't read a poem for you; they won't supply the sort of imagination, creativity, and attention you'll need to read literature closely. But they will help to structure your process of reading and writing, and they can in fact be used to help you analyze any kind of literary work or artistic object, or perhaps anything. Consider for example this concluding paragraph from Michael Atkinson's review of *Napoleon Dynamite*, a bizarre, award-winning film released in 2004 (to understand the paragraph, you should know that Jared Hess is the film's director, and Jon Heder plays Napoleon; also, Atkinson refers in this passage to a Todd Solondz film, *Welcome to the Dollhouse*, that offers a darker view of teen-age angst):

> But the center of Hess's cyclone is Heder and his tetherball-playing monster teen, who is both the film's forbidding hero and its great object of derision. Unlike the Solondz film, *Napoleon Dynamite* exudes little sense of social horror; it struggles to maintain a sunny disposition despite the traumatic social meltdown we witness and the apparent fact that Napoleon is headed not for a tech college but for a long, dire career in food service. He's all too emblematic of too many Americans, and if Hess's movie weren't so funny, it'd be a tragedy.

Even without seeing this movie, or reading the rest of the review, you can see the assumptions that are driving Atkinson's analysis. In the first sentence, Napoleon, played by Heder, is paradoxically both "hero" and "object of derision." The adjective that modifies "hero" is "forbidding," while the adjective that modifies "object of derision" is "great," and this pulling in opposite directions also occurs in the description of Napoleon as a "tetherball-playing monster teen": tetherball is an elementary school game, played by children during recess—not at all what one associates with a "monster teen." The second sentence also celebrates the film's balancing of oppositions, maintaining "a sunny disposition despite the traumatic social meltdown we witness" and Napoleon's apparently dim future. The third and final sentence continues to see the film in paradoxical terms, as Napoleon's weirdness is somehow also "all too emblematic of too many Americans." As an earlier sentence puts it, Napoleon "is such a fantastic creation you can't help seeing him as both a catastrophically extreme case and the common flailing nerd we all still shelter in our deepest memory banks." This kind of both/and vision, unifying oppositions, extends even to the genre of the film, as Atkinson's conclusion asserts that the film is a comedy that would have been a tragedy, if it "weren't so funny."

Clearly Atkinson, like a New Critic, is noticing and valuing paradoxes, ironies, and tensions. Moreover, Atkinson sees how these oppositions are held together: The movie is dismal yet ultimately "sunny," a tragedy that is really a comedy; Napoleon is both heroic and ridiculous, "catastrophically extreme" and everyman. This idea, in fact, is arguably what unifies the film for Atkinson— that at some deeper level, we are like Napoleon. His absurdity is what sets him apart, and at the same what makes him part of us. We laugh at Napoleon but he is constructed in such a way that we are also laughing at some core aspect of ourselves. Although Atkinson is obviously interested in how audiences respond to the film, he tends to view the movie as an artistic object, rather than an experience. He sees the character of Napoleon, for instance, as a coherent thing, "a perfectly conceived and executed battery of melodramatic harrumphs, bruised exhalations, defensive squints, clueless pronouncements, and explosively irate retorts." And the movie as a whole succeeds because its complex ironies and paradoxes are held together in a satisfying unity. Although I seriously doubt that Atkinson considers himself to be a card-carrying New Critic, his assumptions and values are in line with New Criticism— which isn't surprising, when we consider its pervasive popularity over the past century.

This brief look at a movie review suggests how we might reason backward from a finished essay to the strategies employed. To give you a better idea of how to use these principles, let's now work through the process of writing a sample New Critical essay in the next section.

THE WRITING PROCESS: A SAMPLE ESSAY

Literary works are often charming, uplifting, amusing; but they are also often troubling and challenging, confronting difficult and disturbing issues, stimulating our thought. The following poem will probably haunt you. It is a powerful and moving engagement with one of the most controversial and emotional topics of our day. Read it carefully, writing down any questions or comments that occur, looking particularly for tensions or oppositions or ambiguities.

The Mother

Gwendolyn Brooks

Abortions will not let you forget.
You remember the children you got that you did not get,
The damp small pulps with a little or no hair,
The singers and workers that never handled the air.
You will never neglect or beat   5
Them, or silence or buy with a sweet.
You will never wind up the sucking-thumb
Or scuttle off ghosts that come.
You will never leave them, controlling your luscious sigh,
Return for a snack of them, with gobbling mother eye.   10

I have heard in the voices of the wind the voices of my dim
        killed children.
I have contracted. I have eased
My dim dears at the breasts they could never suck.
I have said, Sweets, if I sinned, if I seized
Your luck   15
And your lives from your unfinished reach,
If I stole your births and your names,
Your straight baby tears and your games,
Your stilted or lovely loves, your tumults, your marriages,
        aches and your deaths,
If I poisoned the beginnings of your breaths,   20
Believe that even in my deliberateness I was not deliberate.
Though why should I whine,
Whine that the crime was other than mine?—
Since anyhow you are dead.
Or rather, or instead,   25
You were never made.
But that too, I am afraid,
Is faulty: of, what shall I say, how is the truth to be said?
You were born, you had body, you died.
It is just that you never giggled or planned or cried.   30

Believe me, I loved you all.
Believe me, I knew you, though faintly, and I loved, I
        loved you
All.

(1945)

Preparing to Write

Compare what you've written in your brainstorming to the following list of observations:

(a) The speaker says "Abortions will not let you forget," as if abortions could actively do something. I know what the speaker means, but an abortion is a medical procedure; it can't make *"you"* remember or keep *"you"* from forgetting. Assuming that this phrasing is significant, why doesn't the speaker just say "You can't forget about your abortion"? This question raises another one: why does the speaker say "you" rather than "me," especially since the second section reveals that she has had abortions?

(b) The second line is contradictory, referring to children "you got that you did not get"? Either you got them or you didn't, it would seem.

(c) Why is the poem called "The Mother" if she has had abortions? Does this refer to her other children or to the abortions? This is probably an important tension: it is, after all, the title.

(d) Lines 3 and 4 offer conflicting views. In line 3 "the children" are simply "damp small pulps with a little or with no hair." A "pulp" isn't alive, isn't a person, so removing a hairless (or nearly hairless) pulp isn't a big deal. But line 4 refers to the abortions in a strikingly different way, as "singers and workers that never handled the air." As singers and workers, the children are real, and their loss is tragic: they did not even get a chance to handle the air—which is a wonderful and surprising description of living. We are all, as singers and workers, handling the air.

(e) Another opposition shapes the next few lines. Lines 5–6 suggest that the abortions were in some respects a good thing: "You will never neglect or beat / Them." The next image, never "silence or buy with a sweet," is perhaps faintly negative or even neutral: it doesn't sound good to think of silencing or buying children, and giving them "a sweet" probably isn't the greatest thing to do, but every parent resorts to such strategies. And the next image moves into the realm of tenderness: to "wind up the sucking-thumb" or "scuttle off ghosts that come"—these are acts of kindness. So the lines move from abuse, which places the abortions in a more positive light, to parental care, which makes the abortions seem more tragic.

(f) I notice that the speaker seems to be talking about more than one abortion. But the pain revealed in the poem won't let us easily conclude that the speaker is callous, readily aborting babies without a thought.

(g) The idea of eating up the children in line 10 is strange ("a snack of them, with gobbling mother eye").

It's fine if your ideas aren't similar to those above. In fact, it's great because we'd certainly be bored if everyone thought the same things. But you may find it useful to notice the level of detail involved above and the kind of attention being paid. This kind of preparation will make writing about the poem much easier.

As you think about the poem, putting your ideas on paper, you might reasonably wonder how much you need to know about 1945, when the poem was published; about the history of the debate over abortion; about Gwendolyn Brooks's life; about her career as a poet and about her other poems; and on and on. All these things would be good to know, but you could end up spending a semester on this poem. Further, adopting a New Critical stance, you will assume that the poem itself will reveal whatever it is essential for you to know.

Of course, once you decide to limit your attention to the poem itself as an object, you need some principles to guide your reading. It isn't really that helpful just to say, "Concentrate on the poem itself and read it closely." So, remind yourself specifically what a New Critical reading attempts to expose: unity and complexity. Great works confront us with a unified ambiguity; second-rate works see things simply or fragmentarily.

Shaping

What would you say is the unifying idea of "The Mother"? What holds it together? Those questions are crucial to a New Critical reading because they lead to your thesis, which will shape and control the development of your essay. Even in the few notes I've reproduced above here, it seems clear that the title points us toward the poem's complexity: the speaker, as the title identifies her, is "The Mother," and yet she speaks only of the children she does not have, the children who have been aborted. So how can she be a mother without any children? How can she love her children, or have destroyed them, if they don't exist? That, it seems to me, is one way of saying what the poem struggles through. The theme or unifying idea, holding together the ambiguous status of the speaker, can be stated in any number of ways, and you might try out your own way of expressing it. Here's one way to put it:

Although her children do not exist, and may have never existed, the speaker is a mother because she loves her "children."

In articulating this theme, I've given emphasis to the way the poem ends. Generally that's where the oppositions are resolved. In this case, I would argue, the ambiguity between the speaker as mother and nonmother is resolved at the end of the poem with her declaration of love. She could not love the children if they did not have some kind of existence, and if they exist in some way, then she is some kind of "mother." But her status is by no means simple. Likewise, she "knew" them, she says, even if it was "faintly"; and, again, it would seem she could not know them if they did not exist, if they were not her children.

The strategy of a New Critical reading, then, would involve showing how the details of the poem support and elaborate this complex or ironic unity. Your structure involves arranging this evidence in a coherent way, grouping kinds of details perhaps or moving logically through the poem. That is, throughout the poem, a New Critical reading would find oppositions reinforcing and supporting in some way the poem's central ambiguity. For instance, line 21 would be seen as a reflection of the central opposition. The speaker says, "even in my deliberateness I was not deliberate." Just as the children who are aborted are not children; just as the woman who gives up her motherhood by having an abortion nonetheless retains her claim to the name of "mother"; by the same token, the speaker's "deliberateness is not deliberate."

In other words, her decision to have the abortion was made with "deliberateness," and for such decisions we are more accountable, by some measures anyway, than for impulsive decisions. Premeditated murder, for instance, is in theory a more serious crime than a spontaneous crime of passion. But the mother's culpability is qualified by the rest of the sentence, which says that the deliberateness was not "deliberate." She carefully decided something she did not carefully decide, so it seems.

Drafting

After you've worked your way through the poem, noting oppositions, tensions, ambiguities, paradoxes, and considering how these relate to the poem's unity, then it's time for a draft. Here is a first draft developed out of the annotations above; it's been polished up a bit, and there are annotations in the margin to help you see what is going on.

The Mother Without Children: A Reading of Gwendolyn Brooks's "The Mother"

From (c) in the notes: this tension seemed to unify the poem.

The intro has set up the essay's form: mother vs. not-mother.

This paragraph elaborates on the two possibilities: children or not.

The two possibilities come together in the uncertainty.

This explains how the uncertainty comforts the mother.

This point began to emerge in (f): the mother's pain suggests her love, which is explicitly declared later on.

Gwendolyn Brooks's "The Mother" points to a paradox with its first word, "Abortions." Although the speaker is called "the mother" in the title, she quickly reveals that "the children" have actually been aborted. How can she be a mother if her children never existed? Her opening line asserts that "Abortions will not let you forget," but what is there for her to remember? The rest of the poem shows the "mother's" struggle with this problem: how to remember "the children that you did not get" (2).

On the one hand, the speaker realizes the children are nothing more than "damp small pulps with a little or with no hair" (3), but the rest of this sentence sees them as "singers and workers that never handled the air" (4). If they can be called "singers and workers," then they must have some existence. But if they never "handled the air," they did not work and sing, and so their status as workers and singers is problematic, to say the least. This question is what is distressing the "mother," because if these fetuses were children, then her statement in line 17 is accurate: "I stole your births and your names." But the line begins with an "If," and it is this uncertainty that provides the speaker with some comfort.

The comfort takes two forms. The mother first eases her pain by pointing to the uncertainty of her decision to have the abortions: "even in my deliberations I was not deliberate" (21). Since she is uncertain about the status of what is being aborted, she decided without knowing what she was deciding. In truth, she still does not know what her decision means: no one can say with authority when life begins, or when fetuses become persons and when they are still unviable tissue masses, or "pulps" (3).

More importantly, the speaker is also comforted in the end by declaring her love, even though this expression paradoxically sustains her pain and mourning. She

<table>
<tr><td>

Still relying on
the opposition:
mother/not;
children/not.

From (a) above.

Resolving the
problem set up
in the intro.

</td><td>

clings to the idea of her "dim killed children" (11),
refusing to let them become "pulps," because she can
love them only if they actually existed. So she must say
that she "knew" them, even while admitting it was
only "faintly" (32). She does claim her status as "the
mother," as the title says, even though it causes her
pain. As she says in the opening line, "Abortions
will not let you forget," but perhaps only if you
continue to see yourself as a mother, even though
you have no children. Thus, the poem balances the
speaker's two visions of herself, as murderer
and as mother; and it resolves this conflict in the
final lines, as the mother is able to atone for her
decision, in some measure, by suffering with her
memory always, saying "I loved you, I loved
you / All" (32–33).

</td></tr>
</table>

In the preceding essay I obviously didn't explicate every detail that supports my thesis. Rather, I tried to bring forth enough evidence to be persuasive. How much evidence you need to present to make a close reading convincing will vary depending on the work and your thesis. Follow your common sense and the guidance of your teacher.

Finally, as you apply New Criticism on your own, notice how two factors helped the sample essay develop smoothly.

1. Thorough preparation. The essay, for the most part, arranges and connects the extensive notes on the poem. When I came to write my essay, I had already written a great deal. I had much more material than I could use in my essay, and so I was able to pick and choose which ideas to use. This process, of selecting from an abundance of ideas, is a whole lot more pleasant than struggling for something to say.

2. Theoretical awareness. Since I knew what kind of approach I wanted to take, I knew to look for certain things in the poem: ideas or images in opposition; complexity or ambiguity; the unifying idea or theme. Likewise, I knew what my essay was going to set out to do. I didn't have to worry about whether Brooks might have intended to say this or that, nor did I have to worry about my own attitude toward abortion or even my own reaction to the poem. My job was to focus on the text itself, exposing its complexity and unity. By being aware of the theoretical stance you are

evolving or adopting, you clarify for yourself what you're doing and how to do it.

PRACTICING NEW CRITICISM

It's highly unlikely that one example will make New Criticism crystal clear for you. You'll need to practice it for yourself, see other examples, and (ideally) discuss its workings with your teacher and classmates.

To get you started, I offer here three poems and some sample questions.

forgiving my father
Lucille Clifton

it is friday. we have come
to the paying of the bills.
all week you have stood in my dreams
like a ghost, asking for more time
but today is payday, payday old man,   5
my mother's hand opens in her early grave
and i hold it out like a good daughter.

there is no more time for you. there will
never be time enough daddy daddy old lecher
old liar. i wish you were rich so i could take it all   10
and give the lady what she was due
but you were the son of a needy father,
the father of a needy son,
you gave her all you had
which was nothing. you have already given her   15
all you had.

you are the pocket that was going to open
and come up empty any friday.
you were each other's bad bargain, not mine.
daddy old pauper old prisoner, old dead man   20
what am i doing here collecting?
you lie side by side in debtor's boxes
and no accounting will open them up.

(1969)

QUESTIONS

1. How does the title relate to the poem? (That is, how is the title at odds with what the poem says?) List the statements in the poem that do not sound "forgiving."
2. What is the significance of "collecting" in line 21? How is this word like "accounting" and "open" in line 23? In what sense is the speaker "collecting"?
3. What reasons does the poem offer for forgiving the father?
4. How is the poem's conflict resolved? Is the phrase "forgiving a debt" relevant to this poem?
5. How would you state the theme of this poem in one sentence? (Try a two-part sentence: "Although x, y.")

My Father's Martial Art
Stephen Shu-ning Liu

When he came home Mother said he looked
like a monk and stank of green fungus.
At the fireside he told us about life
at the monastery: his rock pillow,
his cold bath, his steel-bar lifting   5
and his wood-chopping. He didn't see
a woman for three winters, on Mountain O Mei.

"My Master was both light and heavy.
He skipped over treetops like a squirrel.
Once he stood on a chair, one foot tied   10
to a rope. We four pulled; we couldn't
move him a bit. His kicks could split
a cedar's trunk."

I saw Father break into a pumpkin
with his fingers. I saw him drop a hawk   15
with bamboo arrows. He rose before dawn, filled
our backyard with a harsh sound *hah, hah, hah:*
there was his Black Dragon Sweep, his Crane Stand,
his Mantis Walk, his Tiger Leap, his Cobra Coil. . .
Infrequently he taught me tricks and made me   20
fight the best of all the village boys.

From a busy street I brood over high cliffs
on O Mei, where my father and his Master sit:

shadows spread across their faces as the smog
between us deepens into a funeral pyre.   25

But don't retreat into night, my father.
Come down from the cliffs. Come

with a single Black Dragon Sweep and hush
this oncoming traffic with your *hah, hah, hah.*

(1982)

QUESTIONS

1. Where is the poem's speaker located? How does this location relate to what he remembers?

2. What has happened to his father? What does line 25 suggest? Why does it seem especially appropriate that the "smog" comes between them?

3. What do you make of the name of the mountain? What might the oncoming traffic symbolize?

4. In each of the following pairs, which quality is embodied in the poem?

   Closeness, distance

   Presence, absence

   Power, impotence

   Light, heavy

   Spiritual, mundane

5. Do you think the word "Infrequently" in line 20 is significant? How does it contribute to the poem? (Does it simplify things? Make them more complex?)

6. What is the speaker struggling against in the poem? How is the struggle resolved? How is the resolution ambiguous and complex?

On My First Son

Ben Jonson

Farewell, thou child of my right hand, and joy;
    My sin was too much hope of thee, lov'd boy.
Seven years thou wert lent to me, and I thee pay,
    Exacted by thy fate, on the just day.

Oh, could I lose all father now! For why   5
    Will man lament the state he should envy?

escaped   To have so soon 'scaped world's and flesh's rage,
    And if no other misery, yet age!
Rest in soft peace, and, asked, say, Here doth lie
    Ben. Jonson his best piece of poetry.   10
For whose sake henceforth all his vows be such
    As what he loves may never like too much.

(1616)

QUESTIONS

1. Ben Jonson's son was named "Benjamin," a Hebrew name that translates into English as the "child of the right hand." How does this fact help you to make sense of the poem? What does the first line tell us about the person who is being addressed in the poem? And what do you think New Critics mean when they say that we should focus upon the poem itself? (Is the significance of the child's name "in" this poem?)

2. What is the role of Jonson's religious faith in this poem? How is it a source of both comfort and tension?

3. In two places in the poem, Jonson points to "too much" of an emotion, creating an opposition between hope and love in the second line, and between loving and liking in the final line. How does this opposition contribute to the poem's unifying idea? (What, in other words, is the poem's unifying idea? Hint: what is the problem that Jonson is trying to solve in this poem? See lines 5 and 6.)

4. Explain how our understanding of lines 9 and 10 changes as we continue to read. That is, what do readers think when we read "Here doth liecu/Ben. Johnson"? And what do we think as we finish this sentence? What does this shift in reference contribute to the poem? Does New Criticism value this kind of complexity?

5. In the sciences, ambiguity is usually considered undesirable. New Criticism, emerging as part of an alternate culture to the sciences, generally celebrates ambiguity and multiplicity of meaning. In line 11, "For whose sake" seems to have at least three possible references: Benjamin Jonson (the son), Ben Jonson, Jonson's poetry. Is this ambiguity fruitful? Can it be convincingly resolved?

Useful Terms for New Criticism

Let's review briefly the terms introduced in this section:

Voice: The voice is what we don't actually hear, but must imagine that we hear in order to read poetry effectively. In fiction, we are usually given information about who is speaking. In drama, when it is performed anyway, we can actually see and hear the characters speaking. But in poetry, the reader often has to invent the voice out of clues in the work. Oftentimes, readers of poetry are not told directly who is speaking, to whom, from where, on what occasion. We have to figure that out, and that effort helps us to imagine the voices we should hear in the poem.

Speaker: The person speaking in the poem is not equivalent to the author. Even if the poem's speaker has the same name as the author, we should not assume that this speaker is the author. The speaker within the poem is a presentation, a kind of character.

Tone: Tone means pretty much the same thing in critical circles that it means in everyday life. It's the way something is said. What is interesting about texts, again, is that they have no tone until we supply it, and we do so based upon the clues of the text, as we read them. This invention is often not easy, necessitating careful attention. Many readers find it helpful to read a poem aloud, to hear the tone of the work. But note that you cannot simply read the poem aloud in order to create an interpretation of it; you really need an interpretation in order to read it aloud appropriately. Finding the right tone for a speaker in a poem is a process of trial and error. As you read the work, evolve your understanding of the way something is being said. Tone is potentially complex—since there are more ways than one to say what is being said.

Point of View: Everyone has to be somewhere, and point of view is simply that place from which a voice is speaking. Stories may be told by a *first-person narrator*, an "I" who tells us what happened. This "I" may be a participant in what happened, or not. The **narrator** (or speaker, if there doesn't seem to be a story to narrate) can also be a voice standing outside the story. Instead of saying, "I thought John was going" (first person), the narrator could say, "Sam thought John was going" (*third-person narrator*). If the third-person narrator seems to know everything, then we say the narrator is *omniscient*; if the third-person narrator knows more than any person or other entity could (for instance, what other characters are thinking), but not everything, then we have a *"limited omniscient narrator."* Of course, if the narrator is a telepath, then we have a first-person narrator with extraordinary powers.

Irony: Irony calls for the reader to create, in a sense, a certain kind of mask for the speaker. When the reader identifies irony, the reader says, in effect, "I see two of you: a false you who's saying something that I'm supposed to see through; and another more true you who is really saying something different from what you appear on the surface to be saying." The mask may be serious; the face underneath may be kidding. For New Critics, irony is a key term, pointing to the multiple meanings of a single assertion. text with irony is complex, meaning potentially more than one thing.

Works Cited: New Criticism

Atkinson, Michael. "Deadpan Walking: Welcome to the Droll House: American Geekhood Finds a New Icon in a Clueless Idaho Teen." *Village Voice,* June 7, 2004. http://www.villagevoice.com/film/0423,atkinson,54121,20.html.

Brooks, Cleanth. *The Well-Wrought Urn.* New York: Reynal and Hitchcock, 1947; Harcourt, 1975.

Brooks, Cleanth, and Robert Penn Warren. *Understanding Poetry.* New York: Holt, 1938.

Coleridge, Samuel Taylor. *Biographia Literaria.* 1817. Yorkshire, England: Scholar, 1971.

Eliot, T. S. *Selected Essays.* New York: Harcourt, 1932.

Keats, John. *The Letters of John Keats, 1814–1821.* 2 vols. Cambridge: Harvard UP, 1958.

Moore, Marianne. *Collected Poems of Marianne Moore.* New York: Macmillan, 1935.

Ransom, John Crowe. *The New Criticism.* New York: New Directions, 1941.

Richards, I. A. *Practical Criticism.* New York: Harcourt, 1929.

Wellek, René, and Austin Warren. *Theory of Literature.* New York: Harcourt, 1949.

Wimsatt, W. K., and Monroe Beardsley. *The Verbal Icon.* Lexington: U of Kentucky P, 1954.

Recommended Further Reading: New Criticism

Arnason, David. "The New Criticism." Course page. 2002. Dept. of
    English, St. John's College. 26 Nov. 2006 http://130.179.92.25/
    Arnason_DE/New_Criticism.html. A very brief but very rich descrip-
    tion. Arnason's interesting website has a wealth of materials related
    to other approaches also.
Berman, Art. "The New Criticism." In *From the New Criticism to
    Deconstruction*. Urbana: U of Illinois P, 1988. 26–59. A sophisticated
    discussion of the philosophical underpinnings of New Criticism.
Hedges, Warren. "New Criticism Explained." Course page. 1997. Dept.
    of English, Southern Oregon U. 26 Nov. 2006 http://www.sou.edu/
    English/Hedges/Sodashop/RCenter/Theory/Explaind/
    ncritexp.htm. A concise and clear explanation.
Internet Public Library: Online Literary Criticism Collection. 2006. University
    of Michigan, School of Information and Library Studies. 26 Nov.
    2006 www.ipl.org/ref/litcrit. The Internet Public Library is an
    amazing resource, providing links to and assessment of many other
    biographical and literary critical websites. You can search by author,
    by title, by country, by period. There's a "Literary Criticism
    Pathfinder," suggesting strategies for finding criticism in real
    libraries and on the Web. Begun as a class project in 1995, on a
    budget of US$18 per month, the IPL exemplifies the educational
    and scholarly potential of the Internet.
Lynn, Steven. "René Wellek." In *Modern American Critics*. Ed. Gregory Jay.
    Detroit: Gale Research, 1988. 290–303. Discusses the career of a critic
    enormously influential in the development of New Criticism, who
    (interestingly enough) did not consider himself to be a New Critic.
Searle, Leroy. "New Criticism." In *The Johns Hopkins Guide to Literary
    Theory and Criticism*. Ed. Michael Groden and Martin Kreiswirth.
    Baltimore: Johns Hopkins UP, 1994. 528–34. Nice overview.
Sosnoski, James. "Cleanth Brooks." In *Modern American Critics*. Ed.
    Gregory Jay. Detroit: Gale Research, 1988. 33–42. A detailed and
    engaging study of Brooks' stellar career, championing the principles
    of New Criticism and applying them brilliantly.
Tyson, Lois. "New Criticism." In *Critical Theory Today: A User-Friendly
    Guide*. New York: Garland, 1999. 117–152. A lucid and very
    thorough introduction.
Willingham, John. "The New Criticism: Then and Now." In *Contemporary
    Literary Theory*. Ed. Douglas Atkins and Laura Morrow. Amherst: U of
    Massachusetts, 1989. Explores the continued viability of New
    Criticism.

Creating the Text

Reader-Response Criticism

Unless there is a response on the part of somebody, there is no significance, no meaning.

—Morse Peckham

THE PURPOSE OF READER-RESPONSE CRITICISM

New Criticism as the Old Criticism

Reader-response criticism can be seen as a reaction in part to some problems and limitations perceived in New Criticism. New Criticism did not suddenly fail to function: it remains to this day a popular and effective critical strategy for illuminating the complex unity of certain literary works. But some works don't seem to respond very well to New Criticism's "close reading." Much of eighteenth-century literature, for instance, has generally not been shown to have the sort of paradoxical language or formal unity that New Critics have found in, say, Donne or Keats. And New Critics appear to see roughly the same thing in whatever work they happen to read: "This work has unified complexity"; "So does this one"; "Yep, this one too."

Further, if the work is indeed a stable object, about which careful readers can make objective statements, then why hasn't there been an emerging consensus in criticism? Instead, the history of criticism seems to be one of diversity and change, as successive critics provide innovatively different readings of the same work. Developments in literary criticism seem more like changes of fashion than the evolution of science. Even in the sciences, the idea of an objective point of view has been increasingly questioned. Facts, as Thomas Kuhn has argued, emerge because of a certain system of belief, or paradigm. Scientific revolutions occur not simply when new facts are discovered, but when a new paradigm allows these "facts" to be noticed and accepted.

Such ideas about the conceptual and constructed nature of knowledge, even scientific knowledge, call a fundamental assumption of New Criticism into question. In positing the objective reality of the literary work, New Criticism was arguably emulating the sciences; but in the wake of Einstein's theory of relativity, Heisenberg's uncertainty principle, Gödel's mathematics, and much else, it seems clear that the perceiver plays an active role in the making of any meaning and that literary works in particular have a *subjective* status.

In addition, by striving to show how great works balance opposing ideas, New Criticism has seemed to some to encourage the divorce of literature from life and politics, indirectly reinforcing the status quo. By the standards of New Criticism, any literary work that takes a strong position ought somehow to acknowledge the opposing point of view, and criticism ought to point to that complexity and balance. Further, by assuming that literary language is fundamentally different from ordinary language, New Criticism may further tend to support the idea that literary study has little or no practical value but stands apart from real life (a poem should not mean but be, MacLeish says). New Criticism sometimes seems, especially to unsympathetic eyes, like an intellectual exercise.

The perception of these shortcomings of New Criticism—its limited applicability and sameness of results, the questionable assumption of a stable object of inquiry, and the separation of literature from other discourses—no doubt helped open the door for reader-response criticism (and other approaches). But reader-response criticism has its own substantial appeals, as we shall see.

The Reader Emerges

In 1938, while future New Critics were formulating ideas of the text as a freestanding object, Louise Rosenblatt prophetically called for criticism that involved a "personal sense of literature" (60),

The Purpose of Reader-Response Criticism 69

"an unself-conscious, spontaneous, and honest reaction" (67). *Literature as Exploration* was ahead of its day, but by the time Rosenblatt published *The Reader, the Text, the Poem* in 1978, much of the critical world had caught up with where she was forty years before. For instance, the creative power of readers was championed by David Bleich's *Readings and Feelings* in 1975 and by *Subjective Criticism* in 1978. Because "the object of observation appears changed by the act of observation," as Bleich puts it, "knowledge is made by people and not found" (*Criticism* 17, 18).

This insight leads Bleich to embrace subjectivity, even calling his approach "subjective criticism." Writing about literature, he believes, should not involve suppressing readers' individual concerns, anxieties, passions, enthusiasms. "Each person's most urgent motivations are to understand himself," Bleich says, and a response to a literary work always helps us find out something about ourselves (297). Bleich thus encourages introspection and spontaneity, and he is not at all worried that different readers will see different things in a text. Every act of response, he says, reflects the shifting motivations and perceptions of the reader at the moment. Even the most idiosyncratic response to a text should be shared, in Bleich's view, and heard sympathetically.

It is easy to imagine that many students have found such an approach liberating and even intoxicating, and that many teachers have contemplated it with horror. "There's no right or wrong," as one teacher said to me; in Bleich's reader-response criticism, "students can say *anything*." But Bleich actually does not imagine that the student's engagement with literature will *end* with a purely individual, purely self-oriented response; rather, he expects that students will share their responses, and in *Subjective Criticism* he describes the process of "negotiation" that occurs as a community examines together their individual responses, seeking common ground while learning from each person's unique response.

An especially striking illustration of the benefits of Bleich's orientation appears in an essay by Robert Crosman. Crosman recounts a student's response to William Faulkner's famous "A Rose for Emily" that is so eccentric, so obviously "wrong" (if it were possible to be wrong within this approach), that one must begin to wonder if the student really read the story with any attentiveness. The student's response seems in fact to expose the absurdity of letting students say whatever comes into their heads, for she writes that Emily, the mad recluse who apparently poisons and then sleeps with her suitor, reminds her of her kindly grandmother. Crosman's student ignores the horrible ending of the story, which implies that Emily has recently slept with the much-decayed remains of her murdered lover; instead, the student writes about the qualities of her grandmother—"endurance, faith, love"—that she also sees in Emily (360). The student finds that her grandmother and Emily both inhabit houses that are closed up with "relics and mementos of the past"; both her grandmother and Emily seem to think of past events and people as being "more real" than "the world of the present."

The value of this student's response emerges in the way Crosman uses it to modify his own reading. He comes to see that his interpretation, which is much more typical of experienced readers, actually "suppresses a good deal of evidence" (361). Crosman has perceived Emily to be a kind of monster, but he is led by his student to see that such is not entirely the case. Confronting the heroic aspects of Emily's character, Crosman notices that she triumphs, in a sense, over the men (father, lover, town fathers) who are, Crosman says, "ultimately responsible for Emily's pitiful condition" (361). By the same token, just as Crosman is able to see the positive aspects of Emily's character, making her human rather than monstrous, so is his student, by considering Crosman's response, placed in a position to see more than her grandmother's goodness in Emily.

Thus, Bleich sees the reader's response evolving by "negotiation" within a community of readers, and Rosenblatt focuses on the "transaction" between the text and the reader. While she accepts multiple interpretations, as readers actively make different works out of the text, she also considers some readings to be incorrect or inappropriate because they are unsupportable by the text. So the "unself-conscious, spontaneous, and honest reaction" that Rosenblatt encourages ought to be checked against the text and modified in a continuing process, or "transaction": a poem is made by the text and the reader interacting. For both Bleich and Rosenblatt, the reader ought not simply respond and move on. Rather, the reader shares a response, and considers the responses of others, and reconsiders the text, and evolves his or her responses.

The various reader-response critics all share the sense of reading as a process, an activity; their differences stem from this question of how meaning is controlled. Who's in charge? The reader? A community of readers? The text? The case of Stanley Fish is especially interesting in this regard because over his career Fish has taken just about every position. Fish's early work emphasizes how the text controls the reader's experience; the task of criticism is to describe this experience, and Fish's readings seem much like watching a movie in superslow motion as it is being analyzed by an imaginative film critic. Fish moves through a few words or phrases and then considers in brilliant and clever detail what "the reader" makes of it. Fish repeatedly finds that admirable texts continually surprise us, evading our expectations, exposing us to "strains," "ambivalences," "complexity" (*Artifacts* 136, 425). These values, as Jane Tompkins has suggested, are very similar to the values of New Criticism. But the way they are discovered in texts is quite different.

In *Surprised by Sin,* for instance, Fish argues that the reader "*in*" *Paradise Lost* experiences temptations and disorientations that parallel those of Adam and Eve. Thus, the critics who have thought Satan more appealing than God have not spotted a flaw in Milton's achievement; they have simply succumbed to the temptation Milton meant for them to experience. Likewise, in *Self-Consuming Artifacts* Fish shows how the process of reading certain seventeenth-century texts involves creating expectations that are thwarted, complicated, reversed, transformed as the reader goes on.

In his later works, *Is There a Text in This Class?* and *Doing What Comes Naturally,* Fish moves away from the idea of an ideal reader who finds his or her activity marked out, implied, embedded in the text, and he moves toward the idea of a reader who creates a reading of the text using certain interpretive strategies. These strategies may be shared by other readers, and the critic's job is to persuade his or her interpretive community to accept a particular reading. Neither the text's implied activity nor the community's shared reading strategies can be said to determine interpretation, for even when readers inhabit the same interpretive community, they must struggle to persuade one another of the "facts" regarding a particular text. Such persuasion may include information about the author, or the author's audience, or the initial reception of the work, or the history of its reception, or the text itself, or the conventions of interpretation the text draws upon. But the continuing process of discussion begins with the response of the person persuading. More recently Fish has turned his attention to the law and politics, publishing in 1994 *There's No Such Thing as Free Speech: And It's a Good Thing Too,* and in 1999 *The Trouble with Principle*. These books seek to demolish the idea of universal and impersonal principles, arguing that meaning is always created in a particular context by particular people. Our values, in other words, are a kind of reader's response to our culture and history.

HYPERTEXTUAL READERS

The reader's creative role would seem to be especially evident in the case of hypertexts, which are essentially discrete blocks of electronic text (or other media) networked together. By clicking on a link in the text, or inputting a response to the text, readers can determine what will appear before them next. If this book that you are now reading were an electronic hypertext, rather than an old-timey ink and paper one, you might be able to click on the word "hypertext" and be "taken" (in an electronic sense) to more information about hypertexts. "There" you might find links to websites about hypertexts, or links to hypertext novels, or links to Amazon.com and featured books about hypertextuality, or a video clip of me reading my utterly neglected poem, "Ode on a Grecian Hypertext." Reading a hypertextual detective story, for instance, one might be asked which character should turn out to be guilty, and the story would then in some way respond to the reader's response. At first glance, this kind of interactive work seems profoundly liberating for readers, epitomizing the spirit of reader-oriented criticism.

But the extent to which hypertexts blur the distinction between readers and writers—and even between reality and virtual reality—as some theorists have asserted, can certainly be overstated. Let's take the simplest example of a hypertext, one in which the reader can click on one of two options. A character in a story lives or dies, perhaps, or a more detailed explanation of a solution appears, or doesn't. In a sense, the reader confronts two texts: one in which the character lives, and another in which the character dies; one that has a more detailed explanation, and one that doesn't. The reader chooses which text to read—and can even read them both by going back and choosing differently. In this situation, the reader hasn't really interacted with the text or participated in the text's creation: the text's different versions were there all along, just as static as the text you are holding.

A hypertext with dozens or even hundreds of links, and dozens or hundreds of pieces of text, is of course a very complicated text—or bundle of texts. But it remains to be seen whether readers of hypertexts *create* the meaning or the experience of a hypertext in a way that is fundamentally different from an ordinary text.

In any event, the advent of hypertexts underscores the value of reader-response criticism, which authorizes and encourages readers—of whatever sort of text—to begin where, really, readers always must begin: with an individual response. With a hypertext, not only is one reader's experience different from another reader's, but the text itself may be different. The differences in our responses reflect the precious uniqueness of our selves, it seems to me. It is always possible (and often desirable, I think) to evolve a personal response based upon interaction with a community, or further reference to the text, or the employment of a particular political or aesthetic theory, or some other impetus. But you must start with a response. Although you can't click on anything to generate your response, you also can hardly avoid responding. Just read it.

Let's move to a more specific instance of responding.

HOW TO DO READER-RESPONSE CRITICISM

Preparing to Respond

Imagine that you've been asked to write about the following poem, drawing on reader-response criticism. You'll want to read the poem carefully, thinking in terms of the following possible questions:

1. How do I respond to this work?
2. How does the text shape my response?
3. How might other readers respond?

Love Poem #1
Sandra Cisneros

> a red flag
> woman I am
> all copper
> chemical

and you an ax   5
and a bruised
thumb.

unlikely
pas de deux
but just let   10
us wax
it's nitro
egypt
snake
museum   15
zoo

we are
connoisseurs
and commandoes
we are rowdy   20
as a drum
not shy like
Narcissus
nor pale as plum

then it is I want to hymn   25
and halleluja
sing sweet sweet jubilee
you my religion
and I a wicked nun

(1987)

What can you say about this poem? How can audience-oriented criticism help you to understand and appreciate it?

Making Sense

My own response to this poem began when I started to annotate it. I underlined some words that I thought might be especially important or unclear, and then, on a separate sheet, I speculated on their meanings. With any approach, you may need to look up some words. If you're a little hazy on who "Narcissus" is (line 23), for instance, a dictionary definition may be all you need: "A youth who, having spurned the love of Echo, pined away in love for his own image in a pool of water and was transformed into the flower that bears his name" (*American Heritage Dictionary*). Dictionary definitions aren't always sufficient, and (it probably goes without saying) the more you know, the more experience you have as a reader, then the richer and more informed your response is likely to be. Responding to a poem always involves you in creating a context in which the sequence of words makes sense: you must ask, Who is speaking to whom? Under what circumstances would someone say these things?

Still, all responses are potentially worthwhile as starting points. You may want to underline some important or puzzling words and speculate on their meanings before you look at my annotations below. And you may want to share your responses with another reader.

> *a red flag woman*—What does this mean? A red flag means something to watch out for, dangerous, a warning. For instance, "The temperature reading should have been a red flag." So she is dangerous?
>
> *all copper*—Why copper? Because it's cold? Because it turns green?! No, I don't think so. Copper is a great conductor of electrical current and heat. She's hot; she's electrified. That is, she's passionate, emotional, responsive?
>
> *chemical*—Like a chemical reaction?
>
> *an ax and a bruised thumb* — Is he clumsy? He does things aggressively, in an imprecise way. He breaks or splits things like an ax, but he isn't always careful (the bruised thumb).
>
> *pas de deux*—A ballet dance for two, according to *Webster.* The sort of grace and coordination we'd expect from a ballet is indeed unlikely for these two together, a live wire and a wild man.
>
> *nitro etc.*—This is a neat list of unexpected things, each one giving a different aspect of their relationship. Nitro = explosive?; egypt = foreign, exotic, mysterious, enduring (like the pyramids)?; snake = something wicked? a phallic symbol? the garden of Eden? Are "egypt" and "snake" related? "Museum" and "zoo" point us to public institutions. "Museum" suggests their love is rare, valuable, enduring, worth showing off; "zoo" suggests perhaps they're animals?
>
> *connoisseurs and commandoes*—They again appear to be radical opposites: connoisseurs are refined, tasting carefully; commandoes are reckless and go wild.

you my religion—This is about as involved in another person as you can get. There's something troubling about such devotion to another person. No human being should worship another one. But am I taking this line too seriously?

wicked nun—This image continues the religious reference. Being a wicked nun seems especially exciting, or offensive, depending on the responder, combining suggestions of the forbidden and the delayed.

Subjective Response

Thinking about the words, you're already unavoidably beginning to think about the poem as a whole and your own response to it. The next step might be to freewrite about the poem. Just focus on the poem and write quickly whatever occurs to you. Don't worry about grammar, and don't stop writing. If you can't think of anything to say, say whatever is most obvious. The important thing is to keep the pen or keyboard moving. As a last resort, write "I can't think of anything to say" until you think of something. If that fails, then read the poem again and then try once more. Set yourself a time limit for this free response; ten minutes is about right for most people. There's no way to do this exercise incorrectly: just read carefully and respond, being as honest and involved as you can.

Here is my freewriting response:

> This poem reminds me of Carol and Bob's relationship. They are about as unlikely and mismatched a couple as this pair, an "unlikely pas de deux." But instead of "copper" and "chemical," Carol is more like plutonium and nuclear. She's incredibly energetic, especially when you compare her to Bob. He could fit "an ax / and a bruised / thumb," but I suspect the result would be an amputated thumb in his case. They are amazing, like the couple in the poem.
>
> Are Carol and Bob "nitro" together, like this couple? I don't know. There seems to me to be a good bit of energy in their marriage. I don't see Carol wanting "to hymn / and halleluja," perhaps, but I'm really in no position to judge, am I. I don't know what happens when they "wax," whatever that means. Certainly, the two people in Cisneros's poem are not living a dull life, and I think the contrast is also stimulating to Carol

and Bob. There is power in conflict or difference. Opposites not only attract; they make sparks.

Many people find this kind of freewriting exercise very useful: it generates material that you may be able to use in an essay, and it is likely to stimulate your thinking about the work. Just to give you an idea of how individualistic and personal such responses can be, here is another one:

This poem seems to talk about an exciting relationship: she says "it's nitro." That suggests the relationship is great, but I think it's really doomed. I think this relationship, the first time it is shaken, will probably explode, just like nitro. She is emotional; he is rough and clumsy. Where's the long-term interest and compatibility in this set-up? Opposites attract, sure, but when they're so totally opposite, so far apart, the attraction may be volatile. This is after all only "Love Poem #1." I am wondering if there will be #2 and #3 once the relationship matures and cools off.

I think the speaker's comparison of herself to "a wicked nun" is revealing. The comparison supports my feeling that the relationship, despite its current heat, isn't going to make it. I notice that she does not see herself as a nun who has decided to give up her habit. She is just "wicked," doing something wrong and enjoying the extra excitement that doing the forbidden gives her. If her love feels that way to her, then won't that eventually put a strain on the relationship? Will she decide to give up her old life, her old religion, and become devoted to her new religion, her lover? Or will her prior life win out?

In my experience, relationships built on excitement are treacherous and fragile. I bet the nun will repent and reform.

Which of these responses is correct? Both are. Both are thoughtful and well-supported responses to the text. Taken together, these two different responses may suggest a third one that tries to determine whether the poem really does evoke some skepticism on the reader's part or if it is simply a joyous celebration. Are there some elements that would qualify the poem's enthusiasm for most readers?

After engaging the text in a personal way, you can begin to ask such questions about your own response in the context of other readers' responses. Let's see what happens when the reading process is slowed down and an effort is made to imagine how the reader is supposed to respond moving through the poem.

Receptive Response

First, obviously, every reader encounters the title. What response does the title elicit? The poem announces itself as a love poem. What sort of title do we expect from such a thing? Most readers no doubt expect a love poem to have a more romantic or imaginative title than "Love Poem #1," and the reader's initial reaction is to wonder if the poem is in truth a love poem. If it is, then why is the title so bluntly direct? The numbering also creates certain possibilities: will the poem reflect the intensity of love in its first bloom? Will it deflate or satirize infatuation? At this point, the reader cannot know, but the firstness of the poem is perceived to be an important feature, to be taken into account as the poem unfolds.

The first line seems to open further the possibility that the poem is not a love poem in the usual sense: "a red flag" signals a warning, a danger, and seems more appropriate to a poem announcing the end of a love affair. So perhaps the first is the last, and the unimaginative title is ironic? The second line, "woman I am," seems to be an affirmation of the speaker's individuality and her sisterhood. In other words:

Line 1: "a red flag" = Watch out! There's something dangerous here.

Line 2: "woman I am" = The reason you should watch out: a red flag (look out!), I am woman.

But as the reader begins to wonder about these two statements—"a red flag" and "woman I am"—the possibility arises, reading backwards, that these two lines go together in a different way, as a single statement: "a red flag" becomes a modifier of "woman"—I am a red-flag woman.

Without punctuation, the reader cannot decide for sure which syntax is correct, and so both readings continue on: "watch out, I'm a woman," and "I'm a dangerous kind of woman." Do the next two lines support the suggestion of an unromantic, even threatening self-portrait of the speaker? Most readers will think of electrical wiring and plumbing when they read "all copper," which appears to refer back to the speaker; likewise, things that are "chemical" are perceived by most readers as dangerously reactive. Only experts should fool around with plumbing, wiring, chemistry: pipes explode, wires spark, chemicals blow up.

There is of course an element of surprise at hearing the speaker describe herself in this way. "All copper" and "chemical" are not part of the usual vocabulary of love poetry, are they? The reader will find the next three lines equally disorienting, as the speaker's love is described in the decidedly unromantic terms of "an ax / and a bruised / thumb." He or she is potentially destructive and apparently dangerous. (Although some readers may assume the speaker's lover is male, the poem doesn't prescribe that response, does it?) An ax usually isn't used to build things, but rather to cut them, kill them, chop them down. Such wrecking sometimes results, especially if the worker is clumsy, in a bruised thumb, or worse. As a love poem, this one seems to be going nowhere, and the reader may well not be surprised that it is #1. How can there be any more?

Thus, I would argue that the opening of the second group of lines confirms the attentive reader's assessment: they are indeed an "unlikely / pas de deux." This admission also sets the reader up, however, for a turn. By saying they are unlikely as a pair, Cisneros implies that they *may be* nonetheless a couple, somehow. The rest of the poem vigorously fulfills that implication, reversing the reader's inferences, which he or she may have suspected would be reversed. Still, the explanation of their relationship is startling, as the reader encounters a list of unexpected and even puzzling comparisons:

nitro—This one is easy. They are explosive together—and that seems good. But since nitroglycerine is used to blow things up (as well as to prevent heart attacks), an element of danger remains.

egypt—How can the lovers be "egypt"? Perhaps the reference means they are exotic together? Hot, like the deserts? Mysterious, like the pyramids? Alluring, like Cleopatra? Fertile, like the Nile? By not saying how the lovers are like Egypt, Cisneros opens up a space in which the reader can supply all sorts of qualities.

snake—This comparison is as tantalizing and amazing, at least, as "egypt." A snake is of course often considered a phallic symbol, and the reader may think of the lovers' conjunction as a kind of living version of that symbol. But it may also remind us, in the context of a couple, of Adam and Eve, suggesting that they are somehow participating in a return to Eden together; but this time, the lovers are not ruined by the serpent but rather become one themselves? Or, is the snake, in the context of "egypt," supposed to suggest some sort of ancient fertility cult that involved the handling of snakes? We don't know, but the attentive reader will consider these and other possible responses to this rich and startling image.

museum —Another strange and disorienting comparison. How can the lovers be like a museum? Perhaps they create, in their lovemaking, something of enduring value, something so wonderful that future generations would want to preserve it, as in a museum.

zoo —This reference is perhaps the easiest for the reader to respond to: it suggests obviously that they are animals together—a collection in fact of all sorts of exotic and wondrous animals.

The rest of the poem continues to celebrate the lovers in unexpected ways, even though certain ideas reappear. The speaker calls them "connoisseurs and commandoes," which repeats to some degree the oppositions already set up. The reader may connect "connoisseurs" to the cultured reaction of museum goers, but at the same time the lovers are wild "commandoes," which the reader may link to the violence of "nitro" or an "ax." The difference in this third section of the poem is that instead of each lover having distinctly different qualities, they are together "connoisseurs and commandoes," unifying opposing features in their relationships.

If the reader believes, however, that the rest of the poem will fit some sort of pattern set up thus far, the next lines seem designed to thwart that expectation. The lovers are "rowdy / as a drum," which suggests, I suppose, the rowdiness of someone beating a drum. Perhaps this simile reinforces the earlier suggestions of wildness, but it is certainly difficult to see how a drum in itself is "rowdy" or what this comparison is supposed to accomplish. The reader next learns the lovers are "not shy like Narcissus," an allusion that means obviously that they are not self-absorbed, that they don't hold back from love. But is there any deeper significance to this allusion? Why bring in Narcissus and shyness? Would any reader suspect at this point that they *are* shy—these commandoes, who are "nitro"? The next line seems even more elusive, as if the lovers are slowly becoming incomprehensible to the reader: "nor pale as plum"? Perhaps this comparison refers to the color plum and tells us in another way that they are not shy—although the reader surely must hesitate to call "plum" a "pale" color.

But "plum" serves another function beyond befuddling the reader, as it becomes clear at this point, if not before, that a recurrent rhyme is appearing, unobtrusively: "thumb," "museum," "drum," and "plum." And with the appearance of this music, beginning to evade meaning, the poem moves to its climatic ending, comparing the speaker's feelings to a religious ecstasy:

> then it is I want to hymn
> and halleluja
> sing sweet sweet jubilee
> you my religion
> and I a wicked nun

The reader may hear the assertion that she wants "to hymn" as a pun on "him," as if her lover has become an activity in which she can engage or as if the male role is one the speaker longs to adopt. The associations of "hymn" continue for the reader as singing halleluja and enjoying the "jubilee" appear. Immediately these religious comparisons are carried beyond the reader's expectations (which may be, at this point, what the reader does expect), as the speaker declares her lover to be her religion. For most readers, such sacrilege is an exaggeration at the edges of propriety: most readers are all in favor of love, but to make another person one's religion is troubling. The experienced reader probably sees this assertion as exaggeration (hyperbole), but it is nonetheless worrisome in its implications.

But the final line takes even a further step, as the speaker names herself "a wicked nun." This final move completes the effort to convey the excitement of the forbidden, the impossible, the dangerous in the relationship, leaving the reader shaken and stunned—like the speaker herself, it seems—by the power of their love. Their love is itself vigorously direct, like the poem's title; their love is also apparently unadulterated and uncompromised, pure and explosive at its very beginning.

It is quite likely that your own thinking about the reader's reception of this poem is different from mine—perhaps radically different. That's fine with me. Although we could argue over which one of us is insufficiently attentive to the poem's cues, in the context of reader-response criticism it makes more sense to try to learn from each other. For me, even when I'm trying to play the role of the implied reader, I'm continually aware that I'm making choices, filling in blanks and gaps, interpreting in one particular way when several other ways (some of which aren't occurring to me) are feasible. I say "the reader," and I am trying to think of an ideal or implied response, but I'm aware at several points that "the reader" may be only me. Still, it seems helpful to *try* to think of how other readers will respond and to read what other readers say and enrich our own responses. The real beauty of audience-oriented criticism, after all, is that the focus is on our activity: we make the text say whatever it's going to say and then try to persuade others to accept our readings.

You can apply the strategies of reader-response criticism to anything—even to objects or stimuli that we do not literally "read," such as cultural and political events, even paintings and sculptures. You simply need to be able to describe how the "reader" or viewer or listener (hypothetical or real) responds. Think for instance about the sequence of events at a football game, and how the spectators respond as the spectacle unfolds. Why do sporting events typically begin, for instance, with the singing of the national anthem? How are spectators expected to respond? One might argue that the national anthem tends to remind antagonistic fans of the citizenship that they have in common, encouraging them to respond to the game in a better spirit of sportsmanship. Or, perhaps the national anthem lends an air of importance to what follows, suggesting that football is somehow more than just entertainment, but somehow has some significance, and should be taken seriously and passionately. Or perhaps the national anthem marks a boundary, signaling a transition from the real world (before the anthem) to the "play" world, setting aside our concerns and worries while we think only about a game.

Whatever we're analyzing with reader-response strategies, two moves seem especially worth noting here. First, although a response might feel seamless, continuous, flowing, the description of a response must somehow be broken up into parts. Language moves through time, in sentences with subjects and verbs and the rest, and so the description of a response must move through time, forcing us to divide the response up into pieces. The immediate impression that one gets from a painting or sculpture will be difficult to describe, of course, because it feels like an all-at-once experience. You can talk about what one notices first, and second, and third, moving around the canvas or object, or through the event or the text, but you are inevitably making choices about where that first bit of response begins and ends, and the second begins and ends, and so forth. For people who want there to be one right answer, and for everyone to see and experience things the same way, reader-response criticism is bound to be pretty frustrating. (But so will everything else, unless they just stop thinking about things.) For people who rejoice in the diversity of experiences and responses and opinions, reader-response criticism will be especially interesting, not only because of our different orientations and abilities, but also because of the different ways that we partition and perceive our experiences. Texts, films, objects, events generally provide us with cues about how we ought to comprehend their parts, or (depending on the perspective) we ascribe these cues to whatever we interpret. Part of your job in constructing a response, then, will be to determine the segments of whatever you're responding to.

The second move involves understanding how the perception of genre affects the response. If we recognize that a work is a detective story, or a situation comedy, or a sermon, then we have a repertoire of expectations and reactions that come into play. The *Star Trek* television shows, for instance, have all begun in ways that immediately identify the kind of thing that we are watching: The original *Star Trek*, with Captain Kirk, Mr. Spock, and the rest, featured an opening credit sequence that showed the *Enterprise* in space, coming into view in one corner of the screen, zipping across and disappearing from the other corner in an instant. Viewers not only have a response to that scene, identified as a discrete bit of the show, but they also create certain expectations about what will follow. *Star Trek* famously depicted an optimistic vision of the future, in which science and technology will have solved many of our current problems and advanced humankind into space, "the final frontier." This opening scene, displaying a faster-than-light starship, suggests that we should view what follows as science fiction: there will be marvels, but they should be plausible within the terms of what we know and can extrapolate about science today. All the subsequent incarnations of *Star Trek*—*Next Generation, Deep Space Nine, Voyager,* and *Enterprise*—presented some variation on this outer space vista: *Next Generation* showed incredibly beautiful planetary systems and the new *Enterprise* passing by them; *Deep Space Nine* showed us the space station and an amazing interspatial wormhole; *Voyager* depicted strange planets and phenomena, and the ship jumping into warp speed; and *Enterprise* preceded a similar jump to warp speed with various images of human exploration, from the historical past and the imagined future. Viewers familiar with the *Star Trek* series and with science fiction in general are going to respond differently from viewers unfamiliar with either or both. Although educators may tend to think of reader-response criticism as an equal-opportunity sort of approach, allowing every reader (or respondent) to have his or her say about the work's effects, this simple reference to the beginnings of a television franchise emphasizes that our responses depend on what we know: if we understand the genre of a particular work, if we have experience with other similar works, then our responses will be more informed, quite possibly richer. Even those teachers who insist that there are no wrong responses (which is indeed a liberating principle, inviting students to boldly go where their reading and responding has never gone before) still must acknowledge that we become in some sense better at reading and responding with practice. And a key part of what we learn has to do with recognizing, at the outset, the kind of thing we are experiencing.

Let's look more closely at these reader-response strategies by working our way through the evolution of an essay.

THE WRITING PROCESS: A SAMPLE ESSAY

Preparing to Respond

Here is a very short story by Ernest Hemingway, "A Very Short Story," which is actually part of a sequence of stories (for the whole sequence, see *Ernest Hemingway: The Short Stories*).

A Very Short Story

Ernest Hemingway

One hot evening in Padua they carried him up onto the roof and he could look out over the top of the town. There were chimney swifts in the sky. After a while it got dark and the searchlights came out. The others went down and took the bottles with them. He and Luz could hear them below on the balcony. Luz sat on the bed. She was cool and fresh in the hot night.

Luz stayed on night duty for three months. They were glad to let her. When they operated on him she prepared him for the operating table; and they had a joke about friend or enema. He went under the anaesthetic holding tight on to himself so he would not blab about anything during the silly, talky time. After he got on crutches he used to take the temperatures so Luz would not have to get up from the bed. There were only a few patients, and they all knew about it. They all liked Luz. As he walked back along the halls he thought of Luz in his bed.

Before he went back to the front they went into the Duomo and prayed. It was dim and quiet, and there were other people praying. They wanted to get married, but there was not enough time for the banns, and neither of them had birth certificates. They felt as though they were married, but they wanted every one to know about it, and to make it so they could not lose it.

Luz wrote him many letters that he never got until after the armistice. Fifteen came in a bunch to the front and he sorted them by the dates and read them all straight through. They were all about the hospital, and how much she loved him and how it was impossible to get along without him and how terrible it was missing him at night.

After the armistice they agreed he should go home to get a job so they might be married. Luz would not come home until he had a good job and could come to New York to meet her. It was understood he would not drink, and he did not want to see his friends or any one in the States. Only to get a job and be married. On the train from Padua to Milan they quarrelled about her not being willing to come home at once. When they had to say good-bye, in the station at Milan, they kissed good-bye, but were not finished with the quarrel. He felt sick about saying good-bye like that.

He went to America on a boat from Genoa. Luz went back to Pordenone to open a hospital. It was lonely and rainy there, and there was a battalion of arditi quartered in the town. Living in the muddy, rainy town in the winter, the major of the battalion made love to Luz, and she had never known Italians before, and finally wrote to the States that theirs had been only a boy and girl affair. She was sorry, and she knew he would probably not be able to understand, but might some day forgive her, and be grateful to her, and she expected, absolutely unexpectedly, to be married in the spring. She loved him as always, but she realized now it was only a boy and girl love. She hoped he would have a great career, and believed in him absolutely. She knew it was for the best.

The major did not marry her in the spring, or any other time. Luz never got an answer to the letter to Chicago about it. A short time after he contracted gonorrhea from a sales girl in a loop department store while riding in a taxicab through Lincoln Park.

(1925)

*   *   *

How this story shapes the reader's response has already been suggested by Robert Scholes in *Semiotics and Interpretation*. As

Scholes observes, the point of view in the story is technically third person (if it were first-person narration, it would read this way: "One hot evening in Padua they carried me up on the roof . . ."). But the viewpoint, Scholes says, seems to be closer to the unnamed man than to Luz (116–17). If the narrator were equally distanced from both characters, they would both have names. But "he" apparently doesn't need a name. The reader is told in the first and second sentences what "he" could see. Also, as Scholes notes, the assertion "She was cool and fresh in the hot night" really makes sense only from his perspective: *to him,* she seemed cool and fresh. This point of view plays an important role in the reader's response, and I would like to elaborate on Scholes's view of the story by tracing out in some detail "the reader's" experience.

For starters, we might consider how the reader responds to Hemingway's opening paragraph. Our response must be problematic at that point because we know so little: important information is being left out. But we do know something. We know "he" is in Padua, but we don't know what he is doing there or who he is. We learn that "they" carried him to the roof, but we don't know who "they" are or why he has to be carried: is he sick or injured? Does he have a handicap? The reference to searchlights in the third sentence probably suggests to most readers that the story may be taking place during wartime: these are searchlights looking for attacking planes. If that's the case, then perhaps he is being carried because he is wounded. We also learn that he and Luz are somehow close: "they" leave them alone on the roof, and Luz sits on his bed, appearing "cool and fresh."

In this second paragraph, the implied point of view is made clearer, and additional clues are offered. The notion that he is in a hospital is confirmed here. Luz is on night duty, so she would seem to be a nurse—an inference further supported by her preparation of him for the operating table. The reader may notice, as Scholes points out, that the male character's reticence is much like the story's own restraint (119). He doesn't want to blab, and neither apparently does the story's narrator, telling us only the minimum. Letting go is the enemy and the enema; as Scholes puts it, "Logorrhea and diarrhea are equally embarrassing" (119).

Even if the reader finds the male character's fear of talking about anything problematic, the embodiment of a dumb macho stereotype, the strong silent man, we must be softened by his kindness in taking the temperatures. Here he is on crutches, and yet he gets up so Luz won't have to. What is not said by the narrator is what Luz is doing in his bed, but this is a blank that the reader easily fills in. The reader can easily discern that the "it" that the few patients "all knew about" must be an affair "he" and Luz are having. Why else would the narrator present the revelation that "they all knew about it" as if it were a kind of secret?

Recognizing what "it" is, most readers will probably acknowledge that a nurse sleeping with her patient probably does not represent the highest ethical standards. And recognizing this response perhaps makes clear why Hemingway has the narrator immediately tell us "They all liked Luz": their affection for Luz is designed to qualify the reader's disapproval. With the paragraph's final sentence, the reader must also realize, as "he" thinks of Luz in his bed, that she apparently means a lot to a recovering man, perhaps a wounded soldier. Having immersed ourselves in "his" point of view, readers may not notice, without some consideration, that we do not know what Luz is thinking.

In the third paragraph we learn that he is in fact a soldier because he goes back to the front. We learn that he and Luz pray together in church, and the narrator tells us that they wish they could be married and feel as if they are married. If this feeling really is mutual, the reader may wonder about their plan. Why doesn't Luz return with him rather than waiting on his "good job"? Doesn't this condition make her seem a bit mercenary? Also, why are the restrictions on him seemingly so severe? Perhaps it makes sense that he will not drink, especially if he has a problem with drinking. But why does he not want to see his friends? In fact, he doesn't want to see anyone at all, according to their understanding. Does Luz not trust him? Does he not trust himself? The reader cannot be sure, the way this understanding is phrased, whether Luz imposes these conditions or he volunteers them; but since they restrict his behavior, the reader may assume the rules are Luz's idea.

Such subtle shaping of the reader's response prepares us for the bombshell in the sixth paragraph: she dumps him. In thinking about the reader's response here, we might consider (among other things) the effect of the information that "she had never known Italians before." The passage seems to offer this fact as a kind of explanation of her behavior, but it is an excuse that makes Luz seem worse, as if she wants to try Italians the way one might try a new flavor of ice cream. Hemingway does not say this excuse is disgustingly inadequate, but he sets up the story so that the reader easily comes to such a conclusion. Her letter is not quoted, but is filtered through his perspective; from that vantage point, it seems reasonable to assume that Luz has shamefully betrayed him.

There are in fact aspects of the letter, as it is reported, that seem so unfeeling they appear to be cruel. It is difficult for any reader to imagine what could be more devastating than saying what he thought was the love of his life was actually "only a boy and girl affair." To say "she loved him as always" similarly demeans their relationship. "I thought we were in love," she is in effect saying, "but now that I've been with this Italian, I see we were just playing like children." Her love hasn't changed, just her understanding of what that love was. Finally, to say she "believed in him absolutely" after refusing to come to America before he had a "good" job seems the height of hypocrisy and coldness.

How do we respond to the conclusion? Hemingway has led the reader, it may seem, to see Luz's own jilting by the major as just what she deserves. He adds "or any other time" to prevent the reader from assuming that Luz and the Italian had some problems but worked them out. The affair that *she said* she thought was the real thing, in comparison to their boy and girl thing, does not turn out to be real after all. But did she really believe that the Italian was different? Is Luz a "loose" woman? Is that the significance of her name?

By telling us that Luz never got an answer to her letter, Hemingway conveys indirectly the soldier's pain. The reader can imagine he is so hurt and so thoroughly disgusted that he can't even respond to her. The final sentence further deepens the reader's perception of his pain. As Scholes points out, first Luz wounds his heart; then the salesgirl wounds him in a different place. The reader will naturally assume that he wouldn't have been in that taxicab, fooling around recklessly and decadently, in public in Lincoln Park, if it had not been for Luz. The narrator does not say it is Luz's fault that he gets gonorrhea, but that clearly is the implication: when he loses Luz, he loses everything. "A short time after" here implies some connection. First the war wound, then Luz's, then the salesgirl's.

In moving through the story, I am carrying out and elaborating on the reading Scholes suggests. About the reader's response to this story—that is, the implied response that Hemingway marks out—Scholes says the following:

Most male students sympathize with the protagonist and are very critical of Luz—as indeed [the story] asks them to be. Many female students try to read the story as sympathetic to Luz, blaming events on the "weakness" of the young man or the state of the world. This is a possible interpretation, but it is not well supported by the text. Thus the female student must either "misread" the work (that is, she must offer the more weakly supported of two interpretations) or accept one more blow to her self-esteem as a woman. Faced with this story in a competitive classroom, women are put at a disadvantage. They are, in fact, in a double bind. (120–21)

I have thus far essentially agreed with this analysis of the implied reader's response. The text, in Scholes's opinion, makes the case against Luz. Although taking Luz's side is "a possible interpretation," Scholes says, it seems more difficult to him, a misreading. Scholes does, to be sure, place "misread" inside quotation marks, indicating his awareness of alternatives. But in truth, Scholes sees the reader—the male reader anyway—as being pulled toward one best response.

Not only does Scholes implicitly assume the text is a stable structure, marking out a particular response; he also assumes that "most" males will naturally take the soldier's side, and females will naturally try to take Luz's side. But one of the beauties of reader-response criticism is that it takes advantage of the diversity of readers in the world, reminding us of the treacherousness of generalizations about them. Reader-response criticism—by bringing the personal, the individual, even the eccentric responses to our attention—can revitalize texts that we think we have already learned how to read. Having processed the story with considerable care, attempting to play the role of a passive reader, we're ready now to take a more active part as a responding reader, entering into a debate within a community of readers.

Preparing to Write

What seems more difficult to Scholes (that is, taking Luz's side) seems to me in fact more compelling. I felt the first time I read this story that Luz was getting a raw deal, both from the soldier and from the narrator. Does that mean that I am responding from a woman's point of view? And is that point of view necessarily "at a disadvantage"? Even if we assume that women tend to side with Luz, and that the evidence for doing so is weaker than the evidence against Luz, we should still note that what is most obvious is oftentimes not very interesting in literary criticism. Making the case for Luz against the soldier is generally a more interesting endeavor than showing how Luz is cruel to the soldier.

Thus, I argue that Hemingway creates such apparent bias against Luz in order to expose it: that is, the soldier is so obviously being made into a martyr, and Luz into a villain, that the reader's response ought to resist this bias and look more carefully at the text, seeing past the narrator's obscuring point of view.

To give you an idea how I developed this response into an essay, I present below my notes and then the essay that resulted from them. Before examining these documents, you might want to sketch out your own response to Hemingway's story. What does it say to you?

Emphasize that the narrator clearly takes his side: Hemingway is reminding us to consider the source. You can't let the player's coach call the balls in or out, and the narrator in this case is on the soldier's team.

I could make Hemingway into the villain who tries to cover for the soldier, making Luz into an Eve figure. Or I could argue that Hemingway has the narrator make those moves, thus exposing him. I think the latter would be more fun.

What is the absolute worst evidence against Luz? Probably the reason she gives for the breakup. Focus on that reason: "theirs had been only a boy and girl affair." The reader assumes, in the context created by the soldier's spokesman, that this excuse is cruel and cold. But maybe it isn't a rationalization, a way of getting her Italian major. Consider the possibility that Luz is right: they are immature; it is a boy/girl affair. Any evidence?

- The soldier does reveal his immaturity after Luz breaks it off: having sex in a taxicab, getting an S.T.D.—now that's really mature.
- We also must wonder about his decision not to respond to Luz's last letter. If he really loved Luz, wouldn't he consider forgiving her? Doesn't everyone make mistakes? Isn't it possible that Luz just got confused and mistook infatuation with the major for love? At such a distance from the soldier, in such bleak circumstances, she simply erred. But the soldier is such an immature hothead that the idea of forgiving her never occurs to him.
- What is after all the basis of the soldier's relationship with Luz? If she is wrong, if it is more than a boy/girl affair, what evidence is there in the story of his maturity and the depth of his love? The story in fact tells us nothing that suggests any great passion on his part. He seems perfectly willing to leave her behind while he goes to the United States to get a job. What does he think of Luz?

We know only two things, really: She was "cool and fresh" and "he thought of Luz in his bed." So far as we can tell, the relationship is based on sex, which isn't the strongest foundation for marriage.

- What is the evidence that Luz is a bad person? She does have sex with the soldier while he's a patient. She sleeps in his bed. She lets him get up and take the temperatures. But none of this makes her evil. He is a wounded soldier in a foreign country about to go back to the front. She is comforting him. She offers him love and affection. She is the nurse every wounded soldier no doubt dreams of. In letting the soldier get up and take the temperatures, Luz is arguably letting him act as her protector, strengthening his ego, which is likely to be fragile after his injury.

- Why is there an understanding that he won't drink and won't hang around with his friends? Is Luz being mean? Hemingway leaves this meaningful gap in the story, when he could have easily filled it in. Perhaps the soldier has a drinking problem. Early in the story other people do take away the bottles. The story doesn't say that Luz imposed this "no drinking" policy on him; perhaps he imposed it on himself to indicate his seriousness and trustworthiness to Luz.

- What does it mean when Luz breaks it off? Had there been a formal proposal, an acceptance, a ring, an engagement? All the reader knows is that the two are sleeping together and that they come to view each other as married—at least from the soldier's perspective. Hemingway says the understanding is that "he should go home so they might be married." What does "might" mean here? If they wanted to get married before he went back to the front, why didn't they arrange it when he returned? Such unexplained gaps must lead the reader to wonder about the facts. *Has* the soldier come to assume something that just isn't the case? He assumes, because they are sleeping together, they're going to get married? And poor Luz, feeling sorry for his wounds and his inevitable return to danger doesn't have the heart to tell him it just isn't that serious.

- If they really were in love, why might Luz fall for the Italian major? The reader isn't told anything about what things look like from her perspective. Does he write letters? Does he get a job? Does he follow through on his "no drinking" pledge? If he *does* get a job, then why hasn't Luz already come over? It seems likely, in fact, the more one thinks about it, that something is seriously wrong on his end.

Hemingway, by withholding vital information, allows the reader to jump to conclusions—conclusions that the careful reader must eventually withdraw. The reader leaps to conclusions, much like the soldier.

Shaping

Based on these notes, which meditated on the possibility that Luz is being set up and that the reader ought to see through this unfair treatment, I sketched out a draft of the main points I might want to make in articulating my response. Here's what I wrote:

Main point: Luz is right. It was a boy and girl affair.

Evidence:

- Their relationship is apparently based on sex; plus, some questionable ethics are involved in their affair.
- The soldier appears to be unreliable: Luz is afraid he won't get a job but will just drink and run around. Since she doesn't come to the United States, it appears that she may have been right.
- Luz obviously wasn't ready to get married, or she would have married him when he returned to the front, before he returned to the States. She just couldn't break his heart so soon after the war.
- He doesn't respond to her last letter; he doesn't try to win her back. Instead he responds with reckless indulgence. Our first impulse is to feel sorry for him; our more reasoned response is to fault him.

Problems:

- If Luz has no intention of marrying him, it is only momentarily kind to string him along.
- If Luz aims to get him to the States, where he'll slowly forget about her, then why do they have this understanding about his drinking and socializing?

Drafting

At this point, I feel ready to write a draft. After several tries, and some rethinking and rewriting, here is the essay I produced.

The Longer View of Hemingway's "A Very Short Story"

The obvious response described: the set-up.

Why this response occurs (point of view): more set-up for an alternative response.

How third person seems like first.

Transition to a different response, one that looks beyond the point of view.

This focuses on the crucial factor in our response to Luz: she betrays him.

Most readers of Hemingway's "A Very Short Story" will naturally pity the poor nameless soldier. He is wounded in the war, and then his fiancée breaks off their relationship when she falls for an Italian major. Her name, Luz, which might be pronounced like "lose," points to his fate: where women are involved, he will lose. As a final indignity and injury, another woman gives him gonorrhea, emphasizing his status as a victim and a loser—because of women. Although the main villain is Luz, his experience with the salesgirl, who wounds him in a different way, suggests quite simply that women are untrustworthy, evil, dangerous—as bad as the war, it seems.

But this immediate reaction of pity is the effect of our point of view. Although the story is told in third person, Hemingway actually gives us, as Robert Scholes points out in *Semiotics and Interpretation* (Yale UP, 1982), what is essentially the soldier's point of view. Repeatedly in the brief story, we are told what he experiences and what he is thinking. In the opening, for instance, we are told that "he could look out over the top of the town." We learn that Luz "was cool and fresh in the hot night"—a perception that clearly is his. We know his motivation for trying not to talk under anaesthetic (he does not want to "blab"), and we know how many letters he received and what was in them. We never know, however, what Luz is really thinking, and we learn the content of her letters from his perspective, when he reads them. The real context of their writing is hidden from the reader.

But Hemingway gives the careful reader plenty of clues that suggest we should look closer, overcoming the limitations of the narrative's point of view. Is Luz in fact entirely the villain, and the soldier purely the innocent victim?

Our opinion of Luz is of course influenced by the fact that in falling for the Italian major, she betrays the American soldier. There is little question that Luz made a mistake, but it is also clear that she pays for her mistake, for "The major did not marry her in the spring, or any other time." And when Luz writes to the soldier about the major's departure, she is perhaps attempting to resurrect her relationship with the soldier, but he fails to respond. The soldier cannot forgive her, apparently.

The letter is most important in shaping this negative response to Luz.

Nor, it seems, can many readers. The most important reason, I believe, is Luz's letter breaking off her relationship with the soldier. Specifically, her assertion that "theirs had been only a boy and girl affair" seems especially thoughtless and cruel. It is bad enough to be dumped, but it is even worse to learn that your own relationship was, in your partner's view, immature and superficial. But before we damn Luz's insensitivity, we ought to consider the possible validity of her remark. In other words, is she possibly right? Was their relationship only a boy and girl affair?

My response, contrasting the obvious response: Luz may be right.

What in fact is the basis of their relationship? It appears to be only physical. All we know of his view of Luz is that she is "cool and fresh." She sounds more like a soft drink or a vegetable than a partner for life.

I see Luz's immaturity easily.

Luz is after all sleeping in the hospital with one of her patients, and another pronunciation of her name, as "loose," may also be appropriate. When she says their relationship was immature, perhaps she accurately assesses her own behavior. The conditions, to be sure, were extraordinary: it is wartime, and the wounded soldier is returning to the front. I can understand Luz's looseness, but I can also agree that she is immature.

I also see the soldier's immaturity.

Her assessment of the soldier's maturity also seems accurate to me. Just look at his response to her last letter. He goes from hospital-bed sex to taxicab sex. Hemingway provides the tawdry details to emphasize his poor judgment: "A short time after [her letter] he contracted gonorrhea from a sales girl in a loop department store while riding in a taxicab through Lincoln Park." The poor soldier is wounded again in "combat," but surely this problem is his own fault. It is not Luz's fault, nor even the salesgirl's fault, is it? Even if we grant that mature and thoughtful people might contract a sexually transmitted disease, and that things were much different back then, the circumstances here

Most immature: his response to Luz's breakup.

still do not suggest responsible behavior. In fact, it is hard for me to imagine how he could be more immature, unless perhaps he had sex on the sidewalk with a prostitute.

How I respond to earlier evidence of his immaturity.

I also notice the soldier's promise not to drink, nor to see "his friends or anyone." Given the reference early in the story to drinking on the roof, I have to wonder if he has a drinking problem. I wonder why they did not marry when he returned from the front. There was not sufficient time before he left, but surely there is enough time when he gets back. It seems fair to suspect that the lack of time was just a convenient excuse. Likewise, why does he go ahead and leave Luz if he is unhappy with the arrangement? How long does it take him to get a job? Does he in fact get one? If so, then why is Luz still overseas? We are not told many things we need to know to evaluate his responsibility; but what is left out, together with what we do know, does suggest to me that Luz's view may not be thoughtless or cruel, but simply accurate. Theirs was indeed a boy and girl affair. At least Luz is perceptive enough to see it.

I think Luz is right: I can see her side.

PRACTICING READER-RESPONSE CRITICISM

I offer here three works along with some questions intended to stimulate your responses, helping you to develop a reader-response essay. These are just sample questions; other ones will probably occur to you. The important thing is to generate materials that allow you to evolve and articulate your response. Without you, there is no response.

Since There's No Help
Michael Drayton

Since there's no help, come, let us kiss and part,—
Nay, I have done, you get no more from me;
And I am glad, yea glad with all my heart,
That thus so cleanly I myself can free;
Shake hands for ever, cancel all our vows,

And when we meet at any time again,
Be it not seen in either of our brows
That we one jot of former love retain.
Now at the last gasp of Love's latest breath,
When his pulse failing, Passion speechless lies,   10
When Faith is kneeling by his bed of death,
And Innocence is closing up his eyes,—
Now if thou would'st, when all have given him over,
From death to life thou migh'st him yet recover.

(1619)

QUESTIONS

1. As you read the first line, what scene do you imagine taking place? At the end of the first line, what tone do you imagine the speaker is using?

2. How do the next three lines (2–4) affect your perception of the speaker's tone? What do the words "cleanly" and "free" suggest about the speaker's tone?

3. The speaker says about ten times (depending on how you count them) that the lovers should break it off. Why all the repetition? And why the extreme declaration that not "one jot of former love" should remain?

4. Imagine yourself as the person being addressed in this poem. How would you feel after line 8?

5. How does your view of the relationship change in the last six lines? How does presenting "Love" as a dying person affect your response?

6. The poem speaks to "you." Who is this "you"? What clues does the poem give us about the character of "you"?

7. Sometime around 1591 Michael Drayton fell totally in love with Anne Goodere (he said he lost his mind over her). This sonnet was probably written shortly after that, even though it was not published until 1619. Anne Goodere married Sir Henry Rainsford in 1596; Drayton never married. But he did spend every summer at Clifford Hall, the country home of Anne and Henry, his passion apparently turning into a deep friendship. How does this information affect your response to the poem?

Killing the Bear
Judith Minty

1   She has strung the hammock between two birch trees at the edge of the clearing. Now she drifts in and out of the light there and drowsily studies the pattern made by the rope's weaving and the flickering leaves.

2   When she had the dog, he stretched out beneath the hammock. Hackles raised, growling and nipping at flies, he'd meant to save her from shadows. In truth, he startled at noises, even at shifts in the wind, and she ended up more his protector than the other way around.

⌘

3   There were wolves at the little zoo when she was a child. She heard them howling from her aunt's kitchen and went to see them up close.

4   And a bear.

5   Three times she visited, slowly circling the bear pen, but he was always sleeping. He looked like a bundle of clothes by the dead tree. His fence was electrified and posted with signs, and she was afraid to touch the iron bars.

6   The wolves set off a chorus of neighborhood dogs. Their calling floated back and forth all that summer vacation.

⌘

7   She lies in the hammock every afternoon, her life in the rhythm of the woods. Up at dawn to the shrill pitch of bluejays. Logs tossed into the stove, match lit, breath steaming in the cabin's chill. Trip to the outhouse, coffee perking, bucket of water from the river. The rest of the morning, ping of nails driven into boards. Her porch is nearly done. One room and another room. Something inside and something out.

8   The afternoon silence and the sway of the hammock lull her and when she hears a low guttural, she thinks, at first, it is the dog. Then she remembers the dog is gone.

9   She struggles to sit up and makes the hammock sway crazily.

10   A bear stands beyond the pines—small jets of eyes, heavy black coat. He snuffles, then drops on all fours and weaves into the forest.

11   Her hands lift to cover her breasts.

⌘

12   Her favorite doll was a stuffed animal and she slept with it close to her heart. She was nine when her mother said, "Give me your bear for three months. Let's see if you can stop sucking your thumb."

13   She tried very hard to stop, and when the time was up, she asked for the bear again.

14   Her mother said, "Another month."

15   One day, as she sat in the kitchen watching a cake being stirred and poured into the pan and then put into the oven, it came to her that her bear was gone, that it had been thrown down the incinerator.

16   Only a few years ago, her mother told her, misspeaking even then, "I'm sorry for burning the animal in you."

❧

17   Her hammer has stopped its thump and echo. The roof is laid. The porch smells of fresh paint. She has hauled the old sofa out and can sit there in the evenings, if she wants.

18   When the bear understood that she was alone, he came closer. The first time, she was reading in the hammock and heard something like a sigh. She knew it was him, even before she caught a glimpse of black gliding through the woods. The next time, he was so close she smelled him—a terrible, rancid odor. Without looking, she swung out of the hammock and walked to the cabin. Two days later, he stood next to the birch tree, breath rattling his throat. If she'd turned, she could have touched the bristles on his shoulder.

❧

19   The Gilyak tribe honored him. They put his head on a stake outside their doors and made offerings to it. On Yezo Island, the Ainus thought he was a man trapped inside the body of a bear. If a hunter found a cub, he brought it to his wife who suckled it.

20   In Lapland he was King of Beasts. The men lived alone, purifying themselves, for three days after the hunt. At the funeral, after they had feasted, they put his bones back together in the ground.

21   Once she spent an evening with two Swedes. At dinner, their wineglasses held the tint of leaves. Ole, the painter, said, "You live in green light." Gunnar told magic tales. "When a woman meets a bear in the woods, she must lift her skirt. Then he will let her pass."

❧

22   In the travelogue about Alaska, the Kodiak caught a salmon, his claws stretched out like fingers. When the second bear approached, he

reared up. He looked soft and gentle, as if he were greeting a friend, until, with a sweep of his paw, he split open the head of the other.

23   In college, a classmate told about the summer he'd worked at Yellowstone and got too close. He never felt the nick, only knew when blood trickled down his forehead.

24   There was also the news story about the woman dragged from her tent in the middle of the night, crying, "He's killing me. Oh God, he's killing me." The bear carried the woman away, his claws tangled in her hair, ripping at her arm.

25   When she drove to town for supplies, she bought a secondhand rifle. She keeps it loaded now, propped against the doorjamb inside the cabin.

26   The clerk at the hardware store showed her how to fire it, how to aim along the sights. He winked and told her she could get a man with it at twenty yards. She said she didn't need a man, just wanted to do some hunting.

27   She misses the dog. She carries the gun awkwardly over her shoulder when she goes to the woodpile, or to the river.

28   Her calendar hangs on the cabin wall, each day of summer marked with an X, the rest of the year clean and open. She turns up the wick on the lamp and starts to brush her hair, staring at her reflection in the windowpane.

29   She is thinking about leaving. She is thinking about driving out of the clearing.

30   When the scream begins, it breaks against the walls. It shudders in a moan, then rises. Everything, even the wind, holds its breath.

31   It is over so quickly she almost believes it didn't happen and raises the brush again, and barely recognizes herself in the glass. She runs to the lamp and blows out the flame, then to the window, hoping she will not see what must be there.

32   She did not shoot cleanly the first time. When he ripped the screen and tore the siding loose, she stood on the porch, gun leveled.

33   "Go away."

34   He was no more than ten feet from her when she fired. He spun around and fell to the ground, then raised himself up.

35   When she realized she had only wounded him, she ran into the cabin and turned the lock and leaned against the door. She could hear him thrashing and bellowing in the bushes and against the trees.

36   She knew she would have to step onto the porch again, go to the ripped screen, with nothing but night air between them. She would have to take aim and shoot again. And if that didn't stop him, she would have to slip the bolt and reload the rifle and stand there and shoot him again until he stopped bawling and weeping and falling down and getting up and lurching against the trees.

37   When they began this, she never thought she would have to kill him so slow. She never dreamed she would have to hurt him so much.

❀

38   It is nearly dawn when he dies, when she gets up from her chair, when his groans stop pricking her skin. She takes the flashlight and goes out on the porch. She shines the beam around in the gray light and sees the blood dried on the new screen and on the fresh-painted sill and spattered on the leaves around the cabin. She sees the trampled bushes and broken branches and where he crawled into the weeds.

39   She shines the arc out, light bouncing on tree and log, until it lands on a black heap, huddled in the middle of the clearing.

40   As soon as the sun rises, she begins to dig, and by midafternoon she is through with it—the rope tied to him, the car backed up to the hole, the rifle and box of ammunition remembered and dropped in next to him, the musty soil put back, and branches over that.

41   Then she bathes with the last of the water from the river and sweeps the cabin floor, thinking that rain will wash away the blood and that, soon enough, snow will fall and cover it all.

❀

42   It is dark when she gets to the state line. Next summer, she will dig him up to take the claws.

(1991)

QUESTIONS

1. What associations do the first two paragraphs bring to your mind? Can you imagine yourself in a similar scene? How would you feel? How do you react to the suggestion

that she ended up more the dog's protector "than the other way around"?

2. Do paragraphs 3–6 alter the mood created by the first two paragraphs? What contrasting moods are created by the third section?

3. What is your response to the following sentence? "Her hands lift to cover her breasts." For instance, what expectations does the statement create for you?

4. How do paragraphs 12–16 affect the reader's understanding of her attitude toward bears?

5. How does her construction of a porch and the movement of her sofa onto the porch affect your response to the bear's appearance? What does the bear's smell contribute to your response? How about the bear's sex? (The bear is a "him," not an "it.")

6. Paragraphs 19–21 observe how various cultures have honored bears, but it also has its ominous aspects. Explain how the reader's sense of danger builds in the seventh section.

7. Why are the summer days marked with an X? Does that have anything to do with bears?

8. Describe your reaction to paragraphs 32–41.

9. Is the final sentence surprising? Why, or why not?

All Bears

Caroline Fraser

Are Dangerous. Enjoy Them—
say signs—At a Distance. What they want
is huckleberries,
salmonberries, bearberries,
areas of dense brush, heavy   5
forage, golden-
mantled ground squirrels, spawning
salmon full of eggs, corn
spilled from freight cars
on the Continental Divide, canned   10
spaghetti, freeze-dried
beef Stroganoff, anything
you've got. They want to know
whether you're predator
or prey, but what they really   15

prefer is carrion. They like
to roll in it. They may run off
and then return and pull you
out of a tree
like fruit and eat part   20
and stash the rest
for later. But remember:
it's not you
they're after—not the camper lying
zipped in his tent   25
in the rain, hearing the drops splashing
overhead like cloth
tearing, not the girl
cramped on the front seat
of the car, staring   30
into the black, seeing the thick
trunks rear up
and walk bipedally; not your watch,
not your wallet, not your waterproof
down coat. The bears, they could take you   35
or leave you alone
but for the fact
of what they can smell.

[1991]

QUESTIONS

1. Consider how the ending affects your response. Specifically,
   what is suggested by the assertion that "The bears, they could
   take you or leave you alone"? How is that effect altered by the
   last two lines?

2. Is there any logical order to the list of "What they want"
   (beginning in line 2, ending with "anything/you've got")?
   How does the list progress, and how is your response
   affected?

3. How comforting are the lines following the assertion "it's not
   you/they're after"?

4. Consider how the following people might respond to this
   poem: an environmentalist; a hunter; a scoutmaster; a
   comedian; you.

Useful Terms for Reader-Response Criticism

Affect: In discussing your response, you may well talk about how something affects you. Be sure to distinguish the spelling of this word from the following one:

Effect: This word refers (usually) to what the work creates in you: the effect of the work comes from how it affects you. "Affect" is usually a verb, and "effect" a noun—although there are exceptions. Psychiatrists, for instance, talk about the "affect" of someone, referring to that person's emotions and demeanor: "He has a flat affect" means that his emotions appear to be flat. Also, "effect" can be used as a verb, meaning "to bring something into being." For instance, "we are going to effect some changes in the retirement plan" means that we are going to bring about changes.

Expectation, anticipation: In describing your response you're likely to talk about how the text prepares you for something and then surprises or satisfies you.

Implied reader: The reader that you think the author had in mind. In trying to respond as the implied reader, you aim to put aside your own idiosyncrasies and try to play the role of the reader the author was addressing. Obviously, the implied reader is a fiction, a composite of lots of real readers.

Subjective response: This stance involves letting your own personality figure freely into your response. With a subjective response, you're not trying to be the implied reader (as in a receptive stance). Instead, you're trying to respond authentically, honestly, richly, personally.

Works Cited: Reader Response

Bleich, David. *Readings and Feelings: An Introduction to Subjective Criticism.* Urbana, IL: National Council of Teachers of English, 1975.

———. *Subjective Criticism.* Baltimore: Johns Hopkins UP, 1978.

Crosman, Robert. "How Readers Make Meaning." In *Literary Theories in Praxis.* Ed. Shirley Staton. Philadelphia: U of Pennsylvania P, 1987. 357–66. Rpt. from *College Literature* 9 (1982): 207–15.

Fish, Stanley. *Doing What Comes Naturally: Change, Rhetoric, and the Practice of Theory in Literary and Legal Studies.* Durham, NC: Duke UP, 1989.

———. *Is There a Text in This Class? The Authority of Interpretive Communities.* Cambridge: Harvard UP, 1980.

———. *Self-Consuming Artifacts: The Experience of Seventeenth-Century Literature.* Berkeley: U of California P, 1972.

———. *Surprised by Sin: The Reader in Paradise Lost.* New York: St. Martins, 1967.

———. *The Trouble with Principle.* Harvard UP, 1999.

————. *There's No Such Thing As Free Speech: And It's a Good Thing, Too.* Oxford UP, 1994.

Kuhn, Thomas. *The Structure of Scientific Revolutions.* 2nd ed. Chicago: U of Chicago P, 1970.

Rosenblatt, Louise. *Literature as Exploration.* 1938. Rev. ed. New York: Noble and Noble, 1968.

————. *The Reader, the Text, the Poem: The Transactional Theory of the Literary Work.* Carbondale: Southern Illinois UP, 1978.

Scholes, Robert. *Semiotics and Interpretation.* New Haven: Yale UP, 1982.

Tompkins, Jane. "The Reader in History: The Changing Shape of Literary Response." In *Reader-Response Criticism.* Ed. Jane Tompkins. Baltimore: Johns Hopkins UP, 1980.

Recommended Further Reading: Reader Response

Beach, Richard. *A Teacher's Introduction to Reader-Response Theories.* Urbana, Illinois: National Council of Teachers of English, 1993. A very comprehensive overview of the wide range of reader-oriented approaches.

Berg, Temma. "Psychologies of Reading." In *Tracing Literary Theory.* Ed. Joseph Natoli. Urbana: U of Illinois P, 1987. 248–77. A lively discussion of the way personality affects textual reception.

Brenner, Gerry. *Performative Criticism: Experiments in Reader Response.* Albany, NY: State University of New York Press, 2004. In this entertaining variation on reader-response criticism, Brenner brings characters from classic literary works to life, and they respond to works which they inhabit (or rather Brenner responds through them).

Gaillet, Lynee Lewis. "Reading." In *Keywords in Composition Studies.* Ed. Paul Heilker and Peter Vandenberg. Portsmouth, NH: Boynton/Cook, 1996. 196–200. A brief yet expansive view of our current conceptions of making meaning. Includes a concise treatment of reader-response criticism in the context of the teaching of writing.

Holland, Norman. "Hamlet—My Greatest Creation." *Journal of the American Academy of Psychoanalysis* 3 (1975): 419–27. A classic essay, often reprinted and excerpted, arguing that meaning is not discovered, but is actively made as the reader responds.

Iser, Wolfgang. *The Implied Reader.* Baltimore: Johns Hopkins UP, 1974. Influential and still readable, Iser's work convincingly argues that texts provide cues that indicate an implied reader—a role the real reader may assume, play, or reject.

Jauss, Hans. *Toward an Aesthetic of Reception.* Trans. Bahti Hemel. Hempstead: Harvester Wheatsheaf, 1982. A challenging book that places reader-response in historical context: how does a reader's historical position affect his or her response? Should we attempt to respond as the initial readers of a work? Is that possible?

Peckham, Morse. "The Problem of Interpretation." *College Literature* 6
    (1979): 1–17. A compelling and entertaining argument leading to
    the conclusion that the meaning of a statement is the response to
    that statement.
Wimsatt, W. K. "The Affective Fallacy." In *The Verbal Icon: Studies in the
    Meaning of Poetry.* Ed. W. K. Wimsatt, Jr. Lexington: UP of Kentucky,
    1954. The famous essay articulating the New Critical axiom that liter-
    ary criticism is not properly concerned with the reader's response,
    but should focus on the work itself. Reader-response critics would
    embrace this "fallacy."

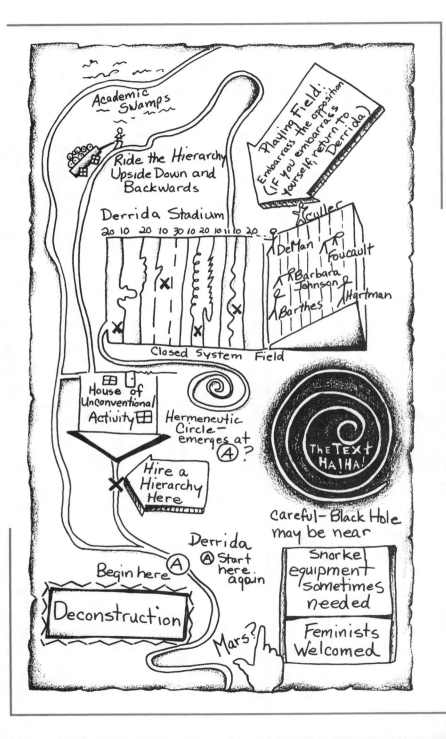

CHAPTER 5

Opening Up the Text:

Structuralism and Deconstruction

Imagine being the first to say, with confidence: uncertainty.

—Michael Blumenthal

THE PURPOSES OF STRUCTURALISM AND DECONSTRUCTION

If New Criticism focuses on the work, and reader response criticism focuses on the reader, then structuralism might be seen as the combination of these two approaches: a structure is something—a pattern, a design—that is somehow "in" a text, but a structure is also something that readers must actively perceive. Without some-one reading, there is no structure; without a structure, there is no one making sense. You have an understanding of the structure of the English language, and that allows you to identify the subjects, the verbs, the modifiers, and so forth of the sentences you are reading—and thereby make sense. This drive to find organization and meaningfulness is so powerful that human beings can find shapes in clouds or the scorch marks of a tortilla. If we can find structure where (most reasonable people would say) there really isn't any, we can also fail to detect structures, as in hidden codes or unknown languages. But when communication takes place, it occurs because these two elements, text and reader, come together: a perceiver sees how the surface experience fits into some underly-ing set of conventions. And if structuralism aims to understand how this conveyance of meaning occurs, deconstruction aims to show

how it doesn't—how the structures that we bring to language and experience inevitably fail, how meaning slips and slides and comes apart. Deconstruction is, in a literal and theoretical sense, what comes after structuralism: to see how something comes apart, one must first see how it went together, so a deconstructive analysis is possible only after some degree of structuralist analysis. Thus, this chapter deals with structuralism and deconstruction, but it focuses on deconstruction. Deconstruction has not rendered structuralism obsolete, but it has, for many people at least, changed our thinking about what structuralism actually does, undermining the scientific exuberance of the early structuralists.

Structuralism and Semiotics

Structuralism grows from Ferdinand de Saussure's series of lectures on language, delivered between 1913 to 1915, but not translated into English or widely known until the late 1950s. Rather than thinking of a particular language in terms of its history, moving through time, Saussure took a "synchronic" view, looking at the relationships of all the parts of a language at a given moment in time. The surface elements of language, which Saussure called *parole* (French for "speech"), may vary widely; it is our understanding of the underlying structure, which Saussure called *langue* (French for "language"), that allows us to make sense of the surface.

Saussure's structural approach to linguistics not only provided a powerful analytical tool, but it also altered the way we think about language and meaning. In particular, the distinction between a "signifier" (a word, an image) and a "signified" (the concept that the signifier is pointing to) is crucial, exposing the arbitrary relationship between the words we use and the ideas in our heads. Anyone who can speak two languages fluently knows that some things that are easy to say in one language may be difficult or even impossible to say in another. Different languages structure the world differently: If one language has eleven different words for fog, and another language has only one, then it's reasonable to assume that speakers of these two languages look at fog differently (and probably spend different amounts of time in fog). It's not that one system of meaning is better than another—that fog either comes in eleven different kinds or one. Fog comes in however many kinds we are able to perceive (and desire to distinguish)—and this organizing of the world is based on underlying structures. Crucially, structure is based on difference: the word "bat" is not "cat" because of the difference in the two initial sounds. At the same time, different languages have some structural features in common. Structuralism seeks to find those underlying commonalities and distinguishing differences, bringing a scientific approach to language.

As a method, however, structuralism can be applied to anything, not just language, and "semiotics" is the term usually employed for this larger enterprise. In the late 1950s, for instance, Claude Levi-Strauss began to demonstrate how structural analysis could be applied to cultures—with fascinating results. Looking for the underlying structures of food preparation, for instance, Levi-Strauss in *The*

Raw and the Cooked (1964) observed that in every culture people divide their food into three classes: raw, rotten, and cooked. This fundamental structure has resulted in some wildly different cuisines that are nonetheless organized in the same way. In one society, moldy clumps of solidified cow's milk are consumed; in another, whale blubber with maggots in it is valued. Specific rules that create systems of meaning allow both these cultures to make sense of their food.

Structuralism, as noted above, shares the assumption of reader-response criticism that meaning is made, not found. But structuralism, rather than focusing on the response itself, seeks to expose the system of meaning that enabled the response. And sign systems are at work, structuralists argued, in all sorts of places that we might not suspect. Football games, for instance, have an underlying structure that allows observers to make sense of what is going on. If all the players are on the field, for instance, then someone who understands the conventions of football knows that it is either before or after the game, or the game has been somehow disrupted. The national anthem and a prayer precede many games, associating the athletic occasion structurally with patriotic and spiritual events.

Post-Structuralism and Deconstruction

Not very long ago, "deconstruction" and "post-structuralism" were used only in what was perceived as radical criticism (or in attacks on such criticism). Now the term "deconstruction" has become so popular and pervasive and has been used in so many different ways and contexts that it is hard to say what it means. As Gregory Jay puts it, "deconstruction has now become an indeterminate nominative" (xi): a name without a reference. If the assumptions of deconstruction are correct, however, "deconstruction" always was an uncertain term, for deconstruction's supposition that all terms are unstable must apply to itself. Few efforts would appear to be more ironic, perhaps even comical, than attempting to define and explain a philosophical position that assumes the inevitability of error and misreading, the impossibility of explaining and defining in any stable way.

There are, however, at least three reasons to attempt to explain deconstruction anyway:

1. The alternative to explaining what in the final analysis cannot be explained is silence. We explain deconstruction, and we practice it, even though something is always left undone, unstated, unclear, unthought of. Another explanation can

supplement this one, and then another one can supplement it. Such is the case with any term, or perhaps with anything human.

2. Deconstruction makes no effort to suppress its own irony or absurdity; instead, deconstructive critics have generally indulged a playfulness that from the perspective of traditional criticism seems at times unprofessional; in the merciless punning of some of the most prominent deconstructive critics, it has seemed occasionally almost juvenile. (I am thinking for instance of Paul de Man's comparison of Archie Bunker [the television character] to "a de-bunker of the *arche* [or origin], an archie De-Bunker such as Nietzsche or Jacques Derrida"[9].)

3. Deconstruction can be learned by students, and it often stimulates a wonderfully imaginative playfulness and scrutiny. In fact, rather than being an esoteric, foreign, abstract, discouraging approach, deconstruction for most students, in my experience, makes tremendous sense: it articulates precisely what they have in fact already assumed in a vague way. Students who understand deconstruction are much more adventurous, questioning, insightful readers.

So, here we go. If the room starts spinning or you find yourself getting dizzy, take a deep breath or put the book on the floor so you can read with your head between your legs. Seriously, the next little stretch is a bit theoretical and even strange, but you'll see several illustrations later on. Just hang in there, and it will get clearer.

Structuralism and semiotics produced many richly revealing and interesting analyses of texts and social phenomena—wrestling matches, detergent boxes, advertisements, anything. But some thinkers started to question just how far structuralist readings could be taken, and they exposed gaps and inconsistencies in the structures they examined. This push beyond structuralism, revealing the failures of systems of meaning, came to be known as post-structuralism. Post-structuralism did not put structuralism entirely out of business: one can still do structuralist analysis, but post-structuralism has altered our sense of what is produced by such readings. And post-structuralism is the set of assumptions and ideas that make deconstruction possible. What is deconstruction? To answer that question, let's turn to Jacques Derrida (1930–2004).

Derrida, a Frenchman, is without question the most important figure for deconstruction. He relentlessly and astonishingly exposed the uncertainties of using language. Derrida starts, we might say, from the recognition that words do not refer directly to things. If they did, all languages would represent the world in the same way, and the meanings of words would be stable. Instead of words referring to things, Derrida argued that the signifier (the word) and the signified (its reference, a concept) are not a unified entity, but rather an arbitrary and constantly shifting relationship. A dictionary only seems to stabilize a language, for what we actually find in a dictionary is the postponement or deferment of meaning: words have multiple definitions, and these definitions require us to seek the meaning of other words, which are themselves defined in the same way.

Even if it were possible to construct instantaneously a dictionary that would be perfectly up-to-date, we would still find ambiguity, multiplicity, and slippage pervading the language. The reason is nicely captured in Derrida's most famous statement, "*Il n'y a pas de hors-tete,*" which is translated as "There is nothing outside the text," and as "There is no outside to the text." (In itself, this uncertainty regarding translation tells us something important about language.) Meaning cannot get outside of language, to reality. Therefore, words always refer to other words.

Deconstruction reveals the arbitrariness of language most strikingly by exposing the contradictions in a discourse, thereby showing how a text undermines itself. As Barbara Johnson puts it, deconstruction proceeds by "the careful teasing out of warring forces of signification within the text itself" (5). Or, as Jonathan Culler says, "To deconstruct a discourse is to show how it undermines the philosophy it asserts, or the hierarchical oppositions on which it relies" (*Deconstruction* 86). This exposure of a text's self-contradictions is possible, deconstruction assumes, because words cannot stabilize meaning: if we choose to say one thing, we are leaving out another thing. And there is always a gap, a space in the text, that the reader cannot ultimately fill in.

Deconstruction is therefore particularly valuable because of its power to open up a text that we may have seen as limited or closed. Popularly, "to deconstruct" seems to be used to mean "to dismantle" or "to destroy," as if "deconstruction" were a fancier form of "destruction." But for most informed critics, deconstruction is not so much a way to obliterate the meaning of a text, as it is a way to multiply meaning. Deconstruction thus encourages us to resist a complacent acceptance of anything and to question our positions and statements in a particularly rigorous way, even reading texts against themselves.

For instance, let's take a very simple text, one appearing beside an elevator: "Seeing Eye Dogs Only." A deconstructive reading of this text might point out that although it appears to extend assistance to the visually impaired, it literally should force them to walk up the stairs, for the sign literally appears to say, "This elevator is reserved for seeing-eye dogs. No other animals or persons can ride it." Or we might argue that the text shifts attention and power to a certain kind of dog, while ignoring the owners of the dogs. Here's a text ostensibly put up to help blind persons, and it actually ignores them. A blind person with a seeing-eye monkey, presumably, must not ride. Plus, blind persons obviously cannot read the sign, which suggests that some other intention does motivate it. Perhaps the sign is intended to make sure that someone who is fully sighted and has a retired seeing-eye dog as a pet, can take such a dog on the elevator? Isn't that what it says? What *is* the point of this sign?

Although such undoing of a text may seem at first glance a bit silly, it actually has the potential for enormous practical value. Imagining all the things a text *might* be saying, including even the opposite of what it may appear to say, will help us to become more creative and careful readers and writers. Some colleagues of mine recently wrote a policy statement that told students "You will fail your Freshman English course if you miss more than three scheduled tutoring sessions." One student read this statement as a prediction rather than a rule, and he elected to skip all his tutoring sessions in order to prove the prediction wrong. As he told me later, appealing his failing grade, "I knew I was smart enough to pass the course without any help, and I resented them telling me I couldn't do it, and I worked twice as hard as I would have otherwise." A deconstructive stance might have anticipated this reading, and precluded it by revising the sentence.

But a deconstructive stance not only may help us anticipate some of the ways that even simple texts can be misread; it may also help us see what is being excluded or suppressed in a text. For instance, the J. Peterman Company advertises a reproduction of "Hemingway's Cap." The point of the advertisement is, of course, that Ernest Hemingway picked out a tough, distinctive, very masculine hat to wear, and now you can have the same. The ad conveys this message by telling us that Hemingway probably bought the cap "on the road to Ketchum," which is where Hemingway's Idaho ranch was located, the scene of hunting, fishing, and other outdoor activities; that he found it "among the beef jerky wrapped in

Hemingway's Cap.

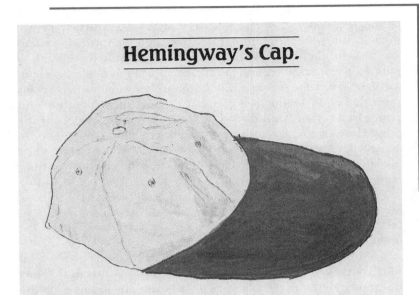

He probably bought <u>his</u> in a gas station on the road to Ketchum, next to the cash register, among the beef jerky wrapped in cellophane. Or maybe in a tackle shop in Key West.

I had to go to some trouble to have this one made for you and me but it had to be done. The long bill, longer than I, at least, ever saw before, makes sense.

The visor: deerskin; soft and glareless and unaffected by repeated rain squalls. The color: same as strong scalding espresso, lemon peel on the side, somewhere in the mountains in the north of Italy.

Ten-ounce cotton-duck crown. 6 brass grommets for ventilation. Elastic at back to keep this treasure from blowing off your head and into the trees.

Sizes: M, L, XL.

Price: $33. (He probably got change from a five when he bought the original.)

cellophane," which also helps create a rustic, macho atmosphere (isn't beef jerky primarily eaten by guys in a duck blind or deer stand—or wishing they were?); that the bill is longer than average, longer in fact than the advertiser has ever seen, and "impervious" to rainstorms; that the cap is the color of "scalding expresso"—a drink for tough men who need a tough cap; that there's an elastic band "to keep this treasure from blowing off your head and into the trees"; and much else. Thus, the advertisement celebrates masculine toughness, durability, endurance, and sensibility, using these values to sell the product.

But a deconstructive stance encourages an acute alertness to rhetorical strategies and even the assumptions these strategies depend upon. Although the cap appears to promote and depend upon a masculine toughness, deconstruction tells us that it also unavoidably promotes and depends upon masculine insecurity. Why would anyone want the longest bill anyone ever saw? For the same reason one might want the fastest car anyone ever saw. Or the biggest ranch. Made of "deerskin," this longest bill becomes a symbol of its owner's power and potency. It may be too much to claim that the bill is a phallic substitute, although it is pretty clear what part of their skin many men would consider most "dear." Certainly, Hemingway was fascinated by potency and its lack: in *The Sun Also Rises,* for instance, Jake Barnes has been emasculated by a wartime injury and loses Brett, Lady Ashley, to a young bullfighter and then to another aristocrat.

Likewise, the idea that Hemingway may have bought his cap "on the road to Ketchum" conjures up scenes of hunting and fishing. But Ketchum is also where Hemingway committed suicide. Seriously ill for some time, he put a shotgun in his mouth and pulled the trigger. Denied the sort of active, impervious masculinity embodied in the cap, Hemingway apparently could not face a compromised life.

How the cap relates to this weakness or insecurity is most startlingly seen in an especially revealing (or especially unfortunate) phrase, referring to the "elastic at back to keep this treasure from blowing off your head." In asserting that the cap is a "treasure," the ad unavoidably raises the danger—the inevitability really—of losing it. This sentence is meant to reassure potential owners, but it also points out how only the elastic (which must age and wear out) stands between the owner and loss of his manly treasure. The advertisement thus helps to foster an insecurity that the cap covers

over; but in such a value system, depending on potency and toughness, the danger of something "blowing off your head" is very real,
as Hemingway's case reveals.

Is such a mischievous, even outrageous, allusion intended in
"blowing off your head"? Although I've had students who insist that
the phrase is a wickedly clever joke, that the ad's author must have
been aware of the implications of "blowing off your head" in the
context of Hemingway, the issue is really undecidable, and from a
deconstructive point of view irrelevant because other conflicting
and contradictory meanings are always available to the attentive,
creative reader. There will always be a trace of "don't buy this hat"
left in any urging to "buy this hat." And this counter-reading can
also be reversed. (I do own one of the caps.)

Let's turn now to some other examples and to the practical matter of how structuralism and deconstruction work on more complex
texts, which often even more readily lend themselves to opening up.

HOW TO DO STRUCTURALISM AND DECONSTRUCTION

In an essay designed to question and criticize, Lawrence Lipking
shows how deconstruction would deal with W. B. Yeats's famous
poem "Sailing to Byzantium." Since deconstruction turns a text
against itself, multiplying its meanings, it seems only appropriate
that Lipking's attack on deconstruction should provide a convenient illustration of deconstruction's value.

Here is Yeats's poem.

Sailing to Byzantium [1]

William Butler Yeats

I

That is no country for old men.[2] The young
In one another's arms, birds in the trees
—Those dying generations—at their song,
The salmon-falls, the mackerel-crowded seas

---

[1] *Byzantium:* Old name for the modern city of Istanbul, capital of the
Eastern Roman Empire, ancient artistic and intellectual center. Yeats uses
Byzantium as a symbol for "artificial" (and therefore deathless) art and
beauty, as opposed to the beauty of the natural world, which is bound to
time and death.

[2] *That . . . men:* Ireland, part of the time-bound world.

Fish, flesh, or fowl, commend all summer long 5
Whatever is begotten, born and dies.
Caught in that sensual music all neglect
Monuments of unaging intellect.

II

An aged man is but a paltry thing,
A tattered coat upon a stick, unless 10
Soul clap its hands and sing, and louder sing
For every tatter in its mortal dress,
Nor is there singing school but studying
Monuments of its own magnificence;
And therefore I have sailed the seas and come 15
To the holy city of Byzantium.

III

O sages standing in God's holy fire
As in the gold mosaic of a wall,
Come from the holy fire, perne in a gyre,[3]
And be the singing-masters of my soul. 20
Consume my heart away; sick with desire
And fastened to a dying animal
It knows not what it is; and gather me
Into the artifice of eternity.

IV

Once out of nature I shall never take 25
My bodily form from any natural thing,
But such a form as Grecian goldsmiths make
Of hammered gold and gold enameling
To keep a drowsy Emperor awake;[4]
Or set upon a golden bough[5] to sing 30
To lords and ladies of Byzantium
Of what is past, or passing, or to come.

(1927)

---

[3] *perne in a gyre:* Bobbin making a spiral pattern.

[4] *such . . . awake:* "I have read somewhere that in the Emperor's palace at Byzantium was a tree made of gold and silver, and artificial birds that sang" (Yeats's note).

[5] *golden bough:* In Greek legend, Aeneas had to pluck a golden bough from a tree in order to descend into Hades. As soon as the bough was plucked, another grew in its place.

Deconstruction requires a norm or a convention to work against. If we don't assume a text is logically coherent, then exposing its incoherence and self-difference is hardly remarkable. In a way, then, a deconstructive reading is like an extension of a New Critical reading: setting aside authorial intention and the reader's response, one first identifies the unity that appears to be present in the text and then divides and dispels it. But a deconstructive reading looks even more like structuralist reading that is pushed beyond the breaking point. I want to illustrate this point by studying the classic New Critical reading of Yeats's poem that is offered by Cleanth Brooks in *The Well-Wrought Urn* (1947). Saussure asserted that language operates by means of binary oppositions: "cold" means something because it is opposed to "hot"; "mean" makes sense because we understand "nice." Brooks's reading of Yeats's poem depends on his perception of a structure of certain tensions or oppositions, which include for instance "nature versus art." By this opposition, Brooks means (among other things) that the first two stanzas talk about "fish, flesh, or fowl" and about aging—aspects of nature. The second two stanzas talk about "gold mosaic," "artifice," "hammered gold"—works of art. Brooks discusses these other oppositions:

becoming	vs.	being
sensual	vs.	intellectual
here	vs.	Byzantium
aging	vs.	timelessness

To unify these oppositions, Brooks focuses on the speaker's "prayer," which begins in the third stanza and asks the "sages" to "come from the holy fire"; and he makes the word "artifice" the crux of the poem:

The word "artifice" fits the prayer at one level after another: the fact that he is to be taken *out of nature;* that his body is to be an artifice hammered out of gold; that it will not age but will have the finality of a work of art. (188)

In every opposition, Saussure said, one element is favored or privileged over the other; and Yeats seems, Brooks says, to favor the second elements in the list above. "Artifice," however, complicates matters:

But "artifice" unquestionably carries an ironic qualification too. The prayer, for all its passion, is a modest one. He does not ask that he be gathered into eternity—it will be enough if he is gathered into the "artifice of eternity." The qualification does not turn the prayer into mockery, but it is all-important: it limits as well as defines the power of the sages to whom the poet appeals. (189)

This move, as I pointed out in the chapter on New Criticism, is typical, as Brooks finds an ironic center that unifies the poem. Here is Brooks's thesis, as it is stated early in the essay, responding to the question of "which world" Yeats commits himself to:

To which world is Yeats committed? Which does he choose?

The question is idle—as idle as the question which the earnest school-marm puts to the little girl reading for the first time "L'Allegro—Il Penseroso": which does Milton *really* prefer, mirth or melancholy. . . .
     Yeats chooses both and neither. (187)

More directly, Brooks articulates his position this way near the end of his essay:

The irony [of the poem] is directed, it seems to me, not at our yearning to transcend the world of nature, but at the human situation itself in which supernatural and natural are intermixed—the human situation which is inevitably caught between the claims of both natural and supernatural. The golden bird whose bodily form the speaker will take in Byzantium will be withdrawn from the flux of the world of becoming. But so with-drawn, it will sing of the world of becoming—"Of what is past, or pass-ing, or to come." (189–90)

This "intermixture" that Brooks finds is for him the force uni-fying the poem's complex oppositions, thereby making possible the poem's greatness.

A deconstructive reading observes the text's structure of oppo-sitions, as Brooks has done, and it notices how the text appears to resolve its oppositions. But it goes further and shows how this reso-lution falls apart. Brooks claims that Yeats chooses both art and nature. But is that really true? In the final stanza, the speaker says, "Once out of nature I shall never take / My bodily form from any natural thing." If he escapes nature and becomes a golden work of art, then he has certainly chosen one member of the opposition. Brooks tries to cover this problem by saying the bird, outside of nature and time, will sing of the world of becoming—"Of what is past, or passing, or to come." But surely singing of something is not the same thing as being in it. Yeats *does choose*—art over nature, being over becoming, the intellectual over the sensual.

Or does he? The final step of deconstruction (after finding oppositions, assessing their hierarchy, positing their resolution, and questioning that resolution) is to call the reversal into question, placing the text in uncertainty. Lipking, employing a deconstructive stance, repeatedly shows how the poem fails to resolve its meaning. He asks, for instance, why should the soul "louder sing / For every tatter in its mortal dress"? Is it singing to distract itself or us from the tatters of its mortal dress? Then the singing is opposed to the tatters, as the soul sings in spite of physical ailments. Or is it singing in celebration of these tatters, because the body's deterioration brings the soul closer to separation from the body? Lipking ponders these alternatives and concludes that "the line does not make sense, if by sense we understand a single unequivocal meaning or even the Aristotelian logic that asserts that nothing can be itself and not itself at the same time. Language goes its own way" (431).

Likewise, Lipking raises the question of whether, in the third stanza, there is a singing school. If "Nor is there singing school" means there isn't one, then how come the speaker wants some singing masters in the next verse? Perhaps the speaker says there is no singing school *unless* it consists of studying monuments of the soul's magnificence. But such activity hardly sounds like a singing school, and it seems unlikely that such soul singing is learned in an academic way. In the final analysis, Lipking suggests that the poem, through a deconstructive lens anyway, is confusing.

Similarly, Lipking asks if the artifice of eternity is "something permanent (an eternal artifice) or something evanescent (an illusion without any substance)" (432). He confesses he can't decide. He also points even to the uncertain syntax of the opening "That" (which, Lipking points out, "Yeats himself said was the worst syntax he ever wrote"). In sum Lipking finds that "the elementary polarities that seem to provide its [the poem's] frame—the dialectic of 'that country' and Byzantium, of young and old, of time and timelessness, of body and soul, above all of nature and art—do not hold up under a careful reading" (432). Thus, "Whatever is begotten, born, and dies" only appears to parallel "what is past, or passing, or to come." The word "lives" would parallel "born" better than "passing," and "begotten" does not clearly relate to "past." Even the word "dies" is not entirely satisfactory because the birds' "song" is one that lives on from generation to generation.

These points may seem rather minor to you. But there is one internal contradiction, as Lipking amusingly says, "so important and obvious that it is noticed by a great many students, and even some critics":

> When the speaker claims that "Once out of nature I shall never take / My bodily form from any natural thing," he seems to ignore the blatant fact that every bodily form must be taken from nature, whether the form of a bird or simply the golden form embodied by an artist. (432–33)

In a famous letter, Sturge Moore did write to Yeats that "a goldsmith's bird is as much nature as a man's body, especially if it only sings like Homer and Shakespeare of what is past or passing or to come to Lords and Ladies" (qtd. Lipking 433). In fact, art seems already to be present in the world of nature that is described so artfully in the first verse. "That" country and Byzantium, Lipking says, "are equally unreal; they acquire significance only by being contrasted with each other" (433). "That" country never appears in the poem; it is always absent. Nor does the poet arrive at Byzantium, as Lipking reminds us: he is only "sailing to" it. And the problem, deconstruction tells us, is that we "swim in a sea of language" (435), where enduring "presence" is impossible: we never arrive where we're going, linguistically. Instead, we find only oppositions and differences that defer meaning.

In making this case, Lipking is depending on, I would argue, the following assumptions:

1. Meaning is made by binary oppositions, *but* one item is unavoidably favored (or "privileged") over the other.
2. This hierarchy is arbitrary and can be exposed and reversed.
3. Further, the text's oppositions and hierarchy can be called into question because texts contain within themselves unavoidable contradictions, gaps, spaces, and absences that defeat closure and determinate meaning. All reading is misreading.

These assumptions, I believe, lead Lipking to something like the following strategies:

1. Identify the pattern of oppositions in the text.
2. Determine which member appears to be favored and look for evidence that contradicts that favoring.
3. Expose the text's indeterminacy.

In its effects, deconstruction is quite comparable to other developments in twentieth-century thought. In mathematics, Kurt Gödel has shown how any mathematical system will contain at least one crucial axiom that cannot be proved within the system itself. There is always, in any interpretation, a loose end, an assumption that cannot be proven, a statement that is called into question by some other statement. Similarly, in physics, Heisenberg's uncertainty principle stipulates the indeterminacy of certain fundamental variables, like the position and momentum of a particle.

Still, we should keep in mind that in his essay Lipking demonstrates deconstruction only to attack it. He is not alone in thinking that deconstruction is disturbing and even dangerous. But many other people find it invigorating and useful. The most damning charge against deconstruction is that it allows a text to mean anything at all—or, as Lipking sees it, ultimately nothing. But deconstruction's supporters, both in Europe and America (who have somewhat different conceptions of the matter), believe that texts *always already* were unavoidably open to interpretation. Deconstruction, in this case, really changes nothing except our awareness of the complexity and "otherness" and openness of our discourse. A text (of any sort) means ultimately whatever people can be persuaded to believe it means, or what the entity with the most power says it means, or what each individual thinks it means. Language is just that pliable and elusive.

We turn now to a closer look at what happens when we adopt a post-structuralist stance and attempt to perform deconstructive criticism—leaving Yeats's golden bird for one of another metal.

THE WRITING PROCESS: A SAMPLE ESSAY

Here's a poem by Amy Clampitt, published on April 12, 1993, in *The New Yorker.*

Discovery
Amy Clampitt

The week the latest rocket went   1
up, a pod (if that's the word)
of manatees, come upriver
to Blue Spring, where it's
always warm, could be seen   5

lolling, jacketed, elephantine,
on the weedy borderline
between drowsing and waking,
breathing and drowning.
As they came up for air,   10
one by one, they seemed numb,
torpid, quite incurious. No
imagining these sirenians
dangerously singing. Or
gazing up yearningly: so much   15
for the Little Mermaid. True,
the long-lashed little ones
could have been trademarked
"Cute" by the likes of Walt Disney.
His world's over that way,   20

suitably for a peninsula where
the cozy mythologies we've
swindled ourselves with, on
taking things easy, might even
come true: sun-kissed nakedness   25
on the beach, year-round, guilt-free
hibiscus and oranges, fountains
welling up through the limestone,
the rumor of Ponce de León, having
found the one he was looking for,   30

living at ease in, some say
Boca Raton, others Cádiz. A last
bedtime placebo? Still, we keep
looking up. That clear morning,
just warm enough for a liftoff,   35
the fabulous itself could be seen
unwieldily, jacket by jacket,
in the act of shedding, as
a snake does its husk, or

a celebrant his vestments: 40
the fiery, the arrowy tip of it,
of the actual going invisible,
trailing its vaporous, ribboning
frond as from a kelp bed,
the umbilical roar of it   45
stumbling behind, while up in

> the belly of it, out of their
> element, jacketed, lolling
> and treading, the discoverers
> soar, clumsy in space suits.   50
>
> What are we anyhow, we warmth-
> hungry, breast-seeking animals?
> At Blue Spring, a day or so later,
> one of the manatees, edging
> toward discovery, nudged a canoe,   55
> and from across the wet, warm,
> dimly imaginable tightrope,
> let itself be touched.

(1993)

Preparing to Write

What does this poem describe? What does it most clearly and obviously say? Do any oppositions or tensions seem to be involved?

It might be helpful to sketch out an initial response to the poem, to show you as fully as possible how a deconstructive essay might be developed. So, I'm going to divide the poem into pieces and try to say what went through my mind as I tried to make sense of it. I'd encourage you to write your own notes before you look through mine.

Discovery

> The week the latest rocket
> went up,   (1–2)

Is the speaker referring to a fictional rocket or a real one? Perhaps the speaker is referring to NASA's space shuttles (they aren't rockets, of course, but they're launched by rockets). Everyone knows one of the shuttles is called "Discovery"; does the title refer to it?

> a pod (if that's the word)
> of manatees, come upriver
> to Blue Spring, where it's
> always warm, could be seen
> lolling, jacketed, elephantine,

> on the weedy borderline
> between drowsing and waking,
> breathing and drowning.   (2–9)

Well, perhaps the poem isn't about the space shuttle or "the latest rocket." Maybe that's just the time frame. I saw manatees when I lived in Florida, and "elephantine" is right—they do seem like armless and legless elephants floating in the water. And they don't seem to swim: "lolling" is a good word for what they do. The idea that they are "between drowsing and waking" also seems just right. But how are they between "breathing and drowning"? And how are they "jacketed"? What does that mean?

> As they came up for air,
> one by one, they seemed numb,
> torpid, quite incurious.   (10–12)

These lines remind me that manatees are mammals, and so they don't breathe under water. They have to come "up for air"—which explains, I guess, the idea that they're between "breathing and drowning": if they don't come up, they'll drown; so they live most of their time in a state between breathing and drowning. I still don't know why they're said to be "jacketed." Perhaps Clampitt is inviting us to see their skin, which looks sort of loose and baggy, as a kind of jacket.

> No
> imagining these sirenians
> dangerously singing. Or
> gazing up yearningly: so much
> for the Little Mermaid. True,
> the long-lashed little ones
> could have been trademarked
> "Cute" by the likes of Walt Disney.   (12–19)

A number of things at this point are puzzling: for instance, why are the manatees called "sirenians"? What is a sirenian, in other words, and why might one imagine them "dangerously singing"? And what's the connection to the Little Mermaid?

Whenever something is puzzling, I usually try doing some research. In this case, a quick look in *The Columbia Encyclopedia* is revealing: the entry for "manatee" refers us to "sirenian," which is the name of a biological order, "Sirenia." (The only other living sirenian, or sea cow, is called a dugong.) Right above "sirenian," we find "Siren," the name for sea nymphs in Greek mythology who sang so beautifully that sailors would crash into the rocks around their island. So, the manatees, although they're sirenians, aren't like the Sirens. So that's one puzzle solved.

The entry also reports the speculation that manatees, "which nurse on the water's surface, are the source of the mermaid legends." Clampitt's speaker finds the manatees so "numb, torpid, quite incurious" that it's impossible to imagine them as Sirens or mermaids. Contrasting them to the Little Mermaid is of course particularly comical given the huge bulk of these floating blobs. They are, according to the entry, "sluggish, largely nocturnal bottom feeders," weighing perhaps one thousand pounds and eating as much as a hundred pounds of vegetation a day. Even so, we must note that the "long-lashed little ones" are "Cute" enough for Disney. So another puzzle is solved.

The entry also may help clear up another question: manatees, we read, have gray skin that is "completely hairless" (except for bristles around the mouth). The skin has folds and wrinkles in it: so maybe that is why it appears to be a jacket to the speaker.

> His world's over that way,
> suitably for a peninsula where
> the cozy mythologies we've
> swindled ourselves with, on
> taking things easy, might even
> come true: sun-kissed nakedness
> on the beach, year-round, guilt-free
> hibiscus and oranges, fountains
> welling up through the limestone,
> the rumor of Ponce de León, having
> found the one he was looking for,
>
> living at ease in, some say
> Boca Raton, others Cádiz. A last
> bedtime placebo?   (20–33)

This section makes clear that the speaker is indeed in Florida at the Kennedy Space Center, where the shuttle launches, near Orlando and Disney World "over that way." We dream, the speaker says, of "taking things easy" in Florida, living in paradise forever

like a successful Ponce de León. Such dreaming doesn't do anything, but it may make us feel better anyway, like a "placebo."

> Still, we keep
> looking up.   (33–34)

What does it mean to say "Still, we keep looking up"? Perhaps it
means that our dreams of contentment ("sun-kissed nakedness on
the beach") aren't entirely satisfying: we still keep looking up, waiting for some discovery—or, in this case, for Discovery. We all want
to see something.

> That clear morning,
> just warm enough for a liftoff,
> the fabulous itself could be seen
> unwieldily, jacket by jacket,
> in the act of shedding, as
> a snake does its husk, or
> a celebrant his vestments:
>
> the fiery, the arrowy tip of it,
> of the actual going invisible,   (34–42)

These lines strike me as a wonderful way of describing a launch:
the shuttle disappearing as it rises is "the actual going invisible."
The shuttle's voyage becomes "the fabulous itself" in the act of
"shedding"—being reborn or transformed like the snake or the celebrant. If you've seen a launch, even on television, you know that the
shuttle does seem to move "unwieldily," rotating slowly as it goes up,
lumbering so it seems, at least at first, toward the heavens.

> trailing its vaporous, ribboning
> frond as from a kelp bed,
> the umbilical roar of it
> stumbling behind, while up in
> the belly of it, out of their
> element, jacketed, lolling
> and treading, the discoverers
> soar, clumsy in space suits.   (43–50)

The comparison of the booster rocket's vapor trail to a "ribboning
frond as from a kelp bed" is very strange, isn't it? What's the point

of such an odd description? It takes us, obviously, to the manatees, who eat such fronds in kelp beds. It begins to link, it seems to me, the astronauts to the manatees. The connection becomes stronger as Clampitt uses "jacketed" and "lolling" to describe the human "discoverers," the same words used to describe the manatees.

In what ways are the astronauts like the manatees? Clampitt suggests that the astronauts are also in a sense "out of their element." They are "treading," not in water, but as if they were. And they appear, like the manatees, to be "clumsy in space suits."

> What are we anyhow, we warmth-
> hungry, breast-seeking animals?
> At Blue Spring, a day or so later,
> one of the manatees, edging
> toward discovery, nudged a canoe,
> and from across the wet, warm,
> dimly imaginable tightrope,
> let itself be touched.   (51–58)

If we had any doubts about what the oppositions are in this poem, and how they're brought together, this final section makes these matters very clear, doesn't it? When Clampitt asks "What are we anyhow, we warmth- / hungry, breast-seeking animals?", who is the "we" here? At the beginning of the poem, it is the manatees who "come upriver" to where "it's / always warm," and it seems clear that the "warmth-hungry" we includes both human "discoverers" as well as manatees (who breast-feed their young on the surface, we recall).

With the final scene of the manatee "edging toward discovery," Clampitt most strikingly unites manatees and humans. The manatees are also "looking up," reaching out. They may seem clumsy, numb, quite incurious, but the astronauts, as they float around "out of their element," also seem clumsy, lolling. Clampitt uses "jacketed" to describe both human and manatee (although I still find this word a bit confusing). In letting itself be touched, the manatee is aligned with humanity, becoming really a courageous discoverer, like the crew of Discovery.

But what is the "wet, warm, / dimly imaginable tightrope" that the manatee reaches "across"? It must be, I suppose, the water, or the surface of the water, and Clampitt's point would seem to be that the manatee, while appearing to be clumsy, is actually pulling off quite a feat. Inhabiting the water, living between breathing and drowning, is like walking a tightrope. Likewise, the astronauts on Discovery may seem clumsy "jacketed" in their suits, but they are in reality "the fabulous itself."

At this point I think I understand the poem fairly well. That is, I understand how the poem's two topics are related. The manatees lolling about in the warm water, and human beings shooting themselves into space: what could be more different? And yet Amy Clampitt brings the two together.

Or does she?

Shaping

Is it possible to turn this reading of the poem around, to tease out another, conflicting meaning? To begin to deconstruct this poem, let's think a bit about the oppositions that seem to be brought together. The worlds of manatees and humans appear to be far apart—as different as "that country" and Byzantium in Yeats's "Sailing to Byzantium." The manatees seem dramatically unlike discoverers: "numb, / torpid, quite incurious." Manatees are even unlike the partly human, the mermaids and sirens. In Yeats's poem, as we just saw, Cleanth Brooks's New Critical reading finds that the golden bird unifies the poem, combining the worlds of nature and art. Likewise, in Clampitt's poem a number of images seem to unify the opposing worlds, as the human discoverers come to seem like the manatees, "lolling," "treading," "jacketed." The closing image of one manatee "edging / toward discovery" most directly shows us how the manatee shares the human urge to "keep / looking up" and to reach out and explore. We are both, manatee and human, "warmth- / hungry, breast-seeking animals." Whereas Yeats's poem unifies art and nature, Clampitt's poem brings together the realms of animal and human. So it seems.

But if the poem appears most obviously to say that manatees and astronauts are similar or linked (out of their elements, awkward, seeking discovery), is it possible to suggest that the poem also undermines this unifying theme? What is being overlooked or suppressed in Clampitt's unifying move? Here are some notes toward a deconstructive reading.

> < > Apparent unity: the manatee is said to be "edging toward discovery," like the Discovery astronauts, it seems.
> > < Reversal: But who really is the discoverer in this situation? The manatee passively "let itself be touched" after it "nudged" the canoe. Although we may think at first that the manatee is "edging toward

[its own] discovery," the more reasonable inference is that the manatee is "edging toward discovery" by the canoe-goers. Does the manatee discover anything? Not that we know. There's really no evidence that the manatee has moved beyond being "numb, / torpid, quite incurious."

< > Apparent unity: "we" are "warmth- / hungry, breast-seeking animals."

> < Reversal: This assertion connects the manatees to us only in a superficial way. More carefully considered, this description actually distances the manatees from "the discoverers" in their "space suits": the astronauts surely aren't seeking warmth or breasts in space. There is something else that drives humanity to explore, to "keep looking up," and that intellectual curiosity is not shared, so far as we can tell, by the manatees.

< > Apparent unity: "jacketed" is used to describe both manatees and astronauts.

> < Reversal: The meaning of "jacketed" as it applies to manatees is never made clear. I can think of two senses in which the astronauts are "jacketed." They're actually wearing jackets; and they're enclosed, in the sense of this definition of "jacket": "a metal casing, as the steel covering around the barrel of a gun or the core of a bullet." I don't see how the manatees are "jacketed" in either of these senses. Applied to both manatees and astronauts, the term really emphasizes the gap between the two when we examine it closely.

< > Apparent unity: The poem says "the fabulous itself could be seen / unwieldily, jacket by jacket, / in the act of shedding, as / a snake does its husk, or / a celebrant his vestments": the reference to a snake and a celebrant again seems to link animal and human activities, subtly implying that the "jacketed" manatees and humans are discovering "the fabulous itself."

> < Reversal: But aren't these two images actually pulling in different directions? A snake shedding its skin is not performing a voluntary, self-conscious act. The celebrant, however, makes the fabulous visible by shedding "his vestments"—a voluntary, self-conscious act. In removing his religious, ceremonial garments, the celebrant reveals somehow, Clampitt says, the mystery and the wonder he has participated in: the fabulous itself. At least, that's how I read these difficult lines.

I would have thought that the fabulous would be glimpsed in the celebrant putting on his vestments and that the act of removing them would reveal the mundane and ordinary world. But Clampitt has imagined the liftoff as an act of shedding, and so images of "shedding" become images of discovery. The gap in meaning results from the difference between a reptile engaging in an automatic, biological function and a conscious human disengaging from a spiritual event.

< > Apparent unity: The notion that the astronauts are "out of their / element" may seem to reflect the manatees' situation, living in water but breathing air.

> < Reversal: But the implicit comparison doesn't hold up because the astronauts really are out of their element, totally unsuited to live in space without the creation of an artificial environment. Manatees, on the other hand, live on the border between air and water: that is their element. Birds fly in the air and build nests in trees and other places. We wouldn't say they're "out of their element" in either situation. Again, we see how the poem's effort to unify animal and human comes apart. Manatees are different: they can't live out of their element; we can, at least for certain periods.

At this point, I'm looking at the phrase "cozy mythologies we've / swindled ourselves with," mythologies that "might even / come true" in Florida, Clampitt says, in the land of Walt Disney. And I'm thinking that the poem itself offers a "cozy mythology" about manatees and humans, suppressing the essential differences. From living in Florida for three years, I remember that a great deal of attention is paid to the manatees—they're endangered, and they're uniquely huge and strange. The state offers a manatee tag for automobiles, and the funds raised go to a "Save the Manatee" campaign. The main threat to manatees in Florida today seems to be from motorboats: as the manatees float up to the surface, boaters fail to see them and run over them, inflicting severe injuries with the propellers. A manatee hospital has even been set up to treat injured manatees, and boat speeds have been restricted in some areas. We are trying to live *with* the manatees; many tourists every year get in the water and swim with them. One could argue that we are forgetting our differences, assuming that manatees are in some crucial way like ourselves, when really perhaps we should leave them alone, banning boats and recreation in the waters they inhabit. At any rate, this reading of Clampitt's poem opens up uncertainties in our understanding of them.

Drafting

At this point I think I have enough ideas to draft an essay. Where should I start? First, I need to set up the task, letting the reader know what I'm trying to do: namely, I'm trying to show how the poem appears to link human and manatee, but really doesn't. I want to start fast, diving right in; and since the ending most dramatically unifies manatee and human, with the two actually touching with the final word, I'm going to try starting with the ending of the poem. The word "discovery" occurs in the final lines, and since it's the title, I need to pay attention to it. The final image occurs in response to a question, it seems, and so it makes sense to move next to the question itself. Then I'll present the other evidence I've generated: "jacketed," "out of their element," and the snake/celebrant problem. That's my tentative plan as I start writing, very much aware that I may change my mind.

Here's the essay that resulted after a draft and a little polishing.

Humanity and Manatee: Amy Clampitt's "Discovery"

This paragraph introduces the issue: why is the poem partly about manatees and partly about humans? The conclusion is crucial, asserting indirectly their unity.

The conclusion of Amy Clampitt's "Discovery" follows a profoundly challenging question: "What are we anyhow, we warmth- / hungry, breast-seeking animals?" Right before this question, the poem refers to astronauts, "discoverers" who are "clumsy in space suits," so it seems reasonable to assume that "we" refers to human beings. But rather than trying to say explicitly what "we" are any-how, answering a question about human nature that has occupied philosophies and religions for centuries, the poem offers instead a little story about a manatee:

> At Blue Spring, a day or so later,
> one of the manatees, edging
> toward discovery, nudged a canoe,
> and from across the wet, warm,
> dimly imaginable tightrope,
> let itself be touched.

While this story might seem at first an evasion of the question, the poem repeatedly links manatees and humans, giving them the same qualities, using the same words to describe them both. Thus, this story implicitly answers the question about human nature by pointing once more to manatees: we are more like them, and they are more like us, than we might have thought. Like the manatee, we are "edging toward discovery," reaching out to other beings.

This paragraph directly presents the thesis: the linking is problematic.

But a careful examination of the implied links between manatees and humans reveals that the similarities are actually questionable. Ultimately, as this paper will show, it is unclear whether the poem's comparison helps us understand the nature of either humans or manatees—or just compounds the mystery.

The strongest evidence for unity, "edging toward discovery," is introduced here.

Let us begin with the strongest unifying agent of manatee and human, the phrase "edging toward discovery." The word "discovery" links the manatee's action to the poem's title and to the space shuttle Discovery. The poem does not say that Discovery in particular is being launched at the time the manatees "come upriver," but "the latest rocket" clearly is one of the shuttles. And the description of the astronauts, "jacketed, lolling and treading," "clumsy in space suits," seems designed to remind us of the manatees, who are described in the first section in the same terms—"lolling, jacketed" and "numb, / torpid" (which certainly suggests clumsiness).

The manatee is not a discoverer, but an object of discovery.

But in what sense is the manatee "edging toward discovery"? Although the same words are used to describe astronaut and manatee, the similarity of their roles in the act of discovery seems uncertain. Whereas the astronauts self-consciously and actively venture out into space, the manatee passively "let itself be touched." Such a surrender may seem essentially different from the behavior of the human "discoverers," either in the shuttle or the canoe. One could argue, of course, that the manatee is discovering how it feels to be touched by human beings. But the astronauts do not rocket into space to deliver themselves to the touch or observation of other beings, and the people in the canoe are not said to be allowing the manatee to see what their hands feel like. There's no solid evidence that the manatee discovers anything or moves beyond being "numb, / torpid, quite incurious." So, "edging / toward discovery" only seems initially to unite manatee and human; upon reflection, it may exhibit their differences or at the least call their likeness into doubt.

The question itself applies better to the manatee.

The question itself—"What are we anyhow, we warmth- / hungry, breast-seeking animals?"—may seem to refer to both manatees and humans. The poem begins by noting how the manatees have "come upriver" to Blue Spring seeking warmth; and as mammals, the manatees do breast feed their young. But this deep question also puts a gap between manatee and human, because the astronauts surely aren't seeking warmth or breasts in space. There is something else that drives humanity to explore, to "keep / looking up," and that intellectual, self-conscious curiosity is not shared, so far as we can tell, by the manatees. Although "we" may be "warmth- / hungry" and "breast-seeking," the suggestion that these are essential qualities limits and narrows what it means to be human.

"Jacket" applies better to humans.

Likewise, "jacket" or "jacketed" appears four times in the poem and would seem to be an important term connecting manatee and human, unifying the poem's two subjects. The term is applied to both manatees, who are "lolling, jacketed, elephantine," and to the astronauts, who are "jacketed, lolling / and treading." But again the link is problematic. The astronauts are "jacketed," it would seem, because they have on jackets, and because they are encased in metal—"jacketed" in the sense of "a metal casing, as the steel covering around the barrel of a gun or the core of a bullet," as Webster's puts it. Are the manatees "jacketed" in either of these senses? The other two occurrences refer to "the fabulous itself" being revealed "jacket by jacket," which seems simply to mean "layer by layer," or "casing by casing." Thus, although the repeated use of the term may seem to bridge the poem and its subjects, it really does not in any clear or direct way. The connection is superficial, and it gives way to a gap: manatees do not really come in jackets in any literal sense; humans do.

More evidence: other gaps.

In a number of other ways the poem's two subjects break apart upon analysis. The notion, for instance, that the astronauts are "out of their / element" may seem to reflect also the manatees' situation, living in water but breathing air. But the astronauts really are out of their element, totally unsuited to live in space without the creation of an artificial environment. Manatees, on the other hand, need to live on the border between air and water: that is their element. Humans do not need to live on the border of space and earth. Or, again, the reference to a snake and a celebrant again seems to link animal and human activities. But aren't these two images actually pulling in different directions? A snake shedding its skin is not performing a voluntary, self-conscious act. The celebrant, however, makes the fabulous visible by shedding "his vestments"—a voluntary, self-conscious act. In removing his religious, ceremonial garments, the celebrant reveals somehow, Clampitt says, the mystery and the wonder he has participated in: the fabulous itself. For the snake, the fabulous itself would seem to be the instinctual act of shedding. The gap in meaning results from the difference between a reptile engaging in an automatic, biological function and a conscious human disengaging from a spiritual event.

Conclusion: the unity may be a myth, or is at least uncertain.

The poem refers to the "cozy mythologies" of paradise and eternal youth that "might even / come true" in Florida. Another myth may be the illusion that manatees and humans are alike in some essential way. The poem asserts that unity, but at the same time it points out the difference, the otherness, of the manatees. We may drive our boats and canoes where they live; we may touch them; but it may be misleading to think we understand them—or even ourselves. The "discovery" may well be the question, what are we anyhow?

PRACTICING STRUCTURALIST AND DECONSTRUCTIVE CRITICISM

I offer here three texts for you to practice on, along with some questions I hope you find helpful.

QUESTIONS

1. What is the most obvious statement the advertisement shown on the following page attempts to make? What sort

of attitudes, feelings, and assumptions does the advertisement attribute to part of its audience? What effect does it strive to create?

2. How might the advertisement tend also to create the attitudes, feelings, assumptions it strives to reduce or remove?

That is, does the advertisement do contradictory things? How does this conflict influence its effectiveness?

3. Look closely at the details of the advertisement and how they reveal (as deconstruction insists all texts must) what is being excluded or suppressed. For example, what does the imperative to "Cut through the anxiety, the unknown, the hassle" acknowledge? If the slogan next to the phone number were to be spoken, what would it say? How does the pun in this slogan divide and complicate it?

London

William Blake

I wander thro' each charter'd street
Near where the charter'd Thames does flow,
And mark in every face I meet
Marks of weakness, marks of woe.

In every cry of every Man,   5
In every Infant's cry of fear,
In every voice, in every ban,
The mind-forg'd manacles I hear.

How the Chimney-sweeper's cry
Every blackening Church appalls,   10
And the hapless Soldier's sigh
Runs in blood down Palace walls.

But most thro' midnight streets I hear
How the youthful Harlot's curse
Blasts the new-born Infant's tear   15
And blights with plagues the Marriage hearse.

(1794)

QUESTIONS

1. What is a charter? What would it mean for a street to be "charter'd"? How about a river (the Thames in this poem)?

2. "Charter'd" is repeated in the first two lines. What other words are repeated in the poem? What might be the purpose of such repetition?

3. In *The Pursuit of Signs* Jonathan Culler reviews some of the many interpretations this famous poem has generated, and he notes that one of two different structures has been perceived to organize the entire poem. The first way of thinking about the poem's structure sees it, as Culler says, as a "synecdochic series, where a list of particulars are interpreted as instances of a general class to which they all belong" (69). What in your opinion might be the "general class" to which the particulars in the poem belong? That is, the chimney sweeper's cry, the hapless soldier's sigh, and the harlot's curse are instances of what? What do they have in common?

4. The second way of thinking about the poem's structure sees it (again following Culler) as an *"aletheic reversal:* first a false or inadequate vision, then its true or adequate counterpart" (69). Where, in your opinion, might the shift from a false vision to a true one occur? How would you describe these two visions? (Hint: where does the poem shift from universal statements—"every," "every"—to more specific ones?)

5. How does the idea of "mind-forg'd manacles" contribute to the structure of the poem? (Your answer to this question may overlap with previous answers.) Is it a particular or a general, a member of a class, or a class?

6. How many examples are offered in the last two verses? What are they examples of? How are they parallel? (You might think in terms of victim—action—institution.) Is there any problem with their parallelism?

No critic, Culler says, takes the statement that the chimney sweep's cry appalls the church at face value (*Signs* 70). How does the structure of the other two examples affect the way we think about the chimney sweep? Again, think in parallel terms. Why would critics find it necessary to explain the example of the chimney sweep?

7. What sense can you make of the last verse? What are the difficulties in understanding it?

8. The speaker of the poem marks (or hears) the sweep cry, the soldier sigh, and the harlot curse. This structural parallelism encourages us to assume a parallelism of meaning. What are the problems with determining such a unity? That is, can you argue that in fact the poem does not make

sense—at least not any one sense, but rather that it goes in conflicting directions?

9. Are the "mind-forg'd manacles" the product of the Church, the Palace, and Marriage? (Most readers seem to assume so.) Can you turn this inference around and argue otherwise? Could the sweep, the soldier, and the harlot create their own manacles?

Ethics

Linda Pastan

In ethics class so many years ago
our teacher asked this question every fall:
if there were a fire in a museum
which would you save, a Rembrandt painting
or an old woman who hadn't many   5
years left anyhow? Restless on hard chairs
caring little for pictures or old age
we'd opt one year for life, the next for art
and always half-heartedly. Sometimes
the woman borrowed my grandmother's face   10
leaving her usual kitchen to wander
some drafty, half imagined museum.
One year, feeling clever, I replied
why not let the woman decide herself?
Linda, the teacher would report, eschews   15
the burdens of responsibility.
This fall in a real museum I stand
before a real Rembrandt, old woman,
or nearly so, myself. The colors
within this frame are darker than autumn,   20
darker even than winter—the browns of earth,
though earth's most radiant elements burn
through the canvas. I know now that woman
and painting and season are almost one
and all beyond saving by children.   25

[1981]

QUESTIONS

1. Consider how these oppositions work within the poem: the adult speaker versus the child in ethics class; the Rembrandt

versus the old woman; accepting responsibility versus avoiding it; the students versus the teacher; the Rembrandt's colors versus autumn's colors; half-imagining versus vividly imagining; childhood versus old age. How are these oppositions related? (Try making a chart with one kind of item on one side, the other kind on the other.)

2. In what sense does the poem itself deconstruct these oppositions? In other words, how does the ending affect the teacher's ethics question?

3. Does the poem itself undermine or support the assertion that woman, painting, and season are "beyond saving by children"? What does Pastan mean when she says that the woman, painting, and season "are almost one"? Do you agree? Does that make sense?

4. What do you think of Linda's "clever" response in line 14? How is it different from the response she would later make as a "nearly" old woman, viewing a Rembrandt herself? (Is it really different?)

5. Perhaps this poem, despite its title, isn't really about "Ethics." What else could it be about? What theme seems to be raised, for instance, by the ending? Is the speaker's age significant? What difference does it make that the three items are "almost one" but not exactly one? What difference does it make that the items are beyond saving by children? Was the teacher literally asking the children to save one or the other?

Useful Terms for Deconstruction

Arbitrariness: Language, deconstruction assumes, is ultimately arbitrary. It could be different from what it is; indeed, languages change and evolve and become different as time goes on. Different languages divide up the universe differently, and each language is itself something constructed: if all English speakers decided that black dogs weren't actually dogs, and should be called "gringats" from now on, then black dogs and other kinds of dogs, according to our language, would be distinct things. Deconstruction wants to highlight this arbitrariness in order to remind us that texts are open to interpretation, and meaning is not fixed.

Binary: Language is based, structuralists and poststructuralists say, on oppositions: "bad" only has meaning because we can contrast it to "good"; "man" takes on its meaning in opposition to "woman," or "animal," or "boy," or some other opposing term. This opposing nature of language means that it is binary—that is, having two parts, two alternatives. Deconstruction recognizes that within this binary nature, one alternative is always suppressed, falsely simplifying reality.

Différance: This difficult term was made up by Derrida to indicate two meanings at once: difference and deferral. "Difference" is an important idea in deconstruction, which seeks to show how a text contains within itself a trace of its own contradiction. The idea that something differs from itself may seem at first insane; but we've all heard someone say, "I'm not myself today." "Difference," as deconstruction sees things, is unavoidable: we are always not entirely and strictly ourselves. The related idea of "deferral" is important too; whereas "difference" seems to be a spatial idea, dividing an apparent unity, "deferral" refers to time—specifically to the idea of putting something off. "I'm going to defer a decision on that matter today," one might say. From a deconstructive point of view, when we move through time we never quite get where we're going: the point in time we aim for is always deferred. Likewise, if we want to see what something means by traveling back to its origin, we can never pinpoint this origin: there is always some prior beginning.

Think of the story of Adam and Eve, for instance: it is a story about "in the beginning," explaining the meaning of evil and suffering, which are (in the traditional reading) the effects of the first man and woman's sin, the fall from grace and innocence. But this story does not reveal the origin of the most important agent in the story: God. Why did God create Eden in the way that he did? What is the origin of the serpent who tempts Adam and Eve? Did God create him? If so, why? If not, where did the serpent come from? Thus, the deeper meaning of the story, the origin of the origin, can always be deferred if the analysis is pressed.

Dispersal: Deconstruction does not suggest simply that meanings can be reversed, end of story. Rather, the reversal of oppositions is a gesture designed to suggest the arbitrariness of meanings. Ultimately, a text could be analyzed until its essential uncertainty resulted in its unraveling—the dispersal or scattering of its meaning.

Opposition: See "binary."

Privilege: In an opposition, one term is unavoidably favored over the other in some way, since a perfect balance in every sense seems unlikely if not impossible. Deconstruction emphasizes how one term is "privileged" over another by reversing or subverting the apparent meaning.

Works Cited: Structuralism and Deconstruction

Brooks, Cleanth. *The Well-Wrought Urn.* New York: Holt, 1947.

Culler, Jonathan. *On Deconstruction: Theory and Criticism After Structuralism.* Ithaca, NY: Cornell UP, 1982.

———. *The Pursuit of Signs: Semiotics, Literature, Deconstruction.* Ithaca, NY: Cornell UP, 1981.

De Man, Paul. "Semiology and Rhetoric." In *Allegories of Reading.* New Haven, CT: Yale UP, 1979. 3–20.

Jay, Gregory. *America the Scrivener.* Ithaca, NY: Cornell UP, 1991.

Johnson, Barbara. *The Critical Difference.* Baltimore: Johns Hopkins UP, 1980.

Lipking, Lawrence. "The Practice of Theory." In *Literary Theories in Praxis.* Ed. Shirley Staton. Philadelphia: U of Pennsylvania P, 1987. 426–40.

Recommended Further Reading: Structuralism and Deconstruction

Barthes, Roland. *Mythologies.* Lavers, Annette (trans). New York: Hill and Wang, 1972. Engaging and influential essays from a structuralist stance on food, toys, cruises, striptease, wrestling matches, and much else.

Borradori, Giovanna, Jurgen Habermas, and Jacques Derrida. *Philosophy in a Time of Terror: Dialogues With Jurgen Habermas and Jacques Derrida.* Chicago: U of Chicago P, 2003. A difficult but often rewarding text for ambitious readers.

Culler, Jonathan. *Structuralist Poetics: Structuralism, Linguistics, and the Study of Literature.* A brilliantly lucid introduction to criticism that analyzes the structure of literary texts, instead of pondering the meaning of the work.

Derrida, Jacques. "Structure, Sign, and Play in the Discourse of the Human Sciences." In *The Structuralist Controversy.* Ed. Richard Macksey and Eugenio Donato. Baltimore: Johns Hopkins UP, 1972. 247–72. Enormously influential essay. Difficult, even exasperating, but also amusing at times. If you lack the stamina to read the entire essay, you should read at least some of it carefully in order to appreciate Derrida's punning, elliptical, tightly packed style.

Eagleton, Terry. "Post-structuralism." In *Literary Theory: An Introduction.* Minneapolis: U of Minnesota P, 1996, 2nd ed. An excellent (but not an objective) introduction.

Hedges, Warren. "Using Deconstruction to Astonish Friends & Confound Enemies (in 2 easy steps)." *The Soda Fountain of Knowledge.* 6 January 2007. <http://www.sou.edu/English/Hedges>.

Krapp, Peter. *Derrida.* Personal webpage. 9 April 2004 <http://www. hydra.umn.edu/derrida/>. All things Derrida are considered on this site. A wide range of materials are gathered, including for example an interesting interview with Derrida from February 2004 about the war in Iraq.

Kent, Thomas. "Deconstruction." In *Encyclopedia of Rhetoric and Composition.* Ed. Theresa Enos. New York: Garland, 1996. Brief explanations of deconstruction abound (check your milk cartons and newspaper inserts), but this one is exceptionally thorough and insightful.

Lynn, Steven. *Samuel Johnson After Deconstruction.* Carbondale: Southern Illinois UP, 1992. Compares deconstruction to other kinds of skepticism, arguing that Johnson anticipates post-structuralism in some important and surprising ways.

Tompkins, Jane. "A Short Course in Post-Structuralism." Eds. Charles Moran and Elizabeth Penfield. In *Conversations: Contemporary Critical Theory and the Teaching of Literature.* Eds. Charles Moran and Elizabeth Penfield. Urbana, IL: NCTE, 1990. 19–37. Aimed at teachers with little or no understanding of deconstruction; helpful for a general audience.

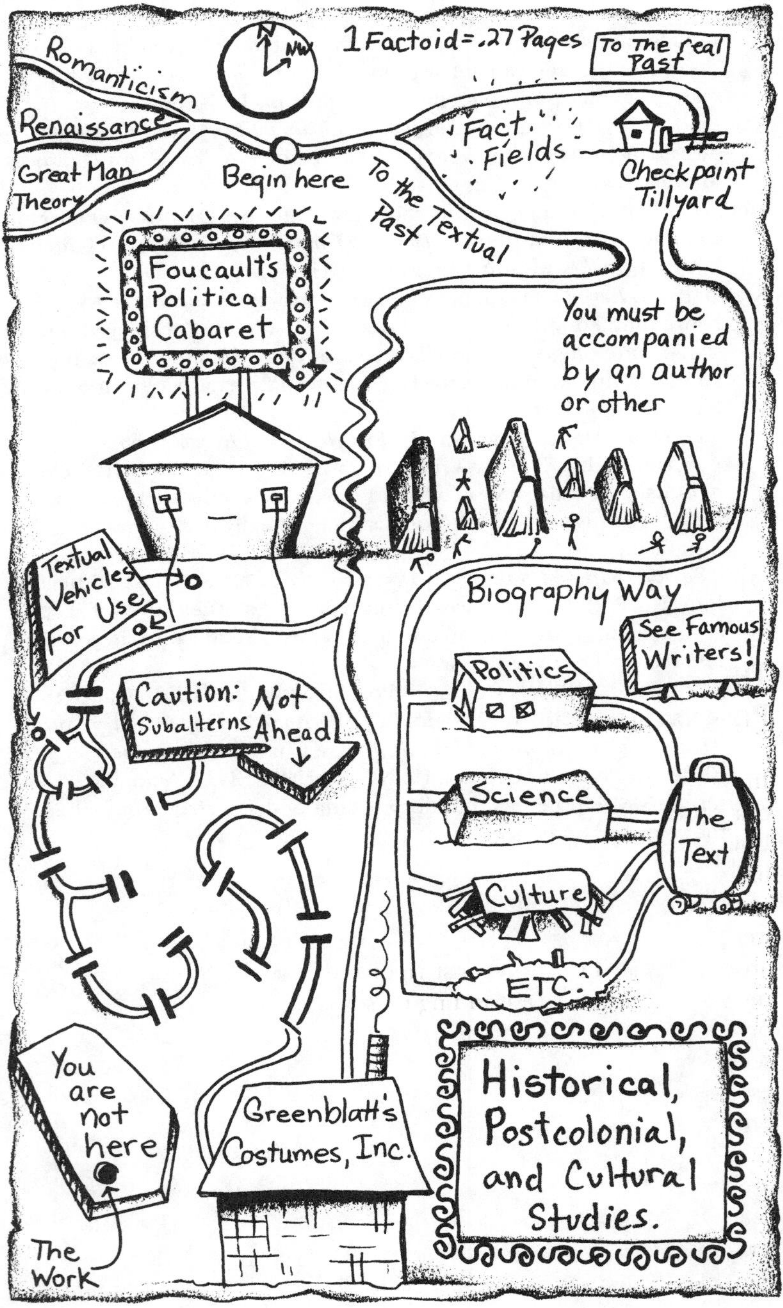

1 Factoid = .27 Pages
To The real Past
Romanticism
Renaissance
Great Man Theory
Begin here
To the Textual Past
Fact Fields
Checkpoint Tillyard
Foucault's Political Cabaret
You must be accompanied by an author or other
Textual Vehicles For Use
Biography Way
See Famous Writers!
Politics
Caution: Subalterns
Not Ahead
Science
The Text
Culture
ETC.
You are not here
The Work
Greenblatt's Costumes, Inc.
Historical, Postcolonial, and Cultural Studies.

Connecting the Text

Historical, Postcolonial, and Cultural Studies

> *We know somewhat, and we*
> *imagine the rest.*
>
> —Samuel Johnson

THE PURPOSES OF HISTORICAL, POSTCOLONIAL, AND CULTURAL STUDIES

In New Criticism, in reader-response criticism, and in deconstruction, our attention is primarily centered on the text itself: how it is unified, how the reader is reacting to it, how it falls apart. But there is more to life, even English professors would admit, than texts. Inquiring minds want to know about authors, what kinds of lives they led, how they were able to create their works, what was going on in the world around them. Even the most rigorously formal New Critics or the most introspectively responding readers may draw upon biographical or historical information to support their analysis or response. It seems obvious that some historical awareness is very useful if not essential for an understanding of many works of literature. And it's often fascinating.

The traditional view of history and biography assumes that there are "facts" that we can know, with some degree of certainty, and as readers we simply need to gather them (if we can), and fit them together (if we can), and cautiously relate them to literary works (if we can). In the last half-century or so, this traditional view of history has become increasingly problematic, as a new way of thinking about language and meaning has challenged our perception of historical and biographical facts. In the wake of post-structuralism and deconstruction, altering our notions of language and knowledge, we also have new conceptions of authorship and historical contexts. "New historicism" (sometimes called "cultural poetics") is the name usually given to this new way of thinking about history and literature. What we really have, according to new historicists, is not some set of stable facts, waiting on discovery, but rather a number of texts waiting on a process of interpretation. Rather than trying to determine what "really" happened, new historicists are interested in exploring how different versions of history are motivated and constructed. At any given moment in a culture, there may be a dominant discourse, a way of thinking and persuading that is assumed to be the norm; or there may be a swirl of competing discourses; or there may be a decaying discourse held by one segment of a culture, but under attack and falling apart, and a rising discourse, gaining adherents. There may well be, in reality, as many discourses as there are people—or even more, since some of us change our minds often, or haven't made up our minds on many things.

The notion that history is somehow up for grabs—that there are competing versions of what has happened, and these stories might be put to different uses—is a crucial idea for postcolonial and cultural studies as well. This chapter will first try to give you some sense of how to do traditional biographical and historical criticism, and then consider how these emerging orientations might further enhance your understanding and your critical repertoire.

Biographical and Historical Criticism

If we think of a literary work primarily as a personal achievement, the accomplishment of a great mind, then biographical criticism offers to help us understand both the work and its creator, as we relate one to the other. Take, for instance, the following poem.

When I Consider How My Light Is Spent
John Milton

When I consider how my light is spent,
   Ere half my days in this dark world and wide,
   And that one talent which is death to hide
Lodged with me useless, though my soul more bent

To serve therewith my Maker, and present   5
    My true account, lest He returning chide,
    Doth God exact day-labor, light denied,
I fondly ask. But Patience, to prevent
That murmur, soon replies, God doth not need
    Either man's work or His own gifts. Who best   10
    Bear his mild yoke, they serve Him best. His state
Is kingly: thousands at his bidding speed,
    And post o'er land and ocean without rest;
    They also serve who only stand and wait.

                                                            (1655?)

    Biographical criticism would insist on the importance of knowing something about the author—perhaps most importantly, in this case, that Milton had lost his eyesight by 1651. Without this fact, it could be argued, the reader might wonder what sense to make of the phrase "how my light is spent," since "going blind" would be only one of many possible meanings (how my day is spent, how my insight is used up, how my lover is tired out, and more). Knowing about Milton's life may also help us to appreciate the poem's significance: the speaker of the poem is not, it may seem, merely a fiction, an assumed character, contemplating some hypothesis; rather, the speaker has some connection to a real man, a writer, contemplating the horror of his own blindness.

    Of course, as one guide to writing about literature puts it, you should "avoid equating the work's contents with the author's life" (Griffith 115); obviously a piece of writing isn't the same thing as a person's life. Still, although the writing and the life "are never the same," are we obliged to conclude that writers do not sometimes try to express themselves truthfully? If we must conclude that "When I Consider" is "fictional" in the same sense that *Star Wars* is fictional, then we may lose some of the poem's power. For most readers this poem is considerably more moving if we imagine that there was someone named "Milton" who is writing about himself in this poem.

    Just as Milton's life may illuminate the poem, the poem may also help us to understand Milton's life. It has been thought by more than one critic that Milton was a misogynist, a "domestic tyrant" as the *Oxford Companion* puts it (654), cruelly ordering his daughters about, sternly dictating to his successive wives (three in all). This poem may suggest perhaps that Milton tended to think of the entire universe in terms of servants and masters, and that he viewed himself as a servant to God. God's "yoke" is light, even though it employs thousands speeding "o'er land and ocean without rest," and the servant's job is simply to serve in whatever capacity. The servant is in fact so inconsequential that "God doth not need / Either man's work or His own gifts." As Milton insists to himself that he must strive to serve even if that serving means simply standing, the submissiveness in the poem reflects the sort of subservience Milton apparently expected (and thought he had earned) from those who served him. He may have treated those around him like his servants, but he also saw himself in the same way, as the servant to another master.

© Hulton–Deutsch Collection / CORBIS

Biographical criticism is the natural ally of historical criticism. We can hardly understand one person's life without some sense of the time and place in which he or she lived, and we can hardly understand human history without trying to think about the individual humans who made it. Historical criticism considers how military, social, cultural, economic, scientific, intellectual, literary, and (potentially) every other kind of history might help us to understand the author and work.

In the case of Milton's poem, the most obvious historical context might well be the political situation of England: in 1655, about the time the poem is supposed to have been written, England was struggling to recover from a civil war that had ended with the beheading of Charles I in 1649. After this regicide, of which he approved, Milton was deeply involved in politics, serving as Latin secretary to the newly formed Council of State and writing on numerous political and religious controversies. Against the backdrop of this political turmoil, the references in the poem to the "one talent" and the urgency of using it might suggest additional meanings. (He is alluding of course to Jesus's parable, in Matthew 25:14–30, of the poor servant who simply buried his talent—literally a very valuable coin, but metaphorically any resource—and the good servants who used their talents for profit.)

For instance: perhaps Milton felt called to straighten out his country by employing his gift for language; the government and the church must have seemed at times to be falling apart before his eyes. With his one talent, his gift for writing, perhaps Milton felt he should be saving the nation. But he puts this self-imposed burden in a new light in the poem when he reminds himself that God does not need his help—that others do God's bidding, and that his own job description may have changed dramatically with his impairment. He is telling himself that all he must do now is "stand and wait," ready to serve when he can. (As it turns out, Milton's accomplishments were prodigious while he "waited" to write his masterwork, *Paradise Lost*.)

The history of literature itself has also been considered especially important for the understanding of particular works. Milton's reader needs to recognize that "When I Consider" is a sonnet, but it would also be nice to know what sonnets Milton had read or might have read, how this sonnet relates to others, and what other poems or other kinds of works Milton knew. Such literary background is almost always helpful and often seems essential.

"It's all about power—getting it and keeping it."

In the study of renaissance literature, for example, students have for decades read E. M. W. Tillyard's *The Elizabethan World Picture* in order to understand the background of Shakespeare, Ben Jonson, Christopher Marlowe, and other Elizabethan writers. Tillyard aimed, as he said, to explain the Elizabethans' "most ordinary beliefs about the constitution of the world" (viii), and he showed clearly and repeatedly how this basic knowledge is essential to our understanding. For example, Tillyard says English citizens who lived during the reign of Elizabeth (1558–1603) believed in "a doctrine of plenitude." They imagined an order in the universe whereby every entity filled a particular position in a "chain of being," stretching from the lowest possible inert element to the highest, from the lowest plant to the highest, and from the lowest creature to the highest (25–33). In *Paradise Lost,* Milton's Raphael, an angel, explains this "chain of being" to Adam, showing him how everything is ranked, and every level of possible being is filled. And Adam explains to Eve one consequence of this hierarchical "plenitude," as Tillyard notes (32):

> Millions of spiritual Creatures walk the Earth
> Unseen, both when we wake, and when we sleep:
> All these with ceaseless praise his works behold
> Both day and night.

Imagining that Milton inherited the Elizabethan idea of the chain of being may help to understand the ending of "When I Consider." Specifically, we get a better sense of the reference to the "thousands" who speed at God's bidding, without rest. They are part of the "millions" of possible creatures existing in the scale between Milton and God; and, if God has a place (but not a need) for those who actively serve him, he also must allow in the scheme of things for some who serve in every other possible way—including standing and waiting. Thus, Milton's passive role is required of him; it is right; it is his current place in the universal chain of being.

As you can see from this small example, historical research can provide us with a richer understanding of what an author is saying.

Cultural Studies

"History" includes, of course, not only those great and obviously influential persons and events that we usually think of, but also the ordinary, the everyday, the apparently trivial. The development of plumbing is clearly very important to civilization, but few people, I would venture, know much about its evolution. And who would think that the history of sewers and toilets would be pertinent to the study of literature? And yet, to take only one example, Jonathan Swift's famous poem "A Description of a City Shower" (1710) makes considerably more sense if we know that the residents of London in 1710, lacking flushing toilets and sewer systems, collected their waste in chamberpots, which were often emptied into open trenches (called "kennels"). Swift's contemporaries, expecting "A Description of a City Shower" to be an idyllic celebration of the beauty of the rain, were no doubt stunned by the poem's grandiose depiction of their smelly reality. The modern reader who is unaware of the sanitary problems in Swift's day may find the poem's imagery incredible. Consider, for instance, the poem's resounding conclusion:

> Now from all parts the swelling kennels flow,
> And bear their trophies with them as they go:
> Filth of all hues and odours seem to tell
> What streets they sailed from, by the sight and smell.
> They, as each torrent drives, with rapid force   5
> From Smithfield or St. Pulchre's shape their course,
> And in huge confluent join at Snow Hill ridge,
> Fall from the Conduit prone to Holborn Bridge.
> Sweepings from butcher's stalls, dung, guts, and blood,
> Drowned puppies, stinking sprats, all drenched in mud,   10
> Dead cats and turnip-tops come tumbling down the flood.

For Swift's reader, or for the modern reader who knows a little something about everyday eighteenth-century life, the poem is not an exaggeration of the city's repulsiveness. Instead, the poem describes in serious and inflated language what everyone saw and tried to overlook every time it rained, and thus Swift's vision becomes both strangely amusing and disturbing. It's funny to think of this mess in such heroic terms; it's also dismaying to see the stinky reality so vividly depicted.

If "history" ought to encompass everything, from international treaties to eating utensils, by the same token "literature" should be seen as more than just the great works that we usually think of. It should include also the second-rate, third-rate, and even too-bad-to-rate writings that actually compose the bulk of literary history. It is in fact probably presumptuous for us to assume the accuracy of our own perspective on what is historically important, in literature or society. The stock of many writers, including Milton, has gone up and down dramatically over the centuries.

Indeed, in the last few decades, many scholars have even expanded their view of literature to include those "texts" that aren't in the usual sense "literary" at all—advertisements, cartoons, films, romances, television shows, popular music, and much more. "Cultural studies," as this ambitious field of research has often come to be called, considers any cultural phenomena to be worthy of serious analysis. Take body piercing, for instance. Have you ever wondered why it has recently become so popular in Western countries? Why are so many people getting their belly buttons, nipples, noses, and/or other parts pierced? What are they trying to communicate through this action? How is this activity related to other cultural events, such as tattooing? While such questions might be investigated by sociologists or anthropologists or psychologists, a "cultural studies" stance would encourage an interdisciplinary and interconnecting approach to such phenomena, relating them to the whole spectrum of popular and literary culture. Cultural studies has thus brought attention to neglected and suppressed writers, providing a richer understanding of the cultural contributions of minorities, the excluded, the oppressed. Cultural studies is in fact often associated with a kind of scholarly activism, as literary and historical study is brought to bear on contemporary concerns.

We have ventured no doubt light-years from Milton (who had no pierced parts whatsoever, so far as I know), but let us adopt a cultural studies stance and imagine the possibility of linking contemporary body piercing to Milton's poem. (You may smile skeptically here if you like.) Body piercing, like tattooing, is surely an effort to draw attention to oneself, to stand out from other people, to say, "I am extraordinary, even doing nothing; I have a unique value; I am myself a work of art." While registering resistance and apartness from the conventional culture, my recent student with purple-striped hair and a large ring in his nose was also declaring his membership in another community. In tribal cultures, such body markings, scarrings, deformations, and ornamental punctures allow for quick identification of one's membership and status.

Although the coding for body piercing in twenty-first century Western culture is not so well established, jewelry through one's nose, or eyebrow, or cheek, or tongue undeniably makes a statement. It says *something*. In his cultural studies classic, *Subculture: The Meaning of Style* (1979), Dick Hebdige noted how the outrageous styles of British lower-class youth—rockers, mods, punks, skinheads, and others—created an alternative value system. By their "style" (in the largest sense), the members of these various groups indicated that they did not belong to the mainstream culture, but that they were clearly part of some different culture. Their personal value might be negligible by the standards of conventional society, but by rejecting that society, making themselves by their very appearance virtually unable to find ordinary employment, they were able to reassure themselves of their value in an alternative community. Body piercing, like other expressions of "style," simultaneously asserts that the practitioner is unique and part of a community.

Milton's poem certainly focuses on the problems of assessing one's own value, and of finding one's place in society. Milton has not purposefully deformed himself, but he did think his eyesight had been weakened by excessive study. He thus finds himself unable to contribute to his community in any ordinary sense. What he is able to do, his "talent," seems "useless" (line 4) in his present physical state. Milton's problem is how he sees, and not how he is seen, but the poem indicates that he considers himself as unemployable as a skinhead applying to be a bank teller. He has become what cultural critics would call a "subaltern" writer—someone who is excluded from power, an "other." But Milton also invokes an alternative value system, for his talent is "useless" only from the point of view of ordinary utilitarian society. For Milton's life to have value in the alternative community, he does not need to make any meaningful contribution. He doesn't need to work or *do* anything to be valuable. His burden of blindness, which is also his warrant for inactivity, he calls a "mild yoke," as if it were no more than a minor inconvenience, like a ring through one's nose or cheek. He has value simply in being his unique self, waiting, serving by doing nothing as one of the community of faithful.

This unlikely conjunction of body piercing and Milton's poem finds, surprisingly enough, some common ground in their analysis. Both Milton and my hypothetical body piercer find themselves rendered physically unfit for work in the conventional sense. Their lives, which might therefore seem to be of questionable value, are made meaningful in terms of an alternative community. For their bodies and their lives to have value, no productive action is required. Milton and the body piercer do appear to differ in one important respect—namely, that Milton comes to see his inactivity as an act of service. Don't people who pierce their bodies act out of self-interest? Or are they, instead, serving by offering a visual entertainment for others?

Cultural studies clearly draws on standard historical work, but in its inclination to leap across the boundaries of disciplines and textual genres, doing subversive work, it also is often drawing on the energies of what has come to be called new historicism. Let's have a look at that now.

New Historicism

The kind of historical background provided by Tillyard depends, as Jean Howard says, on three assumptions:

1. "that history is knowable";
2. "that literature mirrors or at least by indirection reflects historical reality"; and
3. "that historians and critics can see the facts of history objectively" (18)

In the past two decades these assumptions, which seem reasonable enough at first glance, have been persuasively called into question by an outpouring of theory and practice, including deconstruction and reader-response criticism. The starting point for this work is a simple observation: "history" is textual. We read about it; we experience it in words, which are used to explain the physical evidence. We don't have access directly to the past; we have a "story" about it. The Battle of Antietam, for instance, is now a textual phenomenon. It does not exist. Our tendency to separate history and literature—seeing one as fact, the other as fiction, one as the background to the other—is collapsed by this insight. So we cannot directly observe history, nor be scientific or objective about its facts or remains, because history must be interpreted; our reading of it is as subjective as our reading of any other texts.

To see how subjective history is, you probably need only read two accounts of the same event (preferably from newspapers with different political stances). There simply isn't any objective historical "reality" out there, since the past is always absent, gone by, removed. As Hayden White puts it, history becomes "a story of a particular kind" (60). History is shaped by its necessary textuality. The pastness of the past means, again, that it exists now only as an absence, an empty space that is written upon ultimately by language. The crucial insight here, let me emphasize, is that history's content and meaning are open to interpretation. The emerging popularity in recent years of chaos theory has underscored for many people the tentative nature of historical explanations. In the 1960s and 1970s, Edward Lorenz concluded that long-range weather forecasting was unavoidably unreliable because weather patterns were in the final analysis chaotic. Any patterns that we might see in the short term tended to evaporate in the long run—in part because a huge cause may have a tiny effect, and a tiny cause may have a huge effect. The air currents moved by a butterfly's wings, as Lorenz's most famous illustration goes, might set off a chain of meteorological events that would result in a hurricane on another continent. Chaos theory, starting from Lorenz's notion of the strange and potentially unfathomable connections between causes and effects, has been extended to many diverse fields, including literary criticism. For history, chaos theory obviously compounds the problem of history's textual nature by proposing that the reality historians try to describe is itself random, nonlinear, ever-changing, chaotic. But a problem is always also an opportunity, and while one might despair of the uncertainty of historical insight, another might celebrate the wider spaces opened up for innovation and creativity.

History as Text

If history and literature are both texts, then literature is potentially as much a context for history as history is for literature. Elizabethan plays may be seen to "reflect" political events, but Elizabethan politics may also be seen as the consequence of theatrical conventions. We may think of certain political events, the coronation of Elizabeth or state trials for treason, for instance, as being "staged" like plays. We therefore might want to think about how "When I Consider" might have influenced history.

Even the reality of Milton's blindness as a "background" for the poem is produced textually for us, and it must be interpreted. It cannot be taken simply as a freestanding fact. What did blindness mean? Would it have been seen as a punishment? As a special gift or calling? Would Milton see himself as a Homeric figure, in the tradition of ancient Greece's great blind poet? Was Milton's blindness a kind of protection, affording him some exemption from prosecution when the new government failed and Charles II returned to the throne? Why does Milton see himself as essentially helpless, unable to work, to do "day-labor," even though he can still compose—as the poem itself testifies? Was writing not considered work? Is Milton putting forward an image of himself as inactive and helpless, aiming thereby to evade responsibility for Charles I's death?

Although such speculative questions might also be pursued by traditional biographical and historical criticism, new historicism encourages a new way of addressing them. A new historicist critic might elect to examine the whole issue of vision in Milton's day, of "light" versus "darkness," of insight versus sight, of writing versus working, and much more, as a textual matter. Since

Milton's blindness is for us a textual phenomenon, the new historicist would feel free to study medical texts, economic texts, optics texts, rhetoric, and any other texts that might help explain how "blindness" functions in seventeenth-century discourse: how is "blindness" constructed? Whether Milton would actually make such connections could be considered, but it would not necessarily be essential to the significance of the investigation. The new historicist critic would be more likely than the traditional historical critic to consider the possibility that Milton's blindness was psychosomatic, or feigned, or any other hypothesis that might be productive, because the new historicist assumes that history is a story, a construct, necessarily written and rewritten.

One of the most catalytic figures in this rethinking of history has been Michel Foucault, who has persistently attempted, in Eve Bannet's words, "to break down the familiar units, categories, continuities and totalities through which history, society and the symbolic order are traditionally interpreted" (96). We should note that even Tillyard did not himself claim that every Elizabethan endorsed every aspect of "the Elizabethan world picture"; in fact, he repeatedly qualified his position by citing contrary opinions. Still, Tillyard does call his work *"The" Elizabethan World Picture,* and the exceptions are designed to support his generalizations. New historicists, following Foucault, endeavor to expose the complexities, exceptions, divergences, gaps, and anachronisms in our characterizations of any period. While Tillyard sees the chain of being as a reassuring and pervasive principle of order for Elizabethan thinkers, Stephen Greenblatt considers how such myths serve the ideological interests of Elizabethan culture, discouraging dissent and subversion, and he shows how *King Lear,* for example, both affirms and undermines such cultural directives. Greenblatt's argument thus becomes an intervention into the traditional way of looking at Elizabethan England.

In addition to opposing or questioning traditional schemes of history, new historicism also tends to focus on the production of "knowledge" at a particular time and place. Foucault, for example, shows how the modern conception of "the mentally ill" came into being, as the insane are assigned to the same cultural position that those with leprosy had held. Most startling, Foucault argues that "madness" has not been a stable historical event, but is rather an invention, a construct, creating an excluded "other" category. Reversing the idea of asylums as benevolent and rehabilitative, Foucault describes their character as judicial and punitive—judging without appeal and incarcerating without trial. Similarly, Foucault reverses the widespread view that sexuality has been repressed in modern Western culture, arguing instead that sexual behavior has been increasingly discussed, classified, prohibited, authorized, and exposed. Drawing on texts from widely diverse fields, Foucault describes how the categories of the perverse and abnormal have been invented and constructed.

Since new historicists are interested in how historical "knowledge" is produced, they are naturally interested in the effects of power and ideology, whether these appear in "literature" in the usual sense or in any other texts. How we see the "facts"—indeed, whether we see a set of facts—depends (to some degree) upon the controlling system of assumptions and operations (or ideology). This unavoidable interest in power has made new historicism especially appealing to those critics interested in economy and class—often designated as Marxist criticism. Marxist critics see the individual person as a product of society's system of value, and therefore exposing how the individual is constructed by class and economy is vitally important.

Marxist Criticism

While Marxism may be hopelessly flawed as a political philosophy, it is often strikingly useful as an analytical strategy. Certain features of "When I Consider," for instance, can be highlighted by Marxism's drive to see the world in terms of economic classes, to identify who is being oppressed and exploited and by whom. Let's look in particular at the reference to "day-labor" in line 7, which may seem merely a synonym for "work," a longer word for "labor." The line, "Doth God exact day-labor, light denied," appears clearly to be a question, although Milton's text lacks a question mark (some later editors have added a question mark, and sometimes quotation marks too), and the question seems clear enough, once the reader straightens out who is talking—that "I" speaks, and not "He." But "day-labor" is an unusual word, and one might well wonder if Milton intends it to mean something more than just "work."

To find out about the meaning of "day-labor," one could research the history of labor or of economy in the seventeenth century. Or one could see how the term is used by other writers at that time and place. Those investigations could well be fascinating but time-consuming. More directly, we could look in the *Oxford English Dictionary*, which gives the meanings for words at various points in their histories. Or, even more directly, we could see how the term is defined in a dictionary of that time period. The first great dictionary of the English language is Samuel Johnson's famous *Dictionary* of 1755, which defines "daylabour" as "Labour by the day; labour divided into tasks." Johnson then offers illustrations, the first of which, interestingly enough, is the line we are talking about: "Doth God exact *daylabour,* light deny'd, / I fondly ask." Here's the second:

> Did either his legs or his arms fail him? No; but daylabour was but an hard and a dry kind of livelihood to a man, that could get an estate with two or three strokes of his pen.
>
> *Southey*

Johnson's definition and the Southey illustration begin to suggest how "daylabour" differs from "work." Someone who is employed by the day, or part of a day, is more likely to be a worker at the bottom of the social hierarchy than someone who has a position. Today we distinguish between those workers who are paid an hourly wage (they "punch the clock") and those who are salaried. Johnson's illustrations for "Daylabour," which again include an example by Milton, make these hierarchical implications clearer:

> In one night, ere glimpse of morn,
> His shadowy flail hath thresh'd the corn
> That ten *daylabourers* could not end.
>
> *Milton*

> The *daylabourer,* in a country village, has commonly but a small pittance of courage.
>
> *Locke*

A "daylabourer," the Milton quotation implies, is the kind of worker who does such messy, mind-numbing jobs as threshing corn. The pay would be poor for such nonspecialized labor, and the social status would be somewhere below the seventeenth century's equivalent of a hamburger flipper. Locke's quotation further indicates the lowly standing of a "daylabourer" by disparaging the character of that whole group.

From a Marxist perspective, Locke's attitude would also suggest precisely why the working class (the proletariat) should unite and overthrow the middle and upper classes. According to Marx's labor theory of value, the true value of something reflects the amount of labor used to make it. Within a capitalist system, someone who does "day-labor" would be unjustly undervalued: rather than being compensated fairly for "the amount of labor" contributed, the underclass worker would instead be exploited by the private owner. Naturally (as Marxist thinking would go), someone like Locke, a physician and philosopher, certainly not part of the working class, would seek to justify the economic system's suppression of day-laborers by assuming their inferiority: No wonder they're poorly compensated; they have very little courage, for starters.

Such a Marxist stance, focusing on the economic and social implications of "day-labor" alone, certainly deepens and complicates our sense of Milton's poem. Let's consider what happens for a moment, beginning by looking only at the poem's first seven lines:

> When I consider how my light is spent,
>> Ere half my days in this dark world and wide,
>> And that one talent which is death to hide
> Lodged with me useless, though my soul more bent
> To serve therewith my Maker, and present   5
>> My true account, lest He returning chide,
>> Doth God exact day-labor, light denied, . . .

Notice that, observing the poem's original punctuation, we must initially assume on a first reading that it is "my Maker," returning to chide, who says "Doth God exact day-labor, light denied." Spoken by God, the statement would seem to be a rhetorical question: "Does God expect anyone to do the sort of work that day-laborers do, picking crops, threshing corn, digging ditches, etc., when there's no daylight?" The obvious answer in this case would appear to be "no": no day, no day-labor. Of course God wouldn't require such a silly thing.

The beginning of line 8, "I fondly ask," completely reorients our reading, however, assigning the statement to the speaker. Rather than a rhetorical question, line 7 instantly becomes a complaint, and the level of Milton's frustration is indicated by "day-labor." The absurdity of God expecting anything of him, now that his "light is spent" and his talent is "useless," is reflected in the absurdity of the image of one of the most learned men in Europe, who has devoted his life to cultivating his literary talent, engaging in "day-labor." It's as if a rocket scientist has been asked to deliver pizza. Surely God cannot require anything like day-labor of Milton.

The word "fondly," however, necessitates another level of reversal, for in Milton's day "fondly," meant, as Johnson's *Dictionary* defines it, "Foolishly; weakly, imprudently; injudiciously." To be "fond" of something was to be "foolishly tender" or "injudiciously indulgent." The question that Milton asks is, therefore, a really foolish one, as the rest of the poem reveals. Its answer shouldn't be "no"; it should be "yes indeed." In fact, however, as the rest of line 8 begins to disclose, Milton's voice does not ask this question that we have just encountered, because "Patience" is able to "prevent / That murmur" by pointing out that (1) God doesn't need anyone's day-labor or any other kind of labor and (2) some people, even though they may seem incapable of having a job, have the job of simply waiting to see if they have a job of any sort to do. We should all be happy, the poem seems to assert, to serve in whatever fashion we are called upon.

Marxist criticism thus strives to see literature in terms of its relationship to society, and a work is assumed to reinforce the current social structure, or undermine it, or some combination of the two. The reading of "When I Consider" that I have just rehearsed—a reading that considers the experience of moving through the poem (and is probably indebted to Stanley Fish's famous reader-response version of this poem in "Interpreting the *Variorum*")—takes on yet another dimension in this Marxist context: the poem becomes propaganda for the status quo; and the key to this insight is, again, "day-labor." How so? Specifically, the experience of the poem reinforces the emerging capitalist system in Milton's England by undermining any potential resistance by the lower classes to their exploitation. The poem first poses the idea of resisting unreasonable demands for labor, then immediately dispels such opposition. All workers, the poem indicates, need to do their jobs, whatever they might be. Marx says that all should give according to their means and take according to their needs. But Milton stresses the value of work even for those who don't: "They also serve who only stand and wait."

Postcolonial Studies

New historicist critics not only highlight the way power has produced "knowledge" in the past, but they are also often self-consciously aware of the possibility that literary criticism might be used as a political instrument in the here and now. When Greenblatt shows how Elizabethan culture discouraged dissent, he is unavoidably raising questions about how other cultures, including our own, have suppressed, shaped, or encouraged dissent. When Foucault strives to expose the invented status of madness or perversity in the past, he is inevitably challenging the authority of current sexual or psychological norms. Such boundaries, Foucault is implicitly asserting, are based on fictions, not facts; nurture, not nature.

This creative relationship between power and knowledge is especially evident when strikingly different cultures interact. "Knowledge" for a nuclear physicist in California may not be "knowledge" for a Pygmy tribesman in central Africa. Is one form of knowledge better than the other? Wouldn't anyone reading this text agree that the physicist is likely to have a more accurate understanding of the universe than the Pygmy? When I am sick, I think that a virus or a bacterium, not an evil spirit, has probably invaded my body. But isn't it unfair and inaccurate to value one culture over another? Aren't I being ethnocentric, placing my own ethnic group at the center of things, assuming that my own Western worldview is superior, when it is in fact just different? To be sure, characterizing whole groups is always dangerous: some very wacky people live in California, and some very sensible Pygmies no doubt live in Africa. On some issues, the Pygmy and the Californian might agree that *my* ideas are absurd. Such considerations have obviously helped to energize multiculturalism, which seeks to appreciate, understand, and respect the uniquely different viewpoints of different cultures—even if we disagree. Some practices and beliefs, however, seem so obviously unethical and erroneous that a simple multicultural celebration of difference becomes problematic. At the least, a multicultural stance invites us to attempt to understand the subjectivity of our own views—to see where we are standing within our own culture as we look in on other cultures.

The powerful effects of cultural bias were compellingly exposed in 1978 when Edward Said published *Orientalism*, showing how European culture in the nineteenth century created and perpetuated the idea that Middle Eastern and Asian cultures were inferior to their own. The idea that "Oriental" cultures were less advanced was used, as Said demonstrates, to justify European colonization and exploitation. Following Said, in-depth examinations of the various relationships between dominant and subjugated cultures have been carried out by a growing number of scholars. "Postcolonial studies," the name now usually given to such investigations, explores in particular the effects of this history upon formerly colonized peoples. Postcolonial criticism thus considers the role that literature has played as an agent of oppression and resistance, distortion and understanding. What did European imperialists say about the people they colonized? How did the colonized people talk about themselves and their masters?

The playing field for postcolonial studies is huge, as indicated by its ethnic diversity and geographical expansiveness (from Canada to Sri Lanka, from Australia to Jamaica, from India to Senegal) or by its theoretical sophistication and diversity (as suggested for example by *The Empire Writes Back: Theory and Practice in Post-Colonial Literatures,* the landmark 1989 study by Bill Ashcroft, Gareth Griffiths, and Helen Tiffin). Still, as a special kind of historical interpretation, postcolonial studies would appear to be limited in scope, focusing upon certain authors and works (those who write in or about European colonies).

Milton's "When I Consider," for instance, might seem to be an unpromising work from a postcolonial perspective, as it was written well before England's massive global expansion in the eighteenth and nineteenth centuries, and it says nothing at all about colonies or colonizing. Still, one might note that European nations were already striving toward empires well before the mid-seventeenth century. And shouldn't it be possible, in theory, to decipher England's imperialistic aspirations from almost any text, just as any one cell thoroughly analyzed may tell us a great deal about the body it was taken from?

Indeed, if we return once more to "When I Consider" with postcolonial vision, we may notice that Milton does in fact depict God as an autocrat ("His state / Is kingly") who is elsewhere, but who might "returning chide" the speaker for a lack of production, for a falsified account. Milton thus sees himself (or the speaker) as a subjugated person, one who is in fact in servitude, although the absent master's "yoke" is "mild." Milton cannot avoid implicating the idealogy he inhabits, and therefore in his effort to glorify God, he thinks of "Him" as a king who appropriately controls the most extensive empire. With "thousands at his bidding" posting "o'er land and ocean without rest," we can imagine that the sun never sets on His subjects, just as the sun in later centuries would never set on the British empire. Milton's poem thus reinforces concepts essential to justifying British expansion and exploitation, as we see implicitly that the superior being rightly expects complete loyalty and service from an inferior being. The speaker in this poem, the "subaltern" (as Gayatri Spivak would put it), has no business questioning his particular situation. The speaker indeed relinquishes his rights, since his place is simply to do whatever his Maker asks of him—including even to stand and do nothing.

To notice the logic assumed by Milton's poem is to begin to question it, and it is easy to see how the potential for political activism in postcolonial criticism in particular and in new historicism in general would be especially appealing to many scholars who may understandably have wondered through the years if their research is having any real influence on the world beyond academe. From one point of view, new historicism simply acknowledges that some political agenda has always inevitably been involved in historical and critical work; the implications of new historicist work are just more visible and radical—and compelling.

But new historicists have also sometimes been taken to task for allowing their politics to shape their evidence and their conclusions. Foucault, for example, was involved in a variety of radical causes and activities before his death from an AIDS-related illness in 1984, and his work might well be seen as an extension of his personal and political interests. Foucault in fact seemed unaffected by charges that he misrepresented and misinterpreted his data, saying on one occasion, "I am not a professional historian; nobody is perfect."[1] But such a dismissive comment tends to conceal the fact that Foucault's best work, like new historicism at its best, has provided some invigorating and creative ways of looking at texts, history, knowledge, culture. If readers have sometimes been disoriented by the use of unexpected sources to make startling connections and assertions, we have also often been reoriented, challenged to defend our traditional notions or evolve new ones.

In other words, against the assumptions of the traditional history of the sort practiced by Tillyard, we may place the assumptions of the new historicism:

1. History is knowable only in the sense that all texts are knowable—that is by interpretation, argument, speculation.
2. Literature is not simply a mirror of historical reality; history in fact isn't a mirror of historical reality. Literature is shaped by history and even shapes history; it is also distorted by history and is even discontinuous with history.
3. Historians and critics must view "the facts" of history subjectively; in fact, the "facts" must be viewed as their creation.

---

[1] This statement was made at the University of Vermont on October 27, 1982. It is reported by Allan Megill in "The Reception of Foucault by Historians," *Journal of the History of Ideas* 48 (1987): 117.

How To Do Historical, Postcolonial, and Cultural Studies

To do biographical criticism (an individual's history), you need to know as much as you can about the life of the author and then apply that knowledge, being careful not to equate the author with a narrator or character, drawing conclusions cautiously, and supporting them solidly with evidence from the literary text itself, and not only from the author's life. To do historical criticism, you need to know the relevant history and use it in some way. The difficulty here, besides the work of mastering history, is determining just what is relevant. One way to look at this: if the history helps you understand the work, then it's relevant. New historicism complicates things a bit, because you ought to know the author's biography—even though the author's personality is a cultural construct, a textual effect; and you ought to know the history (or histories)—even though the "facts" are always subject to questioning, supplementation, opposition. Thinking from a new historical point of view, you are encouraged to be particularly imaginative in making connections, and to think about how particular documents participate in, or help to create, systems of assumptions and meanings.

To do postcolonial criticism, you need to know the history (social, economic, political, cultural) of the imperial and the colonized peoples, and you want to apply that history somehow to literary texts (or art, music, fashion, whatever). The most influential work in postcolonial theory has dealt with India, Africa, Australia, Canada, the Caribbean and New Zealand, and typical moves involve revealing how the colonial power depicts the native population as in need of domination. The men of India, according to pervasive cultural propaganda, are effeminate and unambitious; Africans are savage and lazy; Oriental people are mysterious and threatening. Postcolonial criticism can show how these images are perpetuated or undermined or transformed in various literary works.

Similarly, cultural studies might be most accurately presented as more of a set of goals than a clear-cut method. The fundamental idea of cultural studies, one could argue, is that the products of a culture are shaped by underlying assumptions and values; and a variety of strategies, ranging from psychoanalysis to deconstruction to feminist criticism and so forth, can be used to explain the artifacts and activities of a culture. A recent book by Richard Lee, *The Life and Times of Cultural Studies* (Duke UP, 2003), notes a shift in cultural studies from issues of working-class culture toward questions involving race and gender. Whatever the object of cultural studies—high culture, low culture, popular culture, elite culture; class, race, gender—"doing" cultural studies means not only attempting to illuminate culture but also intervening in it. Part of the academic popularity of cultural studies no doubt stems from this commitment, allowing scholars and teachers to act on their political allegiances, working for change by producing knowledge. Given the origins of cultural studies in the 1960s in Great Britain's New Left, and particularly in Birmingham University's Centre for Contemporary Cultural Studies, the social change that cultural studies typically advocates is progressive and liberal. In bringing an academic rigor to the analysis of all sorts of things previously ignored or dismissed, such as motorcycle gangs, soap operas, tattoos, advertising, or rock music, cultural studies has indeed made some startling contributions to our understanding.

The whole idea of cultural studies as an "approach" might be questionable for some people, since one could argue that cultural studies is really distinguished by the objects it studies (the products of popular culture and subcultures) or its goals (progressive social change), and not by any distinctive method. But you'll find, I think, that your analytical imagination can be stirred simply by deciding to bring critical analysis to a much larger body of works, or deciding to work from a particular political stance. And so "how to do" cultural studies involves simply looking at certain things with a certain goal—and seeing what happens. Thinking through political stances different from your own can be healthy and invigorating: see what the world looks like from other perspectives. I would therefore encourage the most open version of cultural studies, one that embraces the study of just about any cultural phenomenon from just about any political stance. (But "local programming may vary," as the television networks say.)

The approaches covered in this chapter all direct you to make connections (which can include breaking down fences) between and among the products of history, biography, and culture. Literature, from this perspective or these perspectives, is not something that we study for its own sake. Literature is part of life. And what we call "literature," or at least give a literary sort of attention to, may well be a text (or object or activity) that is not literature in a traditional sense. It is nonetheless possible to give some general guidance about using historical, postcolonial, and cultural studies to write about a literary text, however you define it:

1. Determine the historical setting of the work—when and where was it written and under what conditions. Investigate the author's biography, including of course race, class, gender, and so forth.
2. Consider how the historical background helps us to understand the work, or consider how the work contradicts or stands apart from the consensus historical or biographical background. Are there individuals or groups that are characterized in politically significant ways?
3. Identify other texts of the same time period that might be related to the text under analysis. Identify the ideology (or ideologies) driving these texts, constructing a system of meaning. Expose the cultural significance of the literary text.

Although these approaches require some research and patience, they are interesting and often very rewarding. With the rapid expansion of electronic resources, historical materials are becoming increasingly accessible. There is no substitute for the thrill of examining (carefully) a first edition of Samuel Johnson's great 1755 *Dictionary of the English Language;* but the CD-ROM version of the dictionary, recently released, allows one to search the entire huge work for a particular word or phrase, and anyone seeking the historical meaning of a word will find the electronic dictionary invaluable. Although travelling to London and the British Library to do research on the archives of Parliament can be quite invigorating, not everyone can afford the time and expense; but now those records are available online. You'll miss the soggy weather and charming accents, but you can still get the information you need. Even such basic resources as the *Encyclopedia Britannica* can be accessed online. Museums and libraries now host websites containing informational riches; historical organizations provide links to scholarly journals and primary sources. You need information about railroads in the nineteenth century? Check out the Railroad History Database. Or maybe it's the history of the Air Force: there's the Air Force Historical Research Agency, of course. For anyone interested in history, it's a great time to be alive. Although chat rooms and e-mail and online shopping are nice, the Internet's most stunning potential lies in its power to teach us. The vastness of resources available may seem overwhelming at times, so don't hesitate to seek advice. Librarians and teachers are ordinarily delighted to help. The various search engines, Google and many others, are constantly being refined—but the websites and the information out there must be carefully assessed.

THE WRITING PROCESS: SAMPLE ESSAYS

The work I want to focus on in this section is a compelling short story, first published in the October 27, 1962, issue of *The New Yorker.*

Reunion
John Cheever

The last time I saw my father was in Grand Central Station. I was going from my grandmother's in the Adirondacks to a cottage on the Cape that my mother had rented, and I wrote my father that I would be in New York between trains for an hour and a half, and asked if we could have lunch together. His secretary wrote to say that he would meet me at the information booth at noon, and twelve o'clock sharp I saw him coming through the crowd. He was a stranger to me—my mother divorced him three years ago and I hadn't been with him since—but as soon as I saw him I felt that he was my father, my flesh and blood, my future and my doom. I knew that when I was grown I would be something like him; I would have to plan my campaigns within his limitations. He was a big, good-looking man, and I was terribly happy to see him again. He struck me on the back and shook my hand. "Hi, Charlie," he said. "Hi, boy. I'd like to take you up to my club, but it's in the Sixties, and if you have to catch an early train I guess we'd better get something to eat around here." He put his arm around me, and I smelled my father the way my mother sniffs a rose. It was a rich compound of whiskey, after-shave lotion, shoe polish, woollens, and the rankness of a mature male. I hoped that someone would see us together. I wished that we could be photographed. I wanted some record of our having been together.

We went out of the station and up a side street to a restaurant. It was still early and the place was empty. The bartender was quarreling with a delivery boy, and there was one very old waiter in a red coat down by the kitchen door. We sat down, and my father hailed the waiter in a loud voice. *"Kellner!"* he shouted. *"Garçon! Cameriere! You!"* His boisterousness in the empty restaurant seemed out of place. "Could we have a little service here!" he shouted. "Chop-chop." Then he clapped his hands. This caught the waiter's attention, and he shuffled over to our table.

"Were you clapping your hands at me?" he asked.

"Calm down, calm down, *sommelier*," my father said. "If it isn't too much to ask of you—if it wouldn't be too much above and beyond the call of duty, we would like a couple of Beefeater Gibsons."

"I don't like to be clapped at," the waiter said.

"I should have brought my whistle," my father said. "I have a whistle that is audible only to the ears of old waiters. Now, take out your little pad and your little pencil and see if you can get this straight: two Beefeater Gibsons. Repeat after me: two Beefeater Gibsons."

"I think you'd better go someplace else," the waiter said quietly.

"That," said my father, "is one of the most brilliant suggestions I have ever heard. Come on, Charlie, let's get the hell out of here."

I followed my father out of that restaurant into another. He was not so boisterous this time. Our drinks came, and he cross-questioned me about the baseball season. He then struck the edge of his empty glass with his knife and began shouting again. *"Garçon! Kellner! Cameriere! You!* Could we trouble you to bring us two more of the same."

"How old is the boy?" the waiter asked.

"That," my father said, "is none of your God-damned business."

"I'm sorry, sir," the waiter said, "but I won't serve the boy another drink."

"Well, I have some news for you," my father said. "I have some very interesting news for you. This doesn't happen to be the only restaurant in New York. They've opened another on the corner. Come on, Charlie."

He paid the bill, and I followed him out of that restaurant into another. Here the waiters wore pink jackets like hunting coats, and there was a lot of horse tack on the walls. We sat down, and my father began to shout again. "Master of the hounds! Tallyho and all that sort of thing. We'd like a little something in the way of a stirrup cup. Namely, two Bibson Geefeaters."

"Two Bibson Geefeaters?" the waiter asked, smiling.

"You know damned well what I want," my father said angrily. "I want two Beefeater Gibsons, and make it snappy. Things have changed in jolly old England. So my friend the duke tells me. Let's see what England can produce in the way of a cocktail."

"This isn't England," the waiter said.

"Don't argue with me," my father said. "Just do as you're told."

"I just thought you might like to know where you are," the waiter said.

"If there is one thing I cannot tolerate," my father said, "it is an impudent domestic. Come on, Charlie."

The fourth place we went to was Italian. *"Buon giorno,"* my father said. *"Per favore, possiamo avere due cocktail americani, forti, forti. Molto gin, poco vermut."*

"I don't understand Italian," the waiter said.

"Oh, come off it," my father said. "You understand Italian, and you know damned well you do. *Vogliamo due cocktail americani. Subito."*

The waiter left us and spoke with the captain, who came over to our table and said, "I'm sorry, sir, but this table is reserved."

"All right," my father said, "Get us another table."

"All the tables are reserved," the captain said.

"I get it," my father said. "You don't desire our patronage. Is that it? Well, the hell with you. *Vada all'inferno.* Let's go, Charlie."

"I have to get my train," I said.

"I'm sorry, sonny," my father said. "I'm terribly sorry." He put his arm around me and pressed me against him. "I'll walk you back to the station. If there had only been time to go up to my club."

"That's all right, Daddy," I said.

"I'll get you a paper," he said. "I'll get you a paper to read on the train."

Then he went up to a newsstand and said, "Kind sir, will you be good enough to favor me with one of your God-damned, no-good, ten-cent afternoon papers?" The clerk turned away from him and stared at a magazine cover. "Is it asking too much, kind sir," my father said, "is it asking too much for you to sell me one of your disgusting specimens of yellow journalism?"

"I have to go, Daddy," I said. "It's late."

"Now, just wait a second, sonny," he said. "Just wait a second. I want to get a rise out of this chap."

"Goodbye, Daddy," I said, and I went down the stairs and got my train, and that was the last time I saw my father.

(1962)

In what follows we turn from the primary text to other texts, seeking connections. These connections might be used to argue for the story's unity or disjunction, or to explain the psychology of the characters, or in any number of other ways. But here I am interested primarily in how the story might reflect Cheever's personal history and feelings, in the first example, and then how the story is shaped by a system of ideas regarding prestige, identity, suicide, and alcohol in the second example.

A BIOGRAPHICAL ESSAY

Preparing to Write

A search of the electronic card catalogue at my school's library revealed thirteen books with John Cheever as their subject. I retrieved the seven that weren't checked out and requested the others to be held for me. Then I started skimming and reading, looking especially for materials relating to "Reunion," but also learning as much about Cheever as I could. Here's a sampling of the notes I took:

From *John Cheever* by Lynne Waldeland (Boston: Twayne, 1979):

- "Reunion" is from *The Brigadier and the Golf Widow,* Cheever's "best volume of short stories," according to William Peden (91).
- The stories share a theme of transformation.

From *The Letters of John Cheever,* edited by Cheever's son, Benjamin (New York: Simon and Schuster, 1988):

- Regarding the original publication of "The Brigadier and the Golf Widow," the title story of the volume in which "Reunion" would later appear: Cheever writes to a friend that he went into *The New Yorker* offices to correct the galleys (the trial printing) of the story and found that Bill Maxwell had cut the story "in half." Cheever went along, he says, with the cut in the office but then later called from a bar and cursed Maxwell, who was at home entertaining "Elizabeth Bowen and Eudora Welty" (two famous writers), telling Maxwell that if he cut the story "I'll never write another story for your [sic] or anybody else" (232).
- Cheever's letter concludes this way: "Anyhow the magazine had gone to press and they had to remake the whole back of the book and stay up all night but they ran it without the cut" (232–33).

Maxwell's recollection, reported by Benjamin, is very different: Maxwell says he thought the story had two endings, and so he was going to see how Cheever liked it with only one. He had no plan to cut the story at all without Cheever's approval; the story wasn't about to go to press (Cheever had found it on Maxwell's desk), and there was no all-night reworking; Bowen and Welty had visited his house, but never at the same time (233).

How can Cheever have the story so wrong? Does he have no allegiance to the truth, preferring to spin a good tale? Or does his letter describe the truth, at least as he remembers it? The letter seems to have been written immediately afterward: how could his memory be so immediately faulty? Intrigued by this problem, I turned to the introduction to the volume of letters, written by Cheever's son, Benjamin. Benjamin Cheever makes clear that "my father's interest in telling a good story was greater than his interest in what we might consider the facts" (20). Cheever's letters thus become a kind of rehearsal for his fiction, as he practices shaping reality into better narrative material. Benjamin notes that he has "included excerpts from his journals and his fiction, so that one can see the life—sometimes the same incident—reflected differently through the prism of his prose" (20).

For anyone undertaking biographical criticism, the implications here are clear: we should be particularly cautious regarding the "facts," especially as reported by Cheever; at the same time, we should be aware that Cheever does work his life into his stories, apparently sometimes in rather direct ways.

The following passages also caught my attention:

- Benjamin writes:
  The most difficult part for me, as a son, was the extent of my father's homosexuality. It's impossible for me to be objective about this, or to separate his fears from my own, but he was certainly troubled by the issue. (16)

- Benjamin writes:
  He used to say that I must wish I had a father who didn't drink so much, and I'd always say no. I suppose this makes me what Alcoholics Anonymous would call an enabler, somebody who makes it all right for the alcoholic to destroy himself. Maybe so, but I thought then and think now that you have to take the people you love pretty much the way you find them. Their worst qualities are often linked with their very best ones. (18)

- Also, reminding me of the father's smells in "Reunion," Benjamin writes:
  It remains that while I am not a heavy drinker myself, or a smoker, I still find the smell of gin and tobacco a delicious combination. (18)

Finally, the following passages are especially interesting in the context of biographical criticism:

- Benjamin Cheever says:

    The connection between his life and his work was intimate, but it was also mysterious. My father was fond of saying that fiction was "crypto-autobiography." One obvious reason for this statement is that it protected him from the attacks of friends and family who felt that they'd been libeled in his prose. (21)

From the first chapter of *John Cheever* by Samuel Coale, "Cheever's Life" (New York: Frederick Ungar, 1977):

- Cheever's father was a shoe salesman who was out of work late in life, and his mother opened a shop for the family to survive, selling first their own belongings. Cheever's father resented, apparently, her independence and competence and his own helplessness. (23)

From *Home Before Dark,* a biography of Cheever by his daughter, Susan (Boston: Houghton, 1984):

- e. e. cummings was Cheever's "first model" (59). Susan Cheever remembers attending with her father a poetry reading by cummings. When cummings saw Cheever, "The force and openness of their affection for one another seemed to shake that airless, heavily draped room" (60). Susan remembers particularly, she says, sitting with her father as cummings read "my father moved through dooms of love" (60), the elegy to cummings's father.
- cummings died in 1962, the same year "Reunion" was published.
- A passage that's interesting in the context of the father's use of foreign languages to attract waiters in "Reunion":

    "Although he spoke minimal French, he always called the French classics by their original names: *Les Faux-Monnayeurs, La Chartreuse de Parme, Le Rouge et le Noir.* In his last years—a time when he was so well respected that a lot of people assumed he spoke two or three languages—he began dropping French words into his conversation. When he was sent his own books in French translations, he kept them on the desk or his bedside table. With Italian, he was even worse. He spoke a stilted, conversational Italian, but he used it at every opportunity, and he even insisted on re-Italianizing all

> Americanized Italian words or names. (He always insisted on calling my editor Nan Talese 'Nan Talayzee,' for instance.) 'Che cosa di buona oggi?' he would ask any dark-haired waiter, whether he was at the Four Seasons or the Highland Diner on Route 9 in Ossining. They were always very polite. (113–14)

- Susan Cheever also offers this passage, which reminds me of Charlie's awareness of the smell of his father and suggests that Cheever longed for the sort of father that his character, Charlie, did not have:

> "There is the presence of a father—stern, unintelligent and with a gamey odor—but a force of counsel and support that would have carried one into manhood," my father wrote in his journal. "One does not invest the image with brilliance or wealth; it is simply a man in a salt and pepper tweed, sometimes loving, sometimes irascible and sometimes drunk but always responsible to his son." My father didn't have this ideal, tweedy parent he dreamed of in his journal who would have "equipped him for manhood." He spent much of his life looking for counsel and support from surrogate fathers and ultimately, painfully, rejecting them. (128)

- Late in Cheever's life, according to Susan, when he had achieved some fame:

> He dropped names shamelessly. It was no longer safe to tease him about favorable reviews. In restaurants, he let headwaiters know that he was someone important. Since this kind of behavior was new to him, he wasn't particularly graceful about it. Walking down Park Avenue with him once, after a lunch at the Four Seasons ("Che cosa di buona oggi?"), I noticed that he was smiling his public smile at everyone who passed—just in case they recognized him, I suppose. (210–11)

From Scott Donaldson's biography, *John Cheever* (New York: Random, 1988):

- Cheever's mother told him he was a mistake: "If I hadn't drunk two Manhattans one afternoon, you never would have been conceived" (19). And his father wanted him aborted, even inviting the abortionist to dinner, an event that appears in both *The Wapshot Chronicle* and *Falconer.*
- In the story "National Pastime," the father won't teach the son to play baseball, which causes the son real embarrassment and trauma (20).

From *The Journals of John Cheever,* edited by Robert Gottlieb (New York: Knopf, 1991):

- Cheever writes:

> Having drunk less than usual, having, as my father would say, gone light on the hooch, I find myself, for the first time in a long time, free of the cafard. Quarter to nine. Eastern day-light-saving time. It would be pleasant to consider this a simple matter of self-discipline. Thunder and rain in the middle of the afternoon; the first of the month. Our primordial anxiety about drought and its effect on the crops, the crops in this case being three acres of lawn and forty-two rosebushes. (135–36)
>
> I dislike writing here about boozefighting, but I must do something about it. A friend comes to call. In my anxiety to communicate, to feel the most in warmth and intimacy, I drink too much, which can be two drinks these days. In the morning I am deeply depressed, my insides barely function, my kidney is painful, my hands shake, and walking down Madison Avenue I am in fear of death. But evening comes or even noon and some combination of nervous tensions obscures my memories of what whiskey costs me in the way of physical and intellectual well-being. I could very easily destroy myself. It is ten o'clock now and I am thinking of the noontime snort. (103)
>
> Year after year I read in here that I am drinking too much, and there can be no doubt of the fact that this is progressive. I waste more days, I suffer deeper pangs of guilt, I wake up at three in the morning with the feelings of a temperance worker. Drink, its implements, environments, and effects all seem disgusting. And yet each noon I reach for the whiskey bottle. I don't seem able to drink temperately and yet I don't seem able to stop. (103)
>
> Never having known the love of a father has forced me into love so engulfing and passionate that there is no margin of choice. (177)

At this point I had invested about twelve hours in doing research—skimming, reading, taking notes. I decided to move on to the next phase: organizing this material and relating it to "Reunion."

Shaping

Simply by selecting some observations rather than others, I was already in a sense organizing my materials. But I wasn't quite sure why I was attracted to these materials, and so I spent some time reading over my notes and looking for links and patterns. For each note, I tried to think of some words or phrases that would characterize the material. The following topics seemed the most obvious:

1. Fiction as "crypto-autobiography."
2. The need for the father's love.
3. Alcoholism.
4. The father's smells.
5. The father's coldness.
6. The father's love.
7. The father's failure.
8. Foreign languages (and name-dropping).

Next, I went through the materials again and numbered them according to the list above, thus allowing me to group together all of the materials that dealt, for instance, with the relationship of Cheever's fiction to his life.

At this point, before I could tell how to arrange my organized materials, I needed a main idea: I couldn't tell how to order my materials if I didn't know what I was trying to accomplish. Beginning with Cheever himself, I knew that I was trying to determine how our understanding of Cheever's life enlarges or affects our understanding of his story. In Cheever's case, such an approach seems especially promising, given Cheever's own acknowledgment of the intimate relationship between his life and art.

But how would I characterize that relationship? At this point, before I launch into that speculation, you may want to take a few moments and see where you would go with this biographical information. What would your main idea be?

One striking finding is that Cheever and the father in "Reunion" resemble each other: each is an alcoholic father afraid that he is neglecting or hurting his children. Cheever struggles not to drink before noon and then, losing that battle, struggles not to get out of control. The father in the story also seems to be fixated on his drinking, forgetting apparently about feeding Charlie lunch. After only one drink with Charlie, he orders "Bibson Geefeaters," suggesting perhaps that he has already been drinking beforehand. The father in the story also seems to be like Cheever in his desire to show off his knowledge of foreign languages, and the father also does a bit of name-dropping. Although Cheever and his wife never divorced, they seem to have lived most of their lives on the edge of that gulf. Seeing Cheever in the father, seeing Cheever's awareness of his own shortcomings reflected in the father, I tend to have more sympathy for the father.

But there are also significant ways in which the young boy, Charlie, is like Cheever. Cheever felt distanced from his father, even as he longed for his love. He felt his father to be mysteriously cold—"the greatest and most bitter mystery in my life." Even Cheever's sensitivity to the way his father smelled, recorded in his journal, is a trait we see in Charlie. Cheever did not have a secretary, but his father did, at least until he lost his job. We know that Cheever felt his father neglected him, just as Charlie's father, who has not seen him in three years, is "a stranger." In fact, Cheever believed his father wanted him aborted.

But so what if Charlie's father is like Cheever's father, and like Cheever? And Charlie is also like Cheever and perhaps like Cheever's son? What do these parallels explain? Well, what *needs* to be explained? What do you find most remarkable or puzzling about the story? For me, two things seem obviously strange:

1. Charlie says his father will be "my future and my doom." Why will his father be his doom? How does he know "that when I was grown I would be something like him"?

2. Charlie provides a portrait of his father that is at first perhaps a bit amusing but is ultimately grotesque. In the end Charlie's father seems to be a kind of monster, obsessed with getting "a rise" out of the newsstand clerk while the son he hasn't seen in three years is leaving. Why does Charlie, after telling us how "terribly happy" he was to see his father, reveal nothing of his feelings? We can guess how Charlie felt, but we do not know. Why the absence of feeling—at least in the telling (which may not be truthful)?

Does Cheever's relationship to the two characters offer any sort of explanation to both questions? I think so, and that idea becomes my tentative thesis:

Cheever resented his father's alcoholism and inattention and at the same time longed for his love; he desired to turn away from his father, putting the pain of his neglect behind him, and at the same time he wanted to turn toward his father, to bridge their distance. This love / hate conflict is intensified by Cheever's awareness that he is in certain crucial ways like his father. In "Reunion" Charlie does not directly express his disgust and rage at his father because his position is essentially the same as Cheever's: in hating his father, Charlie (like Cheever) is closing off the possibility of resolution; in hating his father, Charlie (like Cheever) is hating himself.

This thesis, as is usually the case, suggests an organization for the essay:

1. Cheever's fiction meaningfully echoes his life: thesis.
2. Charlie's father and Cheever's father.
3. Charlie and Cheever.
4. Charlie's father and Cheever himself.
5. Conclusion.

Drafting

You might want to sketch out your own draft of an essay based on the plan above before you read the one that follows.

John Cheever's "Reunion" as "Crypto-Autobiography"

The intro sets up the problem: why is Charlie's father harshly portrayed?

In John Cheever's "Reunion," the portrait of Charlie's father seems in the final analysis harsh and unforgiving. Not having seen his son in three years, the father proceeds at their meeting to drink himself into an abusive, obsessive state. He is never overtly mean to Charlie to be sure, but he is also far from attentive. Before the meeting, he did not respond personally to his son's letter asking about the lunch, letting his secretary arrange it instead; and throughout the visit, he seems intent only on getting drinks and exerting his authority over waiters, showing little or no interest in the well-being of his son. As Charlie leaves, his father is unable even to say goodbye appropriately because he is so intent on getting "a rise" out of the newspaper clerk.

Yet Charlie's opinion is not explicitly presented.

And yet, despite his father's distressing behavior, Charlie does not directly express his feelings about the day's events. In the first paragraph he tells us that he was "terribly happy" to see his father, that he even wished they could be photographed together, but at the same time he says he immediately knew, the moment he saw his father, that he was "my future and my doom." Even with this emotional load, Charlie appears simply to report what happened without betraying his own reaction. But much is left out, leaving the reader to guess what Charlie is feeling, how this event has affected him, why this was the "last time I saw my father." Was he so outraged, hurt, saddened, confused, embarrassed, or something else that he determined never to see him again? Or did his father die soon afterward? The story is so brief that it is difficult to speculate with any confidence on Charlie's motivations, or even on his accuracy, yet it is so vividly told that it is difficult not to speculate.

Thesis is introduced here.

Perhaps this distancing is precisely what Cheever wanted: to tell a story about a father and a son, presenting deeply moving events without really exposing what they mean. To understand Cheever's purpose, and thereby understand his story better, we need to look at Cheever's own experience of father-son relationships. The justification for relating life to fiction is particularly strong in Cheever's case since the same incident oftentimes is recounted in his letters and journals and then employed in his fiction. Even when Cheever was supposedly reporting a real event, his "interest in telling a good story was greater than his interest in what we might consider the facts," as his son Benjamin put it (20). As Benjamin wrote, "The connection between his life and his work was intimate," and Cheever was even "fond of saying that fiction was 'crypto-autobiography'" (21). In fact there are obvious autobiographical elements in "Reunion," and decoding them does shed some light on the story.

Cheever's life connects to the story.

Cheever's father and Charlie's father.

First, we should note that Cheever was profoundly troubled by his relationship to his father: late in life he called his father "the greatest and the most bitter mystery in my life," and he revealed that the problem of learning to love a father "appears in all the books and stories" (qtd. Susan Cheever 209–10). We do not need to know much about Cheever's childhood to imagine why he kept trying to sort it out. Not only did Cheever's mother tell him he was a mistake ("If I hadn't drunk two Manhattans one afternoon, you never would have been conceived"), but also, as Scott Donaldson's biography says, "his father wanted him aborted, even inviting the abortionist to dinner, an event that appears in both *The Wapshot Chronicle* and *Falconer*" (19). Charlie's father is in some crucial aspects like Cheever's father: alcoholic, insecure, sarcastic, self-centered. Unlike Charlie's father, Cheever's father was not divorced, but there were tremendous hostilities between his parents, leading to drunken infidelities, threatened suicides, and violent arguments—which formed much of the substance of Cheever's fiction.

Charlie and Cheever.

If Charlie's father is like Cheever's father, Charlie is also a reflection of Cheever. Charlie, like Cheever, wants to love his father, but he finds a man who is apparently uninterested in him and careening out of control. In his hunger for love, Charlie tries to connect with his father on some more primitive level, smelling his father "the way my mother sniffs a rose" and finding "a rich compound of whiskey, after-shave lotion, shoe polish, woollens, and the rankness of a mature male." Cheever was also extraordinarily moved by smells, telling his publisher at one point that he was "a very olfactory fellow," and not to try to remove any of the smells in his book.

Cheever and his father.

But Cheever does not seem to express his rage and disappointment very directly through Charlie. Surely part of the obstruction is Cheever's realization that he is in many ways like his father, Frederick Cheever, a shoe salesman who became unemployed and bitter in the mid–1920s. John Cheever was not technically out of work, but he did not have a regular job, and he struggled for much of his life to make ends meet. Most obviously, like his father—like Charlie's father—Cheever could not control his drinking. In an entry from the early journals (late forties and fifties), Cheever writes, "Year after year I read in here [in his journal] that I am drinking too much, and there can be no doubt of the fact that this is progressive" (103). Although Cheever finds everything about his drinking "disgusting," still "each noon I reach for the whiskey bottle." Cheever was evidently aware of the effect of such behavior on a son, as Cheever's own son, Benjamin, writes (in *The Letters of John Cheever*), "He used to say that I must wish I had a father who didn't drink so much, and I'd always say no" (18).

Cheever and Charlie's father.

In fact, Charlie's father's habit of baiting waiters in foreign tongues may have been modeled on Cheever's own behavior, as a passage from Susan Cheever's biography of her father reveals. After commenting on how Cheever, even though "he spoke minimal French," began "dropping French words into his conversation," she goes on to say, "With Italian, he was even worse," using it "at every opportunity," especially in restaurants (113).

Summary

Thus Charlie's statement that his father was "my future and my doom" resonates on several levels. Cheever, the model for Charlie, had become "something like" his father. And Cheever's father was "something like" Charlie's father, just as Charlie would become "something like" Cheever himself. For Charlie to hate his father would involve hating himself, his own future self; yet he could hardly approve affectionately of his father. But more than that: for Charlie to express his hatred toward his father, Cheever would have to acknowledge his own hatred for his father, which would likewise involve a self-destructive disgust. Cheever could not find a way to love his father, but he could not find a way to hate him either. And so he was driven to write about him endlessly, searching for a way to describe the relationship and resolve it.

Works Cited

Cheever, John. *The Brigadier and the Golf Widow*. New York: Harper, 1964.

———. *The Journals of John Cheever*. Ed. Robert Gottlieb. New York: Knopf, 1991.

———. *The Letters of John Cheever*. Ed. Benjamin Cheever. New York: Simon & Schuster, 1988.

Cheever, Susan. *Home Before Dark*. Boston: Houghton, 1984.

Donaldson, Scott. *John Cheever*. New York: Random, 1988.

A NEW HISTORICAL ESSAY

Preparing to Write

Where could I look for some clues to the ideology shaping Cheever's story? I decided that one place to look, thinking of "Reunion" as part of a cultural system, would be *The New Yorker* magazine in which the story was first published. Knowing the story came out in 1962, I found it in the October 27th issue: the whole story appears on page 45.

I studied the magazine, trying to absorb the culture of 1962, the book and movie reviews, the current events, the articles, the advertisements, time-traveling back a little over thirty years. I did not imagine one issue of one magazine could contain an entire culture, but I did assume that a close inspection of one issue might suggest a great deal about the world *The New Yorker* presented to its readers. I tried to imagine myself as an anthropologist studying a foreign and unknown culture—in this case, the culture of *The New Yorker*'s writers, advertisers, and readers. In reading through the magazine, I was struck very quickly by two messages, which seemed to appear relentlessly in various ways. Both messages arguably still permeate our culture, but they seemed especially prominent in this "foreign" setting. Perhaps I was simply paying close attention to what I ordinarily try to ignore.

Put bluntly, I found the magazine telling its readers again and again to consume—to purchase, to view, to possess, to ingest—and to display the quality of their discerning consumption. Most insistently, it seemed that readers were being told to consume superior alcoholic beverages: directly in some thirty-six ads and indirectly in ads for other products. An ad for Japan Airlines pictured a happy couple in the act of taking drinks from an attentive hostess; another for Caron perfumes depicted a beautiful woman clinking a brandy glass with her lover.

I was also struck by the exhortations to wear superior clothing, urging readers to display their wealth and excellent taste. Such exhibition was motivated, sometimes blatantly, sometimes subtly, by the promise of acceptance and affection. These messages—consume and display—appeared most obviously in the advertisements, but they could also be discerned in the articles and even the cartoons. They often appeared together.

Shaping

If we recognize that Cheever's story appears in a context saturated with recurrent encouragements to drink (for status and success) and to display one's status and success, what difference does it make? How does this context affect our reading of the story? How does the story affect our reading of the context, for that matter?

One effect might be to reconsider our assessment of Charlie's father's drinking. In new historicist fashion, stressing ideology over individuals, I would argue that Charlie's father is not an autonomous agent, fully responsible for his failures. Rather, Charlie's father is to some degree a product of a value system he has learned too well. He has simply learned to seek affection and status in alcohol. His efforts to display his sophistication in languages and to demonstrate his dominance over the various waiters are also the effect of a powerful (but pitiful) desire for status.

This view of the father's fundamental insecurity and loneliness, which he attempts to erase by drinking and asserting himself, reminds me of some passages in Cheever's journal. Writing about his inability to control his drinking, Cheever writes: "I could very easily destroy myself" (103). Charlie's father, like Cheever, is destroying himself slowly. Cheever and his character are being driven by emotional pain and insecurity to seek relief in the way that their culture has prescribed—asserting their status, consuming alcohol.

We do not know in "Reunion" why Charlie's father and mother were divorced, and we may assume that Charlie has not seen his father for three years because his father is uncaring. Cheever's journal may help us to consider other possibilites consistent with the facts of the story—namely that Charlie's mother may have prevented his father from seeing him. Perhaps she considered his father so worthless that she did not want Charlie to see him again. Perhaps Charlie's father feels so guilty that he considers himself unworthy of his son's attention.

Finally, I should mention one more journal entry in which Cheever records the visit of a friend: "in my anxiety to communicate, to feel the most in warmth and intimacy, I drink too much, which can be two drinks these days" (103). The advertisements and cartoons link intimacy and affection to alcohol, and Cheever does the same thing here. Again, Charlie's father's behavior needs to be reconsidered.

At this point, it seems clear that I have way too much material for a brief essay—which means that I'm in good shape. But don't I need to dig further, examining all *The New Yorker* issues of 1962, and *Good Housekeeping* and *Reader's Digest* also, and everything else that can be recovered? Not really, although it's always nice to know as much as you can. My claim is simply that a certain community (the readers of *The New Yorker*) at a certain slice of time (1962) were being exposed to a certain set of messages. Rather than having to dig up a whole city, the new historicist can construct a tentative system of meaning from the close analysis of selected artifacts. The point is not that one document influenced another, but rather that at this moment within this community all documents participated in certain common assumptions.

So, looking over my notes, freewriting, and brainstorming, I come back to my focus on Charlie's father as a reflection of a system of meaning. I try organizing my material in the following way:

> The emotional view: Charlie's father as a deviant jerk.
>
> Thesis: The analytical view: Charlie's father as a product of his time.
>
> Advertisements and cartoons suggest alcohol confers status and affection: manliness.
>
> Cheever and Charlie's father: drowning self and pain in drink.

Drafting

You might wish to draft an essay yourself at this point, then compare your application of the materials to mine.

How to Make an Alchoholic Drink: Cheever's "Reunion" in Its Context

The opening orients the reader to the story and the issue: the father's lack of affection.	In John Cheever's "Reunion," Charlie's father appears to be the worst sort of parent. After three years of separation (following a divorce), the father doesn't respond to his son's letter but rather has his secretary arrange their meeting. He greets his son in a strange way, with no apparent affection:

> "Hi Charlie," he said. "Hi, boy. I'd like to take you up to my club, but it's in the Sixties, and if you have to

catch an early train I guess we'd better get something to eat around here."

Although he puts his arm around Charlie, his subsequent behavior seems to confirm his callous self-
absorption, as he apparently forgets about lunch and
thinks only of drinking and insulting waiters. The visit
ends with Charlie saying good-bye, for the last time, to a
father who seems interested only in harrassing a newsstand clerk.

This paragraph introduces a possible explanation: the father's values are shaped by his culture.

But before we entirely dismiss Charlie's father, we
might consider his motivation. What does he think he is
doing? Where has he learned such behavior? Certainly
Charlie is a victim of his father's indulgent inattention;
but is Charlie's father also a victim in any way? In *The
New Yorker* magazine in which "Reunion" first
appeared, we find a set of directives that helps to
explain the behavior of Charlie's father, which may well
be motivated not by any sort of disregard or animosity
toward Charlie, but rather by the desire for status and
affection. This desire is fueled by a system of values
reflected in and even shaped by *The New Yorker*.

Evidence: Ads for alcoholic beverages focus on status.

Again and again advertisements in the October
26th issue of 1962 convey to the readers the paramount
importance of status, rank, superiority. One of the most
blatant of these ads asks the question "Are you a status
seeker?" If you like "Italian restaurants," the ad continues, "foreign cars," "antique furniture," and finally "Lord
Calvert" whiskey, then you apparently are a status
seeker (as you should be, the ad implies). The association of alcoholic beverages with nobility, and therefore
"status," is a recurrent theme. Grand Marnier is "The
Emperor of Liqueurs," and another scotch is named
"House of Lords." Old Hickory is drunk by "all the nicest
people," and several couples in formal evening attire
are depicted. The drink identifies you as a superior
being, among "the nicest people," which does not in this
context seem to mean the most polite or philanthropic.

Other ads and status.

Other ads for nonalcoholic products also reinforce
this desire for status. One ad pictures an aristocratic
man, sneering slightly, in an overcoat, standing behind a
large, exotic-looking dog, with the caption "Which has
the pedigree?" Of course, it isn't the dog, or the man; it's

the coat. Buying this coat, the ad implies, gives you a pedigree you can wear. This anxiety about the status of one's clothing, or how one's clothing expresses one's status, is also employed by advertisements for alcoholic drinks. One ad depicts a man from the neck down, dressed in a tuxedo, carrying a fur coat with a large label clearly exposed. The caption says, "When a label counts, it's Imported O.F.C.," and we can easily see that the label in the fur coat is the same as the label on the bottle of whiskey to the right of the text.

Clothing and status.

When does a label count? When one is concerned about the display of status and superiority, a concern that this and many other ads serve to amplify and exploit. A tuxedo and a fur coat represent the pinnacle of fashion, and we can imagine that the physically fit man, draping the fur coat over his arm, is waiting for his companion to come claim the coat. The man's head is not pictured because with the right label, his appearance doesn't really matter—and the reader can imagine his own head on that body. Tellingly, the ad says almost nothing about how the whiskey tastes ("Rich. Light.") but stresses rather that it is "In immaculate good taste." This designer whiskey confers status, prestige, and even companionship; who cares what it tastes like?

Here the focus on labels is applied to clothing and whiskey.

This anxiety about one's status and the implication that drinking alcoholic beverages will elevate it, which pervade the advertisements and even the cartoons in *The New Yorker,* arguably shape the character of Charlie's father, and Cheever as well. Charlie's father has his secretary make the arrangements for meeting his son in order to establish that he has a secretary. He wants his son to realize that he has status—because he has absorbed the cultural lesson that his self-worth depends on it. He mentions "my club" for the same reason, I would argue: to convey that he has a club, even though it is conveniently too distant to be used. Likewise, his display of foreign languages and his manic rudeness toward the various waiters are pitiful efforts to impress his son with his sophistication and power. At the end, as he struggles to "get a rise" out of the newsstand clerk, he is trying desperately to show his son how clever and superior he is. That is why he says "just wait a second, sonny": he is putting on this

The claim: Charlie's father is motivated by anxiety, created in part by these cultural values.

performance for his son, not for his own amusement. His interest in his son and his excitement are subtly suggested by his arrival "at twelve o'clock sharp." He's eager to see his son; he simply does not know how to impress his son, and his response is an effort to establish his status.

Even his alcoholism is related.

Even Charlie's father's desperate pursuit of alcohol reflects his anxiety about his status. Not only can we speculate that his nervousness drives him to medicate himself with liquid depressants; we can also see how his pursuit of drinks reflects his awareness of the association, created in advertisements and other cultural messages, between alcoholic consumption and affection. Charlie's father is seeking to create a bond with Charlie in a way that advertisements even today continue to promote. Charlie's father wants to create an "it-doesn't-get-any-better-than-this" moment; when the second waiter refuses to serve Charlie, his father immediately leaves because he wants more than a drink for himself; he hopes the drinks will lead to affection and bonding.

Conclusion: these values are destructive.

But he is really self-destructive, as Cheever makes clear. Charlie's father does not establish his status, and his quest for drinks does not create a bond. Instead, the day's events extinguish the contact between father and son, just as the father's drinking represents a slow self-extinction. Cheever has exposed the lie in the advertisements surrounding his story.

PRACTICING HISTORICAL, POSTCOLONIAL, AND CULTURAL STUDIES

Here are some possibilities to get you started.

1. If you were going to begin today to write a screenplay, a short story, a novel, a poem, or a play, what would it be about? Sketch out a rough draft or outline, or write the work if possible. Then consider how biographical, historical, or new historical criticism might relate to your work.

2. Choose another magazine from 1962 (*Good Housekeeping, Life, Reader's Digest, The Atlantic,* for instance) and compare its system of values to *The New Yorker*'s, as I've described it. How does this

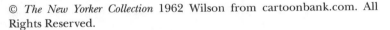

"You're going to get a great summation! He's smashed!"

expanded vision of 1962 affect your view of "Reunion"? What if "Reunion" had appeared in *Good Housekeeping,* for instance?

3. On this page and the next are two cartoons from the same *New Yorker* issue containing "Reunion." Discuss the system of values they imply. How might they be related to "Reunion"?

Useful Sources and Terms for Historical, Cultural, and Postcolonial Criticism

Author: Perhaps the most important thing to gain from this chapter is an awareness of the radically different ways an author is viewed by different critical approaches. Biographical criticism assumes that it matters who wrote something, and under what conditions it was written. Studying the life of a

"He's got this gimmick, see. He's completely honest."

writer is intrinsically interesting and useful—probably anyone's life holds instructive insights; but the purpose of literary biography, ultimately, is to shed some light on an author's work. The risks of biographical criticism are thus fairly transparent, but it is nonetheless important to keep them in mind: First, there's the problem of recovering the author's life and times. For some writers, biographical information is sparse or suspect: for J. D. Salinger (fiercely reclusive) or Homer (perhaps not even a single person), we'd like to know a whole lot more. For other writers, there is a wealth of information, sometimes contradictory and confusing: to understand Samuel Johnson for instance, you'd need to study Boswell's magnificent and massive *Life of Johnson* (five volumes in the standard edition), as well as at least a dozen other biographies and memoirs, not to mention the life and works of those around Johnson (not to mention Boswell's drafts and notebooks, which have some surprising differences with what he published), and so on.

Second, once we think we have biographical information, there's the problem of how to use it to illuminate creative work. We know Hemingway was wounded in World War I, and "A Very Short Story" features a soldier who was wounded, so can we conclude that the soldier is Hemingway? No, we can't. What if the soldier in the story is recovering in the same town in which Hemingway recovered, and is involved with a nurse who sounds a bit like a nurse Hemingway was involved with? We would still diminish the literary work, rather than enhance it, if we assume that Hemingway's story is simply covert autobiography. By insisting on a distinction between the author and his creations, we're in a better position to appreciate the literary work and the artistic choices the author made in crafting it. At the same time, even as we acknowledge the difficulties and risk of recovering an author's life, we can certainly learn much that adds interest and insight to the literary work. We shouldn't naïvely draw a one-to-one parallel between Hemingway and the wounded soldier, but we also shouldn't pretend that literary biography doesn't enrich our understanding of and interest in a work, and vice-versa.

A larger historical perspective sees the work of an author within the context of his time and place. Hemingway and his work can be illuminated by a better understanding of World War I, of its battles, its hospitals and medical practices, and of the values and ideas at work in Hemingway's culture. From a new historical perspective, the author is indeed so much a function of the time and place he or she inhabits, that the author as individual tends to dissolve. From this viewpoint, the language and the patterns of thinking available to an author, at a particular time and place, determine what he or she will say—so thoroughly that it is possible to speak (as Roland Barthes has) of "the death of the author." It's more reasonable, within new historical assumptions at least, to think about an "author" as a part of a system of discourse (language, logic, values, assumptions, etc.), rather than as an individual entity or freestanding agent.

Autobiography: A writer's story of his or her own life—an autobiography—offers (potentially) an especially interesting version of what happened. But it's important to remember that the use of autobiographical material in literary study is subject to the same scrutiny as the use of biographical material. Sometimes we forget what happened, or we only thought we understood what happened, or we decide to place what happened in a certain light, or we may just flat-out lie. Interestingly, autobiographies are rather rare prior to the seventeenth century, when there was a rapid expansion of interest in self-analysis and introspection.

Bourgeoisie: The upper class, the powerful, the privileged. Karl Marx (with Fredrich Engels) uses this term in *The Communist Manifesto.*

Confessional: In some literary works, the writer seems to express his or her strong emotional feelings directly, in his or her own voice and person. We call such works "confessional" because they appear to be about the writer's life, and they often explore uncomfortable, ordinarily private issues (as in a "confession"). The speaker in a poem and the creator of that poem may seem to be united. For some critics, such apparent self-exposure is daring and exhilarating; for others, the work and the life disturbingly collapse into one another, blurring the critic's function. Is the critic judging the writer's life or work? Are we engaging in artistic or aesthetic assessment or psychological analysis? On the other hand, one might argue that confessional works simply expose the personal character that is inevitable in all expressions, insisting that we unite the person and the work, violating the usual critical assumption that the speaker and the author are distinct.

Cultural Materialism: This term is often used for the British counterpart to new historicism, which is generally more political and activist.

Culture: Biographical and historical approaches to literary works assume that it is possible to make some meaningful generalizations, not only about an individual but about the society around him or her. "Culture" refers to the whole of a particular society—the beliefs, habits, facts, laws, values, and more that we may use to distinguish one group of people from another. It certainly makes sense to distinguish one culture from another: early seventeenth-century English culture is different from early twenty-first century English culture; Islamic culture is different from Jewish culture. To understand better a literary work written in an Islamic culture, one should seek a better understanding of that culture. And yet, every individual within a culture does not, of course, embrace every aspect of that culture. Any attempt to describe anything so complicated as a "culture" is bound to be partial—a construct of imagination, to some degree.

Despite such difficulties, the study of literature and culture together is powerfully appealing, as we strive to see how literature and culture shape and influence each other.

Discourse: Literary critics who employ biographical and historical materials have found "discourse" to be a particularly useful term because it allows them to make useful connections between the writer and the work. If one individual is speaking to another one who can be reasonably expected to understand the speaker, then they share, to some degree, a discourse. They are participants in a conversation, which means that they share (for starters) a language. "Discourse" refers to more than just language, including the assumptions and protocols shared by a community. So it's possible for critics to talk about "the discourse of nineteenth-century biology," or "the discourse of the eighteenth-century penal system," or "the discourse of the late twentieth-century capitalism." Particular writers and their works can then be made sense of within these discourses.

Episteme: Michel Foucault's term for the idea that controls a particular historical period. Rather than focus on history as a series of causes and effects, Foucault tries to see particular moments as complex systems of meaning.

Implied Author: This term distinguishes usefully between the real-life person who writes (who may be sitting in his pajamas, worried about his mortgage, with children yelling in the background, with a slight hangover and a sore throat) and the written construction of that person (which might project calm, confidence, energy). This term can be compared to "the implied reader"—an idea distinguishing the reader that the author seems to have imagined from the real-life person who is experiencing the text. The implied reader for some eighteenth-century works, for instance, might well be someone who has some familiarity with the history of armed conflict between France and England, and who has a working knowledge of Latin. A real reader, sitting in his or her twenty-first century living room, might be very different from this implied reader. By the same token, the real author might be very different from the implied author, as he or she is reflected in the text.

Influence: Historical critics are often interested in seeing how some prior work (or body of works) has affected another work (or body of works). Themes, strategies, forms, words, plot devices—anything might be picked up from a prior work and reused by an author. More recently, the idea of influence has gotten renewed attention because of the work of Walter Jackson Bate and Harold Bloom, who drew attention to the way some writers confront "the burden of the past" (Bate) or "the anxiety of influence" (Bloom). Rather than following after a prior writer, accepting an influence, a writer (Bate and Bloom argued) may struggle to hide or overcome an influence, attempting to assert his or her originality.

Intention: Biographical criticism brings the problematic relationship between intention and meaning to the forefront. If the meaning of a text depends on what the author meant to say (a reasonable enough assumption, it would seem), then biographical criticism may hold powerful keys to meaning. As we become removed in time from an author, we face greater difficulties in discerning what he or she might have meant, and biographical information may offer help. Intention is, however, a controversial basis for meaning: how can we know for sure what another person meant? After Freud, how can another person know what he or she meant—there may be unconscious motivations at work. It seems problematic to assume that we can say with any confidence what an author intended. Thus intention is an especially fruitful ground for literary argument and engagement.

Literary History: Literary history not only describes the nature of individual texts but inevitably makes some generalizations about groups of texts. If we have simply a succession of random, unrelated events, then we can't realistically be said to have "history," which connects and relates discrete events. Likewise, literary history aims to connect and relate certain works. In this endeavor, the construction of distinct literary periods is helpful.

Paradigm: This term and any number of related ones ("worldview," "episteme," "ideology") draw our attention to a complex set of assumptions at work within a particular culture at a particular time. A solar eclipse means something very different from within the paradigm of the ancient Egyptians, on the one hand, and the paradigm of a modern astronomer, on the other hand. We may read individual literary works, if we employ historical approaches, in order to make sense of the different paradigms that people have inhabited. At any one moment, in any one place, however, it is quite likely that different people will hold conflicting and overlapping paradigms in their heads—the same person may even have access to conflicting paradigms. A paradigm, in other words, might be thought of as a set of instructions for making meaning. As more people accept this way of making sense, the paradigm grows in importance.

Period: For convenience, we divide history of all sorts, including literary history, into segments or periods. Although these divisions are based on evidence, they are ultimately arbitrary. There are useful generalizations about medieval literature, and about how renaissance literature differs from medieval literature; but like all generalizations, they're subject to exceptions and challenges. The study of eighteenth-century literature has traditionally been distinct from the study of nineteenth-century literature, but it would be unreasonable to think that writers uniformly adjusted their ideas and styles and goals as the calendar shifted. The idea of a period, in other words, is a useful convenience (most useful, perhaps, as you begin to see the limitation of any particular set of generalizations).

Proletariat: The working classes, in Marx and Engels's terminology.

Subaltern: The one below, the other, the dispossessed, the oppressed: these are some of the meanings of this word, invented by the Marxist critic Antonio Gramsci.

Tradition: Just as we divide literary history into distinct periods, we also connect literary works across time with the idea of a "tradition." The most visible sort of tradition is probably that of genre: Milton's *Paradise Lost* can hardly be understood without some sense of the epic tradition, for example. Shakespeare's sonnets are part of a tradition of sonnets. The idea of tradition highlights the limits of formal analysis in New Criticism (and the power of biographical and historical approaches): the text itself is rarely meant to stand by itself. Writers inevitably position their works in one or more traditions of literary effort.

Works Cited: Historical, Postcolonial, and Cultural Studies

Bannet, Eve Tavor. *Structuralism and the Logic of Dissent: Barthes, Derrida, Foucault, Lacan.* Urbana: U of Illinois P, 1989.

Cheever, John. *The Brigadier and the Golf Widow.* New York: Harper, 1964.

———. *The Journals of John Cheever.* Ed. Robert Gottlieb. New York: Knopf, 1991.

————. *The Letters of John Cheever.* Ed. Benjamin Cheever. New York: Simon and Schuster, 1988.

Cheever, Susan. *Home Before Dark.* Boston: Houghton, 1984.

Donaldson, Scott. *John Cheever.* New York: Random, 1988.

Fish, Stanley. "Interpreting the *Variorum.*" *Critical Inquiry* 2 (1980): 465–86.

Foucault, Michel. *Discipline and Punish: The Birth of the Prison.* Trans. Alan Sheridan. New York: Pantheon, 1977.

————. *The History of Sexuality.* Vol. 1. Trans. R. Hurley. New York: Pantheon, 1978.

Greenblatt, Stephen. "The Politics of Culture." In *Falling Into Theory: Conflicting Views on Reading Literature.* Ed. David Richter. Boston: St. Martin's, 1994. 288–90.

Griffith, Kelley, Jr. *Writing Essays About Literature.* San Diego: Harcourt, 1986.

Hebdige, Dick. *Subculture: The Meaning of Style.* London: Routledge, 1993.

Howard, Jean. "The New Historicism in Renaissance Studies." *ELR* 16 (Winter 1986): 13–43.

Montrose, Louis. "Of Gentlemen and Shepherds: The Politics of Elizabethan Pastoral Form." *ELH* 50 (1983): 415–59.

Tillyard, E.M.W. *The Elizabethan World Picture.* New York: MacMillan, 1944.

Waldeland, Lynne. *John Cheever.* Boston: Twayne, 1979.

White, Hayden. *Tropics of Discourse: Essays in Cultural Criticism.* Baltimore: Johns Hopkins UP, 1978.

Woodhouse, A.S.P. "The Historical Criticism of Milton." *PMLA* 66 (1951): 1033–44.

Biographical Research

- For convenient access to essential facts about the life of a major figure—*Encyclopedia Britannica* or another major encyclopedia. As a rule, however, you don't want to cite general encyclopedias in your essay; just use them to get started.

- For more details—the *Dictionary of National Biography* (British), the *Dictionary of American Biography,* or the *Dictionary of Literary Biography.*

- For information on contemporary authors—*Contemporary Authors.*

- Also useful—*Biography Index, Oxford Companion to English Literature, Oxford Companion to American Literature,* and the other *Oxford Companions.* An especially appealing resource is *The Atlantic Brief Lives,* which offers brief and often brilliant biographies of writers and other artists by authoritative scholars.

- For book-length biographies—check the catalogue in your library. Check the publication date of the biography; new facts and resources are coming to light all the time, although a newer biography is not necessarily a better one. Also, book reviews can help you evaluate a particular biography: *Book Review Index* covers the most sources; *Book Review Digest* includes excerpts from the reviews.

Historical Research

- For detailed surveys of literary history—the *Oxford History of English Literature* (13 volumes); F. E. Halliday, *A Concise History of England, from Stonehenge to the Atomic Age;* or Robert Adams, *The Land and Literature of England.* A delightful miniview of American literature appears in the first chapter of *An Incomplete Education.* The standard heavy-duty history of American literature is *The Literary History of the United States,* edited by Robert E. Spiller (2 volumes).

Recommended Further Reading:
Historical, Postcolonial, and Cultural Studies

Auerbach, Erich. *Mimesis: The Representation of Reality in Western Literature.* Princeton, NJ: Princeton UP, 1953. A classic study of the rhetorical devices texts use in order to construct "reality."

Cadzow, Hunter. "New Historicism." *The Johns Hopkins Guide to Literary Theory and Criticism.* Ed. Michael Groden and Martin Kreiswirth. Baltimore: Johns Hopkins UP, 1994. 534–40. A clear, brief, and reliable overview.

Gallagher, Catherine "Historical Scholarship." In *Introduction to Scholarship in Modern Languages and Literatures.* Ed. David Nicholls. 3rd ed. New York: MLA, 2007. 171–193. An excellent survey in a standard reference work.

Harrison, Nicholas. *Postcolonial Criticism: History, Theory and the Work of Fiction.* Oxon: Polity, 2003. Major works (Conrad's *Heart of Darkness,* Camus's *The Outsider,* for example) are used to provide an illustrated introduction to postcolonial studies, while at the same time undermining some established ideas. Challenging, but accessible to students with some critical grounding.

New Historical Research

Some suggestions for places to look for materials:

- Popular or noncanonical literature: children's stories, adolescent fiction, romances, adventure stories, and so forth.
- Primary materials for other disciplines: music theory, psychology, criminology, architecture, and so forth.
- Newspapers and magazines. These can offer you descriptions of events and leads to other texts.
- Artifacts from the period. Think like an archeologist trying to make sense of the physical remains of a particular time. For instance, a delicate and ornate snuffbox from the eighteenth century may illuminate the sort of cultural environment in which, say, Mozart's delicate and ornate music could be written.

Institute of Historical Research. University of London. 15 Jan. 00.
http://ihr.sas.ac.uk. A good example of the wide resources available, this site offers links to research materials, to information about historians, to secondary sources, and much more.

Ryan, Kiernan, ed. *New Historicism and Cultural Materialism: A Reader.* London: Arnold, 1996. A nice selection of important essays.

Thomas, Brook. "The Historical Necessity for—and Difficulties with—New Historical Analysis in Introductory Literature Courses." *College English* 49 (1987): 509–22. A useful introduction to the ideas of New Historicism and a thoughtful consideration of their implications for teaching.

Veeser, H. Aram, ed. *The New Historicism.* New York: Routledge, 1989. A collection of influential essays, theorizing, applying, exploring new historicism.

Young, Robert J.C. *Postcolonialism: A Very Short Introduction.* Oxford: Oxford University Press, 2003. A spirited introduction that uses a series of specific situations (a montage) to explain postcolonialism. Young vividly describes for instance what it would be like to be a refugee, to be African and Caribbean activists who migrated to Harlem in 1924, revealing from the bottom up what it would be like to have a postcolonialist stance.

Kristeva Korner
Chodorow Row
Silverman Springs
Mind the Gap
Jung's Recycling Plant
Home of the Oedipal Complexes
Dreamland
Personal Costume
Hall of Mirrors
Id Caverns
Unconscious Trucking
Entering Id caverns
Ego Center
Freudian Mental Works
slips, stories, jokes, wading boots
made here
Superego Tower
Watch out for
No!
Absolutely No allowed
Stop!
Do not
Former site of the Father
Psychological Criticism
To Skinner Babysitting and Drill School

CHAPTER 7

Minding the Work

Psychological Criticism

*When a member of my family
complains that he or she has
bitten his tongue, bruised her
finger, and so on, instead of the
expected sympathy I put the
question, "Why did you do that?"*

—Sigmund Freud

THE PURPOSE OF PSYCHOLOGICAL CRITICISM

Psychology began in a sense when the first person, rather than just reacting to another person's behavior, wondered instead, Why did you do that? Most people would agree that modern psychology begins with Freud, not simply because he wonders so intensely, but because he offers a compelling answer: we do things, Freud asserted, really weird and silly things sometimes, for reasons that are to some degree hidden, inaccessible, beyond our direct control or awareness. These hidden motivations come from what Freud called *das Unbewusste*, which means literally "the unknown" but is usually translated into English as "the unconscious," that part or activity of one's mind that is unknown even to its possessor. Although both the term "unconscious" and the general concept predated Freud, his theories revolutionized the study of the mind.

There is in fact only one major form of psychotherapy that is not based in some important respect on Freudian concepts: behavior therapy. For a psychological theory, behaviorism seems strangely unconcerned with the mind. Basing their approaches on B. F. Skinner's work, who in turn drew largely on Ivan Pavlov, behaviorists view psychological problems as bad habits: the patient has learned unproductive or destructive behaviors and must unlearn them and take up others. Every other therapy, despite some vast differences, depends in crucial ways on Freud. To understand modern psychology and to practice psychological criticism, you might well start with Freud and particularly with his conception of the unconscious mind.

Obviously, you needn't stop there. Maslow's hierarchy of needs, or Erikson's theory of adult development, or any other psychological theories (including your own) may prove very illuminating. I focus here on Freud because his work is historically the starting point, because his ideas are so familiar to educated people, because his works continue to generate challenge and controversy, and because Freud's work nicely illustrates the application of psychology to literature. His theories in fact were based in significant ways on lit-

"Leon, do you think it's all psychological?"

erary works. There's just no way to survey here the whole field of psychology. So I encourage you to study psychology, expanding your understanding of Freud, and exploring also the theories of others.

The therapeutic procedure Freud developed was designed to help those patients whose conscious lives were being troubled or even overtaken by unconscious fears or desires. It involved having the patient lie on a couch and talk freely about whatever came to mind, roaming back through childhood, dreams, fantasies, whatever, thereby allowing the patient and the analyst to gather enough data to speculate about what was going on in the hidden country of the unconscious. By slowly exposing the effects of the unconscious, peeling back layer after layer of disguised and suppressed fears and desires, Freud's "talking cure" was designed to enlarge the mental "territory" of the conscious mind. When the patient, with the analyst's help, could expose these unconscious materials, Freud believed that their power over the patient would be lessened and even dissipated.

When Freud failed to comfort his injured family members, he was not simply creating work for future therapists (unconsciously?), but he was rather assuming that an apparently irrational action like biting one's own tongue might actually have some important underlying explanation. Freud did not expect his family to express their unconscious motivations ("I bit my tongue because I want to tell you to drop dead, but I know I shouldn't," for instance); rather, he hoped to unearth some evidence of how an unconscious desire was being first covered up or denied and then expressed in a disguised way. He was, in his own way, trying to be a good father.

Freud's theory of the unconscious also revolutionized the study of the mind and launched modern psychology by assuming that the unconscious is inherently sexual. Even children are sexual beings, Freud pointed out, thus scandalizing many of his Victorian contemporaries. Not a few people continue to be scandalized. How this unsettling insight affected Freud's work can be seen in the story of "Little Hans," one of his most famous and remarkable cases. When Hans was brought to Freud at age five, he refused to go outside because he was hysterically terrified that a horse would bite him. Through Hans's father, Freud was able to learn that at age three-and-a-half Hans's mother had tried to discourage him from touching his own genitals by saying that if he didn't stop, the doctor would come to "cut off your widdler and then what will you widdle with?" Freud deduced that Little Hans had noticed that horses had large genitalia and that his mother did not appear to have any, apparently proving that she knew what she was talking about. In the uncanny logic of Little Hans's unconscious mind, castration and horses became all jumbled up with his love for his mother, and the competition with his father for that love. Freud helped the father reassure Little Hans that his own penis was in no danger, curing his irrational fear.

It is, however, incorrect to think of Freud simply as that guy who thought of everything in terms of sex. For one thing, Freud's idea of sexuality includes much more than simply the act of sex. Rather, Freud focused on the entire drive toward physical plea-sure, which he saw as being constantly in conflict with opposing forces. This conflict is necessary for rather obvious reasons: with-out it, we would be unable to function in a civilized society. But our desires, when they cannot be expressed and released, must go somewhere. Hence, the need for an unconscious, a kind of storage vault for psychic energy. In this mental hydraulic system, as Freud sees it, some of the repressed energy does leak out in various dis-guised ways—in dreams, slips of the tongue, jokes, creative writing.

This mechanism for submerging unacceptable desires is well known today as "repression," and it is for Freud an essential activ-ity. Mental illness, then, in which the unconscious is unable to con-tain satisfactorily the repressed material, becomes different only in degree, not kind, from "normal" mental health.

There's already plenty in the little bit I've discussed to make anyone uneasy: we don't know what's going on in our minds even though that activity is influencing our thinking and behavior. The mechanism whereby our fears and desires are being repressed is the same mechanism that leads to mental illness— meaning that "normal" is a relative term, since we're all unavoid-ably a little out of touch; the drive toward pleasure is relentlessly struggling to overpower our grip on the realities of our culture. I haven't even gotten to the Oedipus complex, which, despite its "utter centrality to Freud's work," as Terry Eagleton says (156), is nonetheless outrageous—so disturbingly bizarre that, from a Freudian perspective, there must be something to it.

Freud concisely describes this fundamental sexual phenomenon of early childhood in "The Ego and the Id" (1923). In this accessible paper Freud explains how the young boy invests his desire and affec-tion in his mother, developing an "object-cathexis" for her. The baby's desire for physical contact with his mother obviously begins with the mother's breasts, but the boy will ultimately want to possess his mother entirely. As his "sexual wishes in regard to his mother become more intense," Freud says, his father is increasingly "perceived as an obstacle to them." At this point, desiring his mother, blocked by his father, the young boy has acquired what Freud calls "the simple positive Oedipus complex" (640). Freud is alluding to the ancient myth in which Oedipus, in the course of saving a city, happens unknowingly to kill his father and marry his mother.

Obviously, the desire to do away with the father and join with the mother cannot be acted out without disastrous consequences, and it must therefore be repressed, put out of sight. This "primal repression," as Freud calls it, is in fact what creates the unconscious, making a place for repressed desires. But if nothing more than this repression happens, then the Oedipus complex will persist in the unconscious, exerting its relentless pressure and eventually creating psychological trouble—a "pathogenic effect." This ill effect is avoided, Freud says, when the Oedipus complex is destroyed, a process that is brought about by the boy's perception that his father is superior.

And here is where most readers of Freud tend to drop their jaws or even toss the book across the room, because the threat of the father is focused, Freud believes, in the threat of castration. Fearing that the father may negate his affection for the mother by castrating him, the boy (understandably enough) begins a process of transferring his desires elsewhere. (What Little Hans was experiencing was thus a more intense variation of a "normal" process.) The part of the mind that "retains the character of the father," who comes to stand for the restraints of "authority, religious teaching, schooling, and reading," Freud calls the "superego." In struggling to control the ego, the superego is opposed by the id, the repository of basic instincts and desires. The relationship between the id and ego, as Freud puts it in his *New Introductory Lectures on Psychoanalysis,* is like that "between a rider and his horse" (108). The rider is supposed to direct the horse's energy, but sometimes the rider has "to guide his horse in the direction in which it itself wants to go."

Think of the id as Jack Nicholson or Roseanne—irreverent, indulgent, spontaneous, raucous. Think of the ego as Robert Duvall or Meryl Streep—smooth, adaptable, responsible, an actor. And the superego is like Jimmy Carter or Miss Manners—principled, moral, wholesome, occupied with doing the right thing.[1]

Thus, Freud offers two maps of the mind. First, conscious versus unconscious, then later, this division is refined into the id, ego,

---

[1] In *An Incomplete Education,* Judy Jones and William Wilson compare the id, ego, and superego to Nicholson, Duvall, and Reeve (402).

superego model. The id is largely the territory of the unconscious, and the ego and superego are mostly conscious.

Freud has not been alone in revising his ideas. His earliest followers rather quickly offered major additions, divergences, and rejections of various Freudian features. Melanie Klein, for instance, emphasized the turbulence of the pre-Oedipal period when the child wants to possess and destroy the mother. Harry Stack Sullivan turned from Freud's emphasis on internal conflicts to concentrate on the individual's relationships with important people in his life. The "good" mother, Sullivan says, conveys security and contentment to the child, whereas the "bad" mother communicates her anxiety and distress to the child, who must adjust his or her own behavior to modify the mother's stress. Carl Jung downplayed Freud's emphasis on sex and supplemented the individual unconscious with the idea of a "collective unconscious" that contains themes and images inherited by all humans. Jungian approaches to psychological criticism look for such recurrent themes and images across time and across cultures, seeing them as clues to the structuring of the collective unconscious mind.

Today little of Freud's work is accepted without substantial modification or challenge. Fortunately, in order to do psychological criticism you don't need to wait until the truth of all Freud's particular theories has been settled; and you don't need to understand all the various refinements and refutations and wholesale rethinkings of Freud that continue to appear. The more you know about psychology, to be sure, the more options you're likely to have as a critic. But all you really need to understand in order to do psychological criticism is Freud's fundamental concept of the unconscious—a concept that has remained the unchallenged starting point for most subsequent psychological theories. The purpose of psychology depends on bringing to consciousness the hidden fears and desires that disturb and control our lives. And the purpose of psychological criticism likewise is to direct Freud's question—"Why did you do that?"—to authors, or characters, or readers. Looking at the author, psychological criticism tries to go beyond the biographical facts to expose the underlying motivations—motivations and meanings that the author herself or himself may not have glimpsed. Looking at a character, psychological criticism treats the author's creation as a person whose behavior can be explained psychologically. Looking at the reader, psychological criticism considers how the reader's motivations shape the meaning of the work.

The next section discusses how to carry out such tasks.

HOW TO DO PSYCHOLOGICAL CRITICISM

Psychology and literary criticism have been intertwined from their very beginnings. Plato noted that poets indulge in a kind of madness when they write, stirring up the audience's passions and emotions. A well-ordered republic, Plato thought, would be better off without poets. Aristotle countered Plato's argument with the position that literature has a healthy psychological effect; in the case of tragedy, it purges excessive fear and pity. Longinus felt that literature could cultivate the audience's sense of the sublime, elevating and refining their sensibilities.

Freud's practice of using literary works to illustrate his theories, or test them, or even suggest them, has been continued by psychological thinkers of every variety. Alfred Adler, for instance, one of the earliest theorists to break away from Freud, believed his own psychological insights were drawn largely from literary works; he even asserted that "the artist is the leader of mankind on the road to absolute truth" (329). In "Creative Writers and Day-Dreaming" (1908) Freud lays the foundation for applying psychology to literature. The author's creative production is, for Freud, like the material of a dream: it is a "day-dream," shaped and therefore disguised substantially by the unconscious mind. A work of literature then is like the material the analyst receives from his or her patients. Acts of literary criticism and psychological analysis begin to look very much alike, if they are not in fact the same. In both cases, the interpreter examines a text and reconstructs an underlying meaning and significance. (A text cannot, to be sure, respond to interrogation—at least not in the way that a patient can.)

Since these underlying meanings of the patient's or the author's stories belong by definition to the realm of the hidden and directly unknowable, a certain amount of creativity and imagination on the part of the interpreter are not only authorized but also called for. In addition to creativity, some basic concepts and terms will be useful. These originate with Freud, but they've become part of the psychological vocabulary, and to varying degrees they've even filtered into the common language.

I've already mentioned *repression,* the mind's essential strategy for hiding desires and fears. But out of sight does not mean out of mind in this case. Consider for a moment the following poem, which despite its simplicity has received much critical attention:

A Slumber Did My Spirit Seal
William Wordsworth

A slumber did my spirit seal;
I had no human fears:
She seemed a thing that could not feel
The touch of earthly years.

No motion has she now, no force;   5
She neither hears nor sees;
Rolled round in earth's diurnal course,
With rocks, and stones, and trees.

(1800)

This poem appears in a series of poems about "Lucy," a girl who died young. No historical "Lucy" has been found by researchers, and she appears to have been a fiction. If we ask Freud's question of Wordsworth, Why did you do that?, we will have to make up our own answer: even if he were alive, Wordsworth's own answer could not be trusted because the real reason for the poem might well be hidden in his unconscious. So let us ask ourselves, What wish or fear or desire might Wordsworth be expressing here in a disguised form?

When Wordsworth wrote this poem, he was living with his sister in deep poverty in Germany, enduring an extremely cold winter. His sister, Dorothy, was his lifelong companion, even living with him throughout his marriage. Several of Wordsworth's poems are dedicated to her; several of his poems in fact borrow from her quite brilliant journals. Wordsworth and his sister were very close.

When Wordsworth sent this poem to Samuel Coleridge, Coleridge wrote to another friend that "in some gloomier moment" Wordsworth had "fancied the moment in which his sister might die" (1.479). If the poem is in some way about the death of Wordsworth's sister, then it certainly does represent a profound fear for Wordsworth. And yet, the poem is oddly unemotional. The speaker "had" no fears; "she" feels nothing; the speaker's "spirit" is sleeping and sealed off.

To a psychologist (or a psychological critic), the experience of an event without any of the expected response is called *isolation*. In Cheever's "Reunion," I would argue, Charlie employs isolation to deal with the last time he saw his father. He doesn't overtly deny his emotions, or try to explain them away, or express them; he appears simply to ignore them, disconnecting from them, selectively telling us what happened. One could also argue, I think, that Hemingway's soldier exhibits isolation in "A Very Short Story."

But why would Wordsworth refuse to acknowledge the profound grief one would expect to arise at the idea of his sister's death? A psychological view, looking at the intimacy of Wordsworth's relationship with his sister, would have to wonder if perhaps he isn't protecting himself against desires he cannot acknowledge. If Wordsworth did have, for example, an incestuous desire for his sister, whom he certainly loved deeply, acknowledging that desire would certainly cause him great psychological pain. In fantasy, in his poetry, he could deal with that desire indirectly by imagining his sister, or her surrogate Lucy, as being dead. Channeling an unacceptable urge into some artistic creation or fantasy is called *sublimation.* We see it in Lucille Clifton's "forgiving my father" (see Chapter 3), which transforms her hatred for her father into a work that moves her toward forgiveness. Sublimation is no doubt at work in Mary Astell's *A Serious Proposal* (see Chapter 8), in which her inevitable rage against an oppressive patriarchy becomes the driving force behind her proposal for women to secede.

If Wordsworth is substituting Lucy for Dorothy, he is also engaging in *displacement,* which inserts a safe object of emotion for a dangerous one. We might argue, for example, that Milton's focus on his blindness, in "When I Consider How My Light Is Spent," is a substitute for a more frightening loss of light, his death.

But perhaps we're on entirely the wrong track here, or perhaps there are simply other tracks available. My initial reading of Wordsworth's poem was that "she" is his own spirit. Otherwise, what sense does the initial line make, "A slumber did my spirit seal"? He imagines his own death and depicts his soul as being feminine. "I had no human fears" becomes an instance then of *denial,* in which one simply falsifies reality, flatly and directly refusing to accept it. While repression buries the emotion and other strategies hide or disguise it, denial looks right at it and says it isn't there. Denial can be a more ominous symptom as it signals a break with reality. When Hemingway's soldier in "A Very Short Story" (see Chapter 4) says he doesn't want to see any of his friends, it seems likely he's engaging in denial.

One could also argue, pursuing a different angle, that the critic who claims Wordsworth's poem deals with his incestuous desires is practicing *projection:* "Oh yeah, I see Wordsworth's repressed incestuous desires," the critic says, when it is actually his or her own incestuous desires, projected onto Wordsworth, that are being seen and avoided.

Or one could argue the whole enterprise of criticism is motivated by *intellectualization,* a strategy for avoiding uncomfortable emotions by rationalizing them, analyzing them, talking and talking and talking about them. Intellectualization is isolation for intellectuals.

If we imagine that Wordsworth was terrified of ghosts and spirits, that he feared they were wandering all over the place, and that he was especially convinced that he would become a restless ghoul himself, then we could see the poem as a *reaction formation,* in which one is convinced that the opposite of a terrible situation is actually the case. Although Wordsworth, in this scenario, is convinced that spirits roam the earth, he keeps telling himself insistently that "slumber" actually seals one's spirit, leaving it as dead as a rock. In "My Father's Martial Art," Stephen Shu-ning Liu says his father and his Master are sitting on O Mei mountain (see Chapter 3). To the extent that he believes this statement, he is arguably employing a reaction formation, for the poem makes rather clear that his father is dead. He cannot come down and hush the traffic. He—at least his body—isn't sitting anywhere.

As you're thinking about how to apply psychological theories to literature in specific ways, you might also consider the more general effects of a psychological perspective. I'd like to bring two consequences to your attention.

Students often ask English teachers, "Do you really think the author intended to mean all that?" Which often means, of course, "Aren't you being too clever, reading too much into this, making a big deal out of something that isn't there?" After Freud, such a question becomes irrelevant. The author himself or herself can't really know what was intended because of the inevitable involvement of the unconscious mind. We may think we intend one thing, but our unconscious intentions may be very different and much more complex. Our intention may even be contradictory because the unconscious mind isn't worried about logical consistency. By analyzing the work closely, we may gain some insight into what the author really intended—but we're always just guessing. At the least, we can be confident that the meaning of any statement is richer than it seems.

This point brings me to the second consequence of an awareness of psychological criticism, which is closely related to the first one. After Freud, what idea could possibly be too far out to consider?

Psychological theories ought to encourage you to be creative in speculating about the motivations of characters, authors, or readers. When students write uninteresting papers, it's often because they're too vague on the one hand or too cautious on the other. I would like to think that an acquaintance with psychological criticism will tend to loosen your imagination.

THE WRITING PROCESS: A SAMPLE ESSAY

Hamlet, as you might imagine, has been the subject of considerable psychological analysis, beginning most notably with Ernst Jones's *Hamlet and Oedipus,* which made much of Hamlet's bedroom scene with his mother. In some versions of the play, Sir Laurence Olivier's for instance, Hamlet's physical attraction to his mother is shockingly obvious, as Hamlet pushes his mother onto her bed, holding her down, ranting and raving about her affection for Claudius, his uncle, the murderer of his father, now his step-father. I'm going to look at a passage that seems to me much less promising. If there are psychological analyses of this passage, I'm not aware of them. In fact, I thought at first, after picking the passage at random, that a psychological reading wouldn't work. So, you're going to see the evolution of a psychological reading of this passage.

But first you'll see the passage. In this scene, from Act IV, scene vi, Hamlet has just observed the army of Fortinbras moving to attack a part of Poland. The land the two armies are fighting over is insignificant; Fortinbras's captain says he wouldn't pay "five ducats" to farm it. And yet thousands of men and thousands of ducats will be wasted to fight over it. Hearing this, Hamlet speaks the soliloquy below. Read it carefully and consider what you might say about it from a psychological perspective.

Hamlet 4.4.32–66

William Shakespeare

inform against: accuse	How all occasions do inform against me,
	And spur my dull revenge! What is a man,
market: product	If his chief good and market of his time
discourse: reasoning power, language	Be but to sleep and feed? a beast, no more. 35
	Sure He that made us with such large
	discourse,

Looking before and after, gave us not
That capability and godlike reason

fust: develop
mold
craven:
cowardly
event: the
result

Sith: since

gross: huge,
obvious

Makes mouths:
taunts, scorns

To fust in us unus'd. Now whether it be
Bestial oblivion, or some craven scruple   40
Of thinking too precisely on th' event—
A thought which quarter'd hath but
          one part wisdom
And ever three parts coward—I do not know
Why yet I live to say, "This thing's to do,"
Sith I have cause, and will, and strength,   45
          and means
To do't. Examples gross as earth exhort me:
Witness this army of such mass and charge,
Led by a delicate and tender prince,
Whose spirit with divine ambition puff'd
Makes mouths at the invisible event,   50
Exposing what is mortal and unsure
To all that fortune, death, and danger dare,
Even for an egg-shell. Rightly to be great
Is not to stir without great argument,
But greatly to find quarrel in a straw   55
When honor's at the stake. How stand I then,
That have a father kill'd, a mother stain'd,
Excitements of my reason and my blood,
And let all sleep, while to my shame I see
The imminent death of twenty thousand   60
          men,
That for a fantasy and trick of fame
Go to their graves like beds, fight for a plot
Whereon the numbers cannot try the cause,
Which is not tomb enough and continent
To hide the slain? O, from this time forth,   65
My thoughts be bloody, or be nothing worth!

(1600)

Preparing to Write

One strategy to generate ideas would be simply to run through various psychological concepts and see how each one relates to the play. To see how this heuristic would work, let's first review the concepts that have been mentioned in this chapter (which are by no means all the psychological ideas you might draw on):

- *Isolation:* Understanding something that should be upsetting, but failing to react to it. The person thus *isolates* an event or stimulus, separating it from his or her feelings. "Yes, my uncle murdered my father and married my mother, but so what? I've got a theology exam next Tuesday at the University of Wittenberg, and I just can't worry about it now."

- *Intellectualization:* Analyzing and rationalizing rather than feeling and reacting. The topic isn't forgotten or ignored; it's just turned into an intellectual issue. "I am conducting a study on the incidence of ghost appearances here in Denmark, and I am especially interested in how often the ghost is the father appearing to his son, as in my own case."

- *Repression:* Selectively forgetting about whatever is troubling. "Ghost? What ghost? Oh yeah, *that* ghost. Well, we'd better go get some lunch right now."

- *Projection:* Denying thoughts and feelings by attributing them to someone else. "You know, Horatio is just about paralyzed with uncertainties and doubts. And I think he may be sexually attracted to my mother, too."

- *Displacement:* Shifting an emotion from its real target to another one. Usually, a threatening, powerful target is exchanged for a safer one. "Don't talk to me about Claudius right now. I'm busy plotting to kill those sorry traitors Rosencrantz and Guildenstern."

- *Denial:* Falsifying reality. "I didn't see any ghost. My father is still alive."

- *Reversal:* Asserting the opposite of the truth, turning an emotion around. "I'm not attracted to my mother. I've noticed that she's attracted to me, however."

- *Reaction formation:* A pattern of behavior that repeatedly reverses the truth; an obsessive kind of denial. "First, I'll shine Claudius's boots. Then I'll sharpen and polish his sword. Then I'll dust his desk off and see what else I can do. He's my uncle, and I like him so much."

Now, let's see how these concepts apply to that particular passage from Act IV, scene vi, lines 32–66. The idea here is to think about each term and then brainstorm about the passage in relation to that concept. You may want to brainstorm some on your own before you check out my own meditations below:

Isolation: What is Hamlet not feeling that he should be feeling? This question seems easy to answer. Hamlet himself tells us that he should be feeling bloodthirsty rage, yet his revenge is "dull." So he tries to exhort himself to feel what he should, rather than existing in a "Bestial oblivion," feeling nothing.

Intellectualization: Hamlet offers two possible explanations for his delay in lines 39–41. "Bestial oblivion" (or isolation) is one; "thinking too precisely on th' event" (or intellectualization) is the other. Both these strategies are used to avoid feeling emotions—which is precisely what Hamlet sees himself doing.

Repression: What is Hamlet ignoring? What obvious feeling does he totally pass over? Certainly he recognizes that he should be vengeful but isn't; but Hamlet seems to look right past what would seem most important: he doesn't want to die. If Hamlet kills Claudius, he may lose his own life. He may have, as he says, "cause, and will, and strength, and means / To do't," but he has no guarantee that he can do it safely. This avoidance is, I think, a major repression, and it is bound to express itself somewhere. In fact, this whole passage can be seen as an effort to ignore what he is most pressed to say: that he fears throwing away his life.

Projection: Does Hamlet use projection to disguise his feeling that taking his revenge will mean throwing away his life? There is his reference to the "delicate and tender prince" who is willing to expose "what is mortal and unsure" for the sake of "an egg-shell." Of course Hamlet does not know how the other prince feels, or really whether he is "delicate and tender." The other prince may well believe that the upcoming battle is a small but glorious part of an epic campaign—not that he is fighting for an eggshell, but that the battle is strategically, symbolically, historically, personally of major proportions. It is in fact Hamlet who, deep inside, feels that he, a delicate and tender prince, a student and theater-goer, is being asked to act like a warrior and throw away his life for an eggshell. He says, "That guy is throwing his life away for an eggshell." His unconscious meaning: "I'm throwing my life away for an eggshell."

A problem here: Can we really say that Hamlet views his cause as an eggshell? He has "a father kill'd, a mother stain'd."

These would seem to be more than an eggshell. But his revenge will not alter his father's death. He'll be just as dead after Hamlet acts. Nor will Hamlet's revenge undo the stain on his mother. Although men will "find quarrel in a straw / When honor's at the stake," her honor has already been tarnished by Claudius, hasn't it? Early in the play Hamlet has referred to his world as "an unweeded garden / That grows to seed, things rank and gross in nature / Possess it merely" (1.2.135–37). So perhaps the world and his cause are no more than an eggshell for Hamlet.

Displacement: Instead of venting his anger at Claudius, who is dangerous, Hamlet is attacking himself.

Denial: Hamlet says he does not know why he hasn't acted, but the reason is right in front of him: he doesn't want to be like the twenty thousand men already marching to their meaningless deaths. He is denying that he knows.

Reversal: Hamlet says that the twenty thousand men are marching to their "imminent" deaths "to my shame." Isn't he turning that around, however? Isn't it really to their own shame? Hamlet acknowledges that their deaths will not mean anything significant; shouldn't they be ashamed of such senseless slaughter? The ground won't even be able to hold them, Hamlet says; but that has already been true of the bodies Hamlet has encountered: his father won't stay put; Polonius's body eludes the court; Ophelia's body floats away and surfaces again in her grave. One must wonder if the ground can ever contain the bodies put into it.

Reaction formation: Does Hamlet convince himself that the exact opposite of something bad, something that he doesn't want to confront, is going on, and that it is good? Hamlet knows that he must eventually carry out his revenge, giving in to a need for revenge that does not make conscious sense to him. His ego is being pressed by the superego, who is literally his father figure, calling for justice. His ego is also being pressed by his id, which hungers for violence, indulgence. He wants to give in to something bad: the violent energy of his id. But he tells himself he doesn't want to.

Let's try that again. Hamlet knows unconsciously that he must behave violently, like an animal, a savage, in order to carry out his revenge. He must become a beast. Yet, he tells himself the opposite. He is a beast, he says, if he doesn't carry out his revenge.

The conflict in Hamlet's mind over whether he should be a beast or not, whether he should exercise "godlike reason" or not, seems designed for relating to the id, ego, and superego. So those terms could also be used as prompts in the invention phase.

> **Id**—Hamlet says all occasions "spur" his revenge—as if it were a horse. Freud in fact compares the id to a horse. It is Hamlet's id that will have to motivate his revenge: logically, he can't do it. But Hamlet doesn't want to be "a beast," in "bestial oblivion." If he lets the id's horse run, however, that's exactly what he'll be.
>
> **Ego**—So his ego is caught in the middle, driven to commit suicide without any consciously satisfying reason.
>
> **Superego**—Justice, the moral code, the stand-in for the father: in this case, the ghost of the father isn't just in his head; he's walking about. Like the id, Hamlet's superego calls for revenge, which the ego recognizes as requiring its own extinction. No wonder Hamlet is caught in the middle, unable to act. He says at the end his thoughts will be bloody—but he doesn't say anything about his actions.

Is this enough material for an essay? How would you organize it?

Shaping

Is there a thesis floating around in the brainstorming above? It seems clear that I'm returning again and again to the question of why Hamlet is not taking his revenge. Why is he standing there talking rather than doing something? He thinks he should be killing people, or at least one particular person, yet he hasn't done it. And the conclusion of his speech, which seems to announce his action, on closer analysis just says his thoughts will be bloody. The next scene in the play isn't Hamlet bursting in on Claudius and cutting his throat.

So, my thesis might be that this passage helps us understand Hamlet's hesitation—his mental conflict. How? Why? First, I list what I think I know:

1. Hamlet's father and his superego (one stands in for the other) call for justice. Morality has been violated and it must be set right. "Honor's at the stake," as Hamlet says.
2. For some reason, this call to violence is insufficient. Hamlet avoids coming to terms with it for much of the play. How?

3. I said when I was developing ideas that Hamlet's unconscious wants to be bloody. But that really doesn't make sense, does it?

Let us imagine that Freud's comparison of the id to a horse is very appropriate. Let us further imagine that when Hamlet says the occasions should "spur" his revenge, he is speaking about the kinds of urges and passions that Freud assigns to the unconscious. So why is Hamlet's unconscious unwilling to kill Claudius? For the reader who assumes Hamlet's behavior is motivated—that "Hamlet" can be discussed as if he were a personality and not a set of lines in a play, a fiction—this unwillingness is the nub of the problem.

Acting as a psychological critic, I want to persuade my audience to accept my explanation of Hamlet's behavior. To do that, I need to look some more at the text and ask a few more questions.

Why would anyone be unwilling to kill someone who deserved it? I've already noted above that Hamlet doesn't want to throw away his life. He's not convinced, even though his superego or his father tells him he should be, that killing Claudius is worth it. But this stuff is logical: this is the "thinking too precisely" that Hamlet mentions. The other reason, the "bestial oblivion," is more primitive.

I haven't yet drawn on Freud's crucial Oedipal complex, and it finally occurs to me that here's where it comes into play: Hamlet doesn't want to kill Claudius because at some level he can't blame Claudius. When Hamlet says he stands with "a father kill'd, a mother stain'd," he is in exactly the Oedipal position that Freud says the unconscious desires to be in. Hamlet calls these events "Excitements of my reason and my blood," and they are exciting, but not in a way that he consciously recognizes. He finds at some deeper level himself excited and unable to be enraged at Claudius for carrying out his own deep-seated wish.

At this point, I think I have a rough plan for an essay:

The problem: how can this passage be used to help readers understand Hamlet's hesitation?

The answer: we see him using some classic strategies to avoid two realities: (1) killing Claudius will probably involve getting himself killed, and he just can't justify that; (2) killing Claudius will involve killing himself in a symbolic sense because Claudius has done what he wanted to do, unconsciously: kill his father and sleep with his mother.

Drafting

And here's a draft, worked out from this plan.

The Psychology of Hamlet's Hesitation: A Reading of 4.4.32–66

Introduces the problem: why does Hamlet hesitate?

Possible explanations.

Shakespeare's *Hamlet* would be a simple case of king-killing and revenge except for one thing: Hamlet hesitates. Like Mona Lisa's smile, Hamlet's delay in carrying out his revenge is puzzling because we do not know his motivation. Some possible reasons are obvious. Perhaps he is not sure that the ghost is telling the truth. Perhaps he is waiting for the perfect revenge, when Claudius is doing something evil rather than praying, thus increasing the near-certainty that he will go to hell. Perhaps he wants to survive his revenge-taking. Perhaps he just wants to be sure he can succeed.

But Hamlet himself doesn't agree with these.

Any or all of these reasons might well be sufficient to explain Hamlet's delay, but Hamlet does not himself accept these reasons. In Act IV, scene iv, after repeated efforts at self-analysis, Hamlet can still say:

> I do not know
> Why yet I live to say, "This
> thing's to do,"
> Sith I have cause, and will, and
> strength, and means
> To do't.　　　　　　　　　　(43–46)

Oedipus complex extended to hesitation.

If Hamlet does not know by this time why he is waiting, then perhaps the cause of his delay is not conscious or rational.

Hamlet's psychology has often been examined. The idea that Hamlet's attitude toward his mother is motivated by an Oedipus complex is well known. But Hamlet's hesitation to revenge his father's death can also be profitably connected to his unconscious psychology as an examination of his soliloquy in Act IV, scene iv will show. Hamlet is unable to admit to himself that "honor" is not a sufficient reason for self-sacrifice; nor is he able to understand that he identifies with Claudius, despite his detestation of him.

A problem:
revenge equals
the bestial.

After observing Fortinbras and his army advancing to fight and die for a small piece of worthless ground, Hamlet exclaims: "How all occasions do inform against me, / And spur my dull revenge!" (32–33). When Hamlet says that all occasions "spur" his revenge, he compares his mind to a horse being spurred. But the next few lines clash with this metaphor: "What is a man,/If his chief good and market of his time/Be but to sleep and feed? a beast, no more" (33–35). Hamlet wants his revenge to be bestial, yet he censures those who act like beasts. He's caught in a dilemma: how to be "spurred" without becoming less than human?

Hamlet's denial of the realm of Freud's id, the realm of bestial desires, is expanded upon in the next few lines:

> Sure He that made us with such
>   large discourse,
> Looking before and after, gave
>   us not
> That capability and godlike
>   reason
> To fust in us unus'd. (36–39)

In saying that we are made "with such large discourse," Hamlet is pointing out the vastness of man's reasoning ability, which makes him, Hamlet believes, "godlike." Unlike the id, man's ego is able to look to the future and the past, "Looking before and after." We should use that reason. But using our reason does not promote violent action, as Hamlet's next few lines indicate:

> Now whether it be
> Bestial oblivion, or some craven
>   scruple
> Of thinking too precisely on
>   th' event—
> A thought which quarter'd hath
>   but one part wisdom
> And ever three parts coward—I do
>   not know
> Why yet I live to say, "This
>   thing's to do,"

> Sith I have cause, and will, and
> strength, and means
> To do't. (39–46)

Humankind ought not be bestial.

Neither bestial oblivion nor the rational mind seem conducive to revenge. After asserting that he should use his reason, rather than letting it get moldy, Hamlet says that reasoning blocks decisive action. To kill Claudius, Hamlet must assume a "godlike" role, handing out justice; yet his godlike faculty does not support such dangerous action any more than his bestial instincts support it.

Reasoning works against revenge.

Consciously unaware of this conflict, Hamlet continues to berate himself, saying "Examples gross as earth exhort me." That is precisely the problem: his reason obstructs his action, and the examples exhorting him are "gross as earth." The kind of primitive, bestial violence required of Hamlet is foreign to him. He has suppressed his bestial self even as he recognizes on one level that it needs spurring. Hamlet seems to think he is exhorting himself to action when he points to the massive army, which is "Exposing what is mortal and unsure / To all that fortune, death, and danger dare, / Even for an eggshell" (51–53). But the logical absurdity of the example actually works against Hamlet's desire: anyone who thinks about it at all will realize that it is stupid for men to die for an eggshell.

Further support.

Hamlet's cause is not an eggshell, and the next few lines indicate further just how deluded Hamlet is in his comparisons:

> Rightly to be great
> Is not to stir without great
> argument,
> But greatly to find quarrel in a
> straw
> When honor's at the stake.   (53–56)

His case is not a straw, and the idea that one should not stir "without great argument" actually justifies his delay, even though Hamlet consciously believes he is talking himself into taking action. What is perhaps most intriguing here, however, is the question of how Hamlet's "honor" is involved. The play would seem to be about murder, regicide, and justice. Compared to these, honor would seem to be a minor concern.

Honor and revenge.

But the relevance of honor emerges in the next lines:

> How stand I then,
> That have a father kill'd, a
>   mother stain'd,
> Excitements of my reason and
>   my blood,
> And let all sleep, while to my
>   shame I see
> The imminent death of twenty
>   thousand men,
> That for a fantasy and trick of
>   fame
> Go to their graves like beds,
>   fight for a plot
> Whereon the numbers cannot try
>   the cause,
> Which is not tomb enough and
>   continent
> To hide the slain?   (56–65)

Honor and the Oedipal urge.

Hamlet feels that his mother is "stain'd," even though it is unclear that she knows anything about Claudius's murder. But Hamlet has already shown himself to be obsessed with his mother's sexuality, especially in the bedroom scene. And the lines following the mention of his mother's stain demonstrate Hamlet's subconscious expression of his own desire. He refers to the "Excitements of . . . my blood," and to "sleep," to "fantasy" and a "trick," and to "beds." While Hamlet is consciously focused on burying the dead in an insufficient tomb, his bestial self is concerned with his mother's womb and dying in a sexual sense.

Thus we can see that Hamlet fails to take action because his rational ego and his bestial id block his revenge and because his own Oedipal desire to do what Claudius has done—kill his father and possess his stained mother— tends to defuse his resolve. We may notice that the

Conclusion: Hamlet's psychological conflicts account for his hesitation.

conclusion of his soliloquy does not call for bloody actions. Instead, he says, "O, from this time forth, / My thoughts be bloody, or be nothing worth!" (65–66). Hamlet's psychological conflicts block his action. He cannot actively seek revenge; revenge must come to him, and when it does, his hesitation will be justified by his own doom.

PRACTICING PSYCHOLOGICAL CRITICISM

Freud's theories, as numerous critics have observed, take the male sex as the norm. How does the Oedipus complex apply to little girls? Their first physical pleasure is also contact with the mother; do little girls wish to sleep with their mothers and kill their fathers? Freud was himself mystified by the problem of applying his theories to women, the "dark continent" as he once called them, but he did try to explain how girls passed through the Oedipus complex. Instead of "castration anxiety," which causes the little boy to submit to reality and his father, turning his desires elsewhere, the little girl perceives that she is already "castrated." Is there then no reason that the little girl should turn her affections from her mother? Freud's solution was the notorious concept of "penis envy"—an idea that continues even today to drive people up the wall. The little girl turns to her father, Freud said, because she realizes that her mother also has been "castrated." This envy is hardly as powerful as the fear of castration, it would seem, and Freud did believe that the superego of women was not as powerfully formed as that of men and that women consequently had weaker ideas of justice and authority. The complementary idea of womb envy apparently did not occur to Freud, but it seems equally if not more plausible.

If this all seems too bizarre, let me briefly suggest once more why I'm bringing this up here. Freud's thinking is the foundation of psychological criticism, and the Oedipus complex is central to Freud. Freud's struggles to make this complex work for little girls resulted in his concept of penis envy. And this concept can be interestingly tested with the following poem.

A Narrow Fellow in the Grass
Emily Dickinson

A narrow Fellow in the Grass
Occasionally rides—

You may have met Him—did you not
His notice sudden is—

The Grass divides as with a Comb—   5
A spotted shaft is seen—
And then it closes at your feet
And opens further on—

He likes a Boggy Acre
A Floor too cool for Corn—   10
Yet when a Boy, and Barefoot—
I more than once at Noon

Have passed, I thought, a Whip lash
Unbraiding in the Sun
When stooping to secure it   15
It wrinkled, and was gone—

Several of Nature's People
I know, and they know me—
I feel for them a transport
Of cordiality—   20

But never met this Fellow
Attended or alone
Without a tighter breathing
And Zero at the Bone—

                                          (1866)

QUESTIONS

1. This poem was one of the few poems published while
   Dickinson was alive. It appeared under the title "The Snake,"
   which was not Dickinson's title, but the addition of an editor.
   Does that title detract from the poem?
2. Which words in the poem seem odd in the context of a
   snake?
3. From a Freudian perspective, paraphrase the poem: that is,
   narrate what happens.
4. Why does Dickinson make the speaker of this poem "a Boy"?
5. What might "Zero at the Bone" mean? What fear or desire
   might be expressed by this phrase?

O to Be a Dragon

Marianne Moore

If I, like Solomon, . . .
    could have my wish—
my wish . . . O to be a dragon,
a symbol of the power of Heaven—of silkworm
size or immense; at times invisible.   5
Felicitous phenomenon.

(1951)

QUESTIONS

1. Can this poem be related to Dickinson's "narrow Fellow" poem?
2. In what way does a psychological perspective alter your reaction to this poem?

Dover Beach

Matthew Arnold

The sea is calm tonight.
The tide is full, the moon lies fair
Upon the straits;—on the French coast the light
Gleams and is gone; the cliffs of England stand,
Glimmering and vast, out in the tranquil bay.   5
Come to the window, sweet is the night-air!
Only, from the long line of spray
Where the sea meets the moon-blanched land,
Listen! you hear the grating roar
Of pebbles which the waves draw back, and fling,   10
At their return, up the high strand,
Begin, and cease, and then again begin,
With tremulous cadence slow, and bring
The eternal note of sadness in.

Sophocles long ago   15
Heard it on the Aegean, and it brought
Into his mind the turbid ebb and flow
Of human misery; we
Find also in the sound a thought,
Hearing it by this distant northern sea.   20

The Sea of Faith
Was once, too, at the full, and round earth's shore
Lay like the folds of a bright girdle furled.
But now I only hear
Its melancholy, long, withdrawing roar,   25
Retreating, to the breath
Of the night-wind, down the vast edges drear
And naked shingles of the world

Ah, love, let us be true
To one another! for the world, which seems   30
To lie before us like a land of dreams,
So various, so beautiful, so new,
Hath really neither joy, nor love, nor light,
Nor certitude, nor peace, nor help for pain;
And we are here as on a darkling plain   35
Swept with confused alarms of struggle and flight,
Where ignorant armies clash by night.

[1867]

QUESTION

Nancy Chodorow (in *Feminism and Psychoanalytic Theory*) notes that girls are able to identify with the adult they spend the most time with; but boys, who cannot identify with the mother, must separate and withdraw themselves from the mother. Thus girls, according to Chodorow, feel more connected to the world and to their caregiver. Girls typically engage in *cooperative* play, while boys typically engage in *competitive* play, Chodorow says. Girls think in terms of relationships, and boys think in terms of rules and rights. Girls cultivate intimacy; boys may find it uncomfortable.

How might Chodorow's work be related to "Dover Beach"?

Useful Terms for Psychological Criticism

As you're employing psychological criticism, the following list of commonly used terms may be helpful. The illustrations refer to Shakespeare's *Hamlet* and specifically to the passage discussed on pages 216–220.

Isolation: Not feeling what one ordinarily would be feeling. Hamlet should be feeling rage, yet his revenge is "dull."

Intellectualization: Explaining away emotions rather than feeling them. Hamlet acknowledges the possibility that he is "thinking too precisely on th' event."

Repression: Submerging an idea or emotion, putting it out of the conscious mind. Hamlet should at least consider the possibility that he is delaying because he fears losing his own life. He doesn't—a major repression.

Projection: Assigning one's own emotions to another person. Hamlet thinks Fortinbras feels the same injury he does, yet Fortinbras takes action. In reality, Hamlet doesn't know what Fortinbras is thinking or feeling.

Displacement: Shifting one's emotions from a threatening target to a less threatening one. Hamlet, rather than getting mad at Claudius, gets mad at himself.

Denial: Refusing to acknowledge what one knows. Hamlet says he doesn't know why he acts, but the answer is right in front of him: he doesn't want to end up like the 20,000 men marching to their meaningless deaths.

Reversal: Turning a situation around; saying the opposite of what is the case. Hamlet says the 20,000 men march to their meaningless deaths to his shame, but isn't the shame really their own?

Works Cited: Psychological Criticism

Adler, Alfred. *The Individual Psychology of Alfred Adler.* Ed. Heinz and Rowena R. Ansbacher. New York: Anchor Books, 1978.

Coleridge, Samuel Taylor. *Collected Letters.* Ed. Earl Leslie Griggs. 6 vols. Oxford: Clarendon, 1956–71.

Eagleton, Terry. "Psychoanalysis." *Literary Theory: An Introduction.* Minneapolis: U of Minnesota P, 1983. 151–93.

Freud, Sigmund. "The Dissolution of the Oedipus Complex." In Gay, 661–66.

———. "The Ego and the Id." In Gay, 628–58.

———. *New Introductory Lectures on Psychoanalysis.* Vol. 22 of *The Standard Edition of the Complete Psychological Works.* London: Hogarth, 1933.

Gay, Peter, ed. *The Freud Reader.* New York: Norton, 1966.

Recommended Further Reading: Psychological Criticism

Freud, Sigmund. *The Interpretation of Dreams*. 1900; Oxford: Oxford UP, 1999. A fascinating work, fairly accessible, enormously influential.

Holland, Norman. *The Brain of Robert Frost: A Cognitive Approach to Literature*. New York: Routledge, 1988. An impressive use of psychological approaches to reading Frost.

———. *Holland's Guide to Psychoanalytic Psychology and Literature-and-Psychology*. New York: Oxford UP, 1990. Useful handbook on psychology and literature.

———. "Norman Holland's Homepage." May 5, 2004. http://www.clas.ufl.edu/users/nnh. December 15, 2003. A wealth of resources here, including much that is related to Holland's teaching and is accessible for students. Available online, linked to this site: *Holland's Guide to Psychoanalytic Psychology and Literature-and-Psychology* (1990).

Jones, Judy, and William Wilson. "Psychology." In *An Incomplete Education*. New York: Ballentine, 1987. 398–431. An entertaining introduction to some basic psychological concepts. Sub-chapters include "Eleven Ways to Leave a Mother" and "Hello, Jung Lovers."

Meltzer, Francoise. "Unconscious." In *Critical Terms for Literary Study*. Ed. Frank Lentricchia and Thomas McLaughlin. Chicago: U of Chicago P, 1990. 147–62. A stimulating discussion of this fundamental idea.

Noel-Smith, Kelly. "Harry Potter's Oedipal Issues." *Psychoanalytic Studies* 3 (2001): 199–207. Available online at http://human-nature.com/free-associations/harrypotter.html. An entertaining and suggestive application of Freud's theory to the popular series.

Sarup, Madan. *Jacques Lacan*. London: Harvester, 1992. Explains the extremely difficult but influential theories of Lacan, comparing them to Freudian ideas and relating the Freudian/Lacanian tradition to feminism.

Willbern, David. "Reading After Freud." In *Contemporary Literary Theory*. Ed. G. Douglas Atkins and Laura Morrow. Amherst: U of Massachusetts P, 1989. 158–79. An excellent introduction to Freud's impact on literary study.

Zizek, Slavoj. *How to Read Lacan*. New York: Norton, 2007. A lively introduction to Jacques Lacan's influential but very challenging psychoanalytical theories.

CHAPTER 8

Gendering the Text

Feminist Criticism, Post-Feminism, and Queer Theory

> *I am already performing a feminine critical act, namely refusing to speak from a position of supposed neutrality and pseudoscientific objectivity.*
>
> —Naomi Schor

My daughter, age five, trips and falls on the driveway, skinning her knees. I'm there quickly, patting her on the back, saying, "Let's go inside and get that fixed up." My daughter looks up at me, tears flowing, and says in amazed disgust, "What can you do? You're just a literature doctor! I want mom, the real doctor!"

What indeed can literature doctors—and their students—do? What does literature itself do, for that matter? Is there any practical value in doing literary criticism? With all the skinned knees in the world, not to mention hunger, disease, poverty, oppression, racism, sexism, child abuse, isn't the study of poetry, fiction, and drama a huge self-indulgence? Don't we have much better things to do?

To be sure, nothing I could say, however insightful, would disinfect and bandage my daughter's knee (although she did laugh as I recited Carroll's "Jabberwocky" while she was getting cleaned up). We say "The pen is mightier than the sword," but I'd rather have a sword sometimes. Still, as Christopher Hitchens puts it in his recent book on the political impact of literature, *Unacknowledged Legislation,* "there are things that pens can do, and swords cannot" (xiv). Hitchens's title refers to Percy Bysshe Shelley's famous claim that "Poets are the unacknowledged legislators of the world"; and for Hitchens, a good example of literature's legislative power is the collapse of the Soviet Union's empire, the consequence in large part, especially in Eastern Europe, of "a civil opposition led by satirical playwrights, ironic essayists, Bohemian jazz players and rock musicians, and subversive poets."

The approaches discussed in this chapter in fact all insist that literature and literary study can have enormous practical value, raising our awareness of oppression and bias, showing us how all sorts of exclusions, suppressions, and exploitations are invented, reinvented, and perpetuated. Whether we are talking about gender, sexuality, economic status, ethnicity, or race, we may reasonably assume that literary works not only unavoidably reflect the politics of the world we inhabit, but they also inevitably influence that world. There are obvious examples of literary works that have had a direct and dramatic impact upon society: Harriet Beecher Stowe's Uncle Tom's Cabin clearly fueled anti-slavery sentiments leading up to the American Civil War. When Abraham Lincoln met Ms. Stowe, he remarked, "So this is the little lady who made this big war!" But the political significance of a particular literary work is often more subtle, complex, and dependent upon interpretation.

Literary critics have sometimes naively imagined that their work has no political implications, as if the reading of literature and culture were somehow beyond the shaping and wielding of power and influence. Among those strategies that have been openly and avowedly political, feminist criticism has been one of the most visible and influential over the past few decades. Indeed, key figures in the struggle for women's equality have been academic scholars of literature: Germaine Greer, for instance, who published a classic bestseller *The Female Eunuch,* in 1970, wrote her doctoral dissertation on Shakespeare's early comedies; Kate Millet, whose 1969 *Sexual Politics* is another classic of the women's liberation movement, deals extensively with literature.

This chapter aims to illustrate the creative power of politically self-conscious reading by focusing on feminist criticism, post-feminism, and queer theory—with the understanding that race,

ethnicity, economics, class, and many other political issues provide fertile interpretive grounds. Political criticism in all its varieties is concerned with identifying and opposing the ways that a particular portion of a culture is excluded, suppressed, and exploited. Feminist criticism, like feminism itself, is concerned of course with the status of women. Jonathan Culler in fact argues that "feminist criticism" is "the name that should be applied to all criticism alert to the critical ramifications of sexual oppression, just as in politics 'women's issues' is the name now applied to many fundamental questions of personal freedom and social justice" (56). In this expansive sense, interestingly enough, the examination of masculine roles and stereotypes, men's (or masculinist) studies, would be considered a branch of feminist criticism.

Post-feminism, as you might imagine, also grows out of the feminist movement. The term has sometimes been used to describe a reactionary stance, occupied by such figures as Naomi Wolf, Camille Paglia, and Rene Denfield, who reject the idea that women today are inevitably victims oppressed by men—an assumption that they attribute to mainstream feminism. In this sense, post-feminism is akin to "antifeminism." But another way of thinking about "post-feminism" is that it refers to what comes *after* feminism, suggesting that feminism has substantially done its work, and men and women have pretty much become equals—in the most important respects, in modern cultures anyway. From this "post-feminist" perspective, the main goal of what is sometimes called "the first wave" of feminism—equality—has been achieved, at least in the sense that women have the freedom to determine their lives. They can vote, own businesses, defer childbearing, be elected to office, pursue any career they're physically and mentally capable of. Sure, prejudice against women still exists (and in many parts of the world is regnant), but it is pervasively dying out in first-world countries as quickly as its adherents can pass away (or evolve).

Post-feminism can also be seen as an extension of feminism, in the sense that post-structuralism is an extension of structuralism, or post-modernism pushes beyond modernism. If the first wave of feminism sought equality for women, then the "second wave" of feminism (it's generally agreed) focused on the distinctive needs of women. Equal opportunity is good, but if women are still primarily responsible for childrearing, housekeeping, socializing, and so forth, then equal opportunity is not really equal. Therefore, some second-wave feminists (Mary Daly, Andrea Dworkin, for instance) have argued that we should reverse the established patriarchy. Such a reversal does not lead, of course, to the end of prejudice and oppression; an elephant upside-down is still an elephant. Beyond such a reversal, post-feminism becomes the next step in feminism: a liberating deconstruction of the whole business of gender and sexuality. The historical progression here does fit the classic structure of deconstruction: first, notice the binary relationship (men and women) and which element is privileged (the first wave); second, expose the arbitrariness of this privileging by reversing it, advocating matriarchal values (the second wave); and third, deconstruct the binary, dismantling the very oppositional structure that makes oppression and prejudice possible (post-feminism, which has sometimes been called the third wave).

What does such a deconstructive move amount to in practice? A commitment to disrupting comfortable patterns of thinking leads inevitably, it seems, to a pluralistic outlook. For instance, by rejecting the idea of women as victims, and at the same time embracing the self-determination of women, post-feminists (in this third wave incarnation anyway) might well be reluctant to condemn pornography. Whereas first and second wave feminists have typically seen pornography as a dramatic instance of the exploitation of women, a post-feminist theorist might ask what happens when women are involved in the writing, directing, and producing of pornography? If women enjoy watching pornography, are they still being exploited? (In the same way?) Or, if pornography is inherently exploitative, is there any intrinsic reason why women are exploited more gravely than men? As Ann Brooks argues in *Postfeminisms: Feminism, Cultural Theory, and Cultural Forms* (1997), the opposition of man versus woman is just too simple, and too unhealthy: post-feminism replaces dualism with diversity, and consensus with variety. It sets aside assumptions. One might well decide that pornography is singularly exploitative of women, or that men are equally exploited, or that no one is exploited; that pornography actually serves a useful purpose, or that it is profoundly evil—or all of the above. The point of post-feminism, or of feminism's third wave, is that our comfortable assumptions ought to be destabilized, opening up our thinking.

Such a rethinking of traditional cultural values has been the goal of a related critical effort, gay and lesbian studies. This expanding field has much in common with feminist criticism, striving to identify, recover, and appreciate work by gay and lesbian authors, as well as expose the means by which gay and lesbian people have been culturally represented. Homosexuals have certainly suffered discrimination and oppression; gay and lesbian studies works to reverse that prejudice. The most dramatic development in this field has taken the name "queer theory," transforming a harshly insulting word into an academic descriptor. The progress from gay and lesbian studies to queer theory parallels the development from feminism to post-feminism: just as post-feminism seeks to deconstruct the oppositional thinking of feminism (male versus female), so does queer theory seek to destabilize the binary of heterosexuality versus homosexuality.

Specifically, queer theory challenges the idea that there is a gay identity (just as post-feminism questions the notion of a feminist identity). There is no one way to be gay or lesbian. In fact, finally, queer theory undermines the very idea of stable sexual oppositions. Things are just much more complicated than the oppressive categories we have inherited. And the shared political aim of these stances—feminism, post-feminism, and queer theory—is to break down our preconceptions and prejudices.

It is possible, most obviously by denying the historical reality of sexual oppression, to resist the premises of feminist criticism. One can argue, for instance, that Western society has actually been structured to protect women from the brutalities of war and commerce, allowing them to be nurturers, mothers, and homemakers. Rather than exploiting or suppressing women, this line of thinking goes, Western society has celebrated and cherished them. While I have no doubt this idea may be sincerely held, and even to some degree supported, it will not stand up to analysis. It is at best too simple; and at worst, flat-out wrong.

It overlooks the way that insulation and honor are themselves a kind of suppression and exclusion. (If a woman is put on a pedestal, she can't *do* much of anything up there.) And it assumes that women are the weaker sex (emotional, unstable, passive, irrational), needing protection, unable to compete with men. But all women are not weaker than all men in any way. Many women are taller, stronger, smarter, and more aggressive than many men. These qualities are in fact the yardsticks of a man-oriented, or patriarchal, culture, but even by those values, which certainly may be questioned, generalizations about "men" and "women" are troublesome.

In fact, as queer theory emphasizes, even dividing humankind into men and women can be problematic since there is no simple genetic or physiological test that will clearly divide all humans into "male" and "female." Determining clear *psychological* differences between the sexes appears to be even more complex and elusive. Although we can articulate certain stereotypical ideas of "masculine" or "feminine," hetero or gay thinking, we could not use these features to sort males and females, straight or gay perfectly—any more than we could use height, or weight, or muscle mass.

A particular individual may have the external appearance of a female and the biochemistry of a male, or vice versa, or an infinity of in-between states. We can, of course, like the Olympic authorities, impose a definition of "male" and "female," prescribing, for example, a certain maximum level of testosterone for a "female" body, but such limits are ultimately arbitrary and (as the East German women swimmers formerly proved) subject to tampering. Racial categories are similarly subject to arbitrary definition. Even if there were some essence of "Indian" or "Negro" blood (the biological consensus is that there isn't and that the concept of "race" is inherently problematic), where should one draw the line? Is an "Indian" someone who has two Indian parents, or is one sufficient, or one grandparent enough, or even a great-grandparent? Historically, in various cultures, individuals have been assigned to a particular racial minority with as little as one-twentieth of their genetic material purportedly coming from that race, which means, given my grandmother's Cherokee heritage, that in some places at some times I would be considered an American Indian. Am I a Native American? I don't know. It depends on what the term is being used to mean, I suppose.

Political criticism of every variety has struggled with such essential questions of identity: What is an African American? What is a "woman"? What is the "working class"? What is a "bisexual" person? Such difficulties have led to the idea that it would be more useful to think in terms of a continuum rather than two totally distinct opposites. This insight allows us to distinguish "sex" (the biological status of male and female) from "gender" (our conceptions of "man" and "woman"). As Simone de Beauvoir puts it, "One is not born a woman, one becomes one" (301). An individual, in other words, may be born female (sex), but that status does not entail the attributes of "woman" as our culture has defined them (gender). Our conceptions of femininity (and masculinity), Beauvoir is saying, are social constructions that are imposed on individuals. Or as Thomas Laqueur puts it in his detailed history of the ways we have invented our ideas of gender, sex "is situational; it is explicable only within the context of battles over gender and power" (11); and "two sexes are not the necessary, natural consequence of corporeal difference" (243). Or as Barbara Johnson says, "The question of gender is a question of language" (37). Or, as Judith Butler argues in *Gender Trouble,* gender is "performative," created by what one does, not what one is.

In fact, the more one considers the sexual diversity of human beings and the way that biological "sex" is fashioned into social "gender," the more inadequate seems the idea of a continuum stretching from "male" to "female." Such a continuum still depends upon the idea of "male-ness" and "female-ness," categories from which particular individuals may differ to one degree or another. And a male-to-female continuum also ignores questions of sexual preference, which suggest another continuum ranging from heterosexual to bisexual to homosexual. Unsettling our various sexual categories has provided a rich opportunity in the arena of literary criticism for all kinds of redefinition and debate, about what it means to be a man or a woman, about how one becomes such an entity (or not), about what such processes reveal about our culture.

It is of course always possible that you just don't agree that women have been oppressed and that generalizations based on sexual orientation or gender are dumb. What would be the purpose of feminist criticism for such a person? Can such a nonfeminist even do feminist criticism? For that matter, is it even possible for a man to do feminist criticism? At the risk of irritating or even outraging some of my readers, I think the answer is that *anyone* can do feminist criticism—a male, even a male chauvinist—and do it "honestly" in a sense. One of the wonderful things about words is that we can use them to try out ideas, to speculate, to put on roles and explore. We construct arguments and conduct analyses not only to persuade others but also to investigate things for ourselves—if we have an open, critical mind, that is. Writing is a process of learning.

If you already inhabit a feminist outlook, then applying it to literature may help you understand both the work and your outlook better. And if this way of thinking isn't where you find yourself today, it won't hurt you to visit and try to think like a native for a while. You'll enlarge your vision, you may even decide to stay. At the least you'll have a better understanding of feminist thinking. Your performance as a feminist critic (or any other sort of critic) may be an act, a role you've taken on, but it need not (and ought not) be an *insincere* performance. One can *pretend* to play Macbeth or Willie Loman, or one can sincerely *play* these characters. Your job is to immerse yourself in feminist criticism, genuinely attempting to appreciate its insights, regardless of whether you finally accept them.

And when is some form of feminist criticism appropriate? It's always a possibility, an available option. The way to see if a feminist approach is appropriate is to try it out. Even if the text isn't obviously dealing with feminist concerns, a feminist approach may be revealing. In fact, the absence of women or their concerns may be quite significant. For some texts, admittedly, a feminist reading may require considerable care and imagination. But, again, the pervasiveness of sexual bias in our society ensures, I would argue, that most texts will readily provide ample materials for a feminist response. Just as we expose the presence of a virus by assuming its existence and then running tests to establish its effects, we ought likewise to assume the existence of bias and prejudice and make efforts to expose its effects. When feminist criticism can find nothing to talk about, when all its tests come out negative, then its work will be done. Then we can assume that traditional literary studies will sufficiently include issues of sex and gender; then we can neglect to consider the implications of our actions in the context of such issues. Then we will live in a very different world.

HOW TO DO FEMINIST CRITICISM, POST-FEMINISM, AND QUEER THEORY

According to Cheryl Torsney, feminist criticism is not a single method, but rather a patchwork or "a quilt" of different methods stitched together with a common conviction: "that one can read, write, and interpret as a woman" (180). This plurality of approaches is one reason that Robert Con Davis says it may well be "that the future of literary studies is being decided in current feminist theory and criticism" (161), as various ways of reading are woven together, blended, contrasted, and questioned. My survey of critical approaches ends with feminist criticism because it can draw on each of the theories described here, as well as on others. Any act of criticism, to be sure, is likely to draw on various strategies, blending together complementary and sometimes even contradictory assumptions and practices. But feminist criticism, post-feminism, and queer theory are perhaps uniquely positioned to benefit, and benefit from, other approaches.

I'll focus here then on two illustrative concerns of feminist criticism: how women have written and how women have been written. The first of these concerns deals significantly with the status of women writers, and its most influential formulation is probably Virginia Woolf's *A Room of One's Own*, published in 1929. Woolf's impetus can be seen in her revealing thought experiment: what if, Woolf asks, Shakespeare had a sister, equally as brilliant and talented as Shakespeare himself? What would have become of her? She would not have had the same educational opportunities, the same financial independence, the same social freedom or professional access. Obviously, her career would have been strikingly different from Shakespeare's. In fact, Woolf doubts that she would have had a career at all. In "Professions for Women," Woolf explains how her own career has been obstructed by narrow conceptions of womanhood, which offered virtually no role for serious women writers. In calling for "a room of one's own," Woolf is asking for the freedom and the space for all Shakespeare's sisters to speak honestly out of their own experiences, without assuming male pseudonyms or adopting masculine voices.

Some extraordinary women, as Woolf makes clear, somehow did manage to write, and this tradition of women's writing is extremely important because "*we think back through our mothers if we are women*" (79). Without some sense of these "mothers," the woman writer will be unable to make a creative room of her own, being forced instead to suppress her unique voice and attempt to fit into the mansions of the male tradition. Literary history—a *new* literary history that includes women—thus becomes a vital action, making it possible for women to write as *women,* whatever that means. (For Woolf it appears to have included the freedom to transcend gender.)

The effects of the effort to recover women's writing have been dramatic: most obviously, the canon of honored, "serious" literature has been enlarged to include more works by women (an alternative canon of women's writing has also arisen), and certain genres long considered minor or secondary have received serious attention. Women did write in the major genres (fiction, drama, poetry), but their creative energies also found outlets in letters, journals, diaries, and other long-neglected forms. In recovering this work of their "mothers," feminist critics have often invoked Woolf, attempting to describe the "precious speciality" (in Woolf's words) of this nearly lost tradition of women's writing. For Elaine Showalter, this engagement with women's writing calls for a "distinctly female vision." In *A Literature of Their Own* (1977), obviously building on Woolf's project, she uses the term "gynocriticism" to refer to this study of women by women.

The second concern has to do with the way women have been written—that is, with the image of women in literature. The most influential work here, without question, is Simone de Beauvoir's *The Second Sex,* published in French in 1949. Beauvoir's point is simple but powerful: females have been depicted in literature and culture as either Mary or Eve, the angelic mother or the evil seductress. Such a representation of women, especially in works by men, serves to make women unreal, other, the absence of maleness, rather than anything positively female or mutually human: this vision is especially pernicious when it is unnoticed and is perceived to be "natural" or "realistic." The work of the reader, then, is to expose this opposition—misogyny (woman seen as monster) or idealization (woman seen as saint)—thereby undermining its power by exposing its artifice. Notable followers of Beauvoir's tradition include Mary Ellman, whose *Thinking About Women* (1968) argues that gender stereotypes in literature are applied not only to characters but to *everything;* and Sandra Gilbert and Susan Gubar, whose *Madwoman in the Attic* (1979) argues that women writers both accept and reject the angel vs. seductress stereotypes, thereby creating their own distinctive vision.

These two concerns—woman as writer, woman as written—can be illustrated by looking briefly at Mary Astell's *A Serious Proposal to the Ladies,* published in 1692. We should note first that merely reading Astell's work verges on a feminist act. Her *Proposal* certainly has not held a secure place in the traditional canon. In Tillotson, Fussell, and Waingrow's popular *Eighteenth-Century Literature,* published in 1969, Astell's work does not appear (the volume covers 1660–1800). Representative works of some ninety men do appear, spread over 1538 pages. Women writers are virtually ignored: three are represented, occupying less than two pages. Let's recap that score: men—1538; women—1 and a fraction. In John Mahoney's anthology for the same period, *The Enlightenment and English Literature,* published about eleven years later (1980), we might expect to see more women writers, especially given the surge of interest in feminist criticism in the 1970s. But there are in fact no women at all in Mahoney's anthology.

Such neglect points to the need for alternative collections, such as Sandra Gilbert and Susan Gubar's *Norton Anthology of Literature by Women,* which covers the middle ages (fourteenth century) to the present, and presents fifteen women writers (including Astell) in its eighteenth-century section; or Roger Lonsdale's *Eighteenth-Century Women Poets,* which offers the work of over one hundred women; or Robert Uphaus and Gretchen Foster's *The 'Other' Eighteenth Century: English Women of Letters,* which presents in some depth the work of twenty-two women, including Astell. But merely offering alternatives to the traditional surveys seems to many people entirely inadequate, leaving the writing of women in a secondary, supplementary position. It is no longer plausible, after the advent of feminist criticism, to argue that women writers are justifiably omitted from the standard anthologies ("the canon") because their writing is inferior to the writing of men. For one thing, women's writing has gone largely unread, even in graduate survey courses, so that even "experts" in eighteenth-century literature may know little about Astell or any other female writer; one cannot say that the writing of men is better without having read the writing of women. For another thing, the standards used to construct "the canon" are the invention of mostly male critics and scholars, who are themselves the product of the exclusion of women: women aren't included now because they haven't been included in the past, and the cycle perpetuates itself. Feminist criticism therefore may show how some works by women meet the traditional standards of excellence, but it may also challenge the arbitrariness of those same patriarchal notions of excellence.

Consider the following two passages from Mary Astell's *Serious Proposal*. In the first Astell announces precisely what her proposal is; in the second she summarizes her plan. As you read these two passages, labeled A and B respectively, pay attention to how women are presented. What images of "woman" do the passages convey? (I have numbered the sentences for easy reference.)

(A)

1. Now as to the proposal, it is to erect a monastery, or if you will (to avoid giving offence to the scrupulous and injudicious, by names which though innocent in themselves, have been abused by superstitious practices), we will call it a religious retirement, and such as shall have a double aspect, being not only a retreat from the world for those who desire that advantage, but likewise, an institution and previous discipline to fit us to do the greatest good in it; such an institution as this (if I do not mightily deceive myself) would be the most probable method to amend the present, and improve the future age. . . .

2. You are therefore ladies, invited into a place, where you shall suffer no other confinement, but to be kept out of the road of sin: You shall not be deprived of your grandeur, but only exchange the vain pomps and pageantry of the world, empty titles and forms of state, for the true and solid greatness of being able to despise them. . . .

3. Happy retreat! which will be the introducing you into such a paradise as your mother Eve forfeited, where you shall feast on pleasures, that do not, like those of the world, disappoint your expectations, pall your appetites, and by the disgust they give you put you on the fruitless search after new delights, which when obtained are as empty as the former; but such as will make you truly happy now, and prepare you to be perfectly so hereafter.

4. Here are no serpents to deceive you, whilst you entertain yourselves in these delicious gardens.

5. No provocations will be given in this amicable society, but to love and good works, which will afford such an entertaining employment, that you'll have as little inclination as leisure to pursue those follies, which in the time of your ignorance passed with you under the name of love, although there is not in nature two more different things, than true love and that brutish passion, which pretends to ape it.

6. Here will be no rivalling but for the love of God, no ambition but to procure his favour, to which nothing will more effectually recommend you, than a great and dear affection to each other.

(B)

7. The ladies, I'm sure, have no reason to dislike this proposal, but I know not how the men will resent it to have their enclosure broke down, and women invited to taste of that tree of knowledge they have so long unjustly monopolized.
8. But they must excuse me, if I be as partial to my own sex as they are to theirs, and think women as capable of learning as men are, and that it becomes them as well.
9. For I cannot imagine wherein the hurt lies, if instead of doing mischief to one another, by an uncharitable and vain conversation, women be enabled to inform and instruct those of their own sex at least; the holy ghost having left it on record, that Priscilla as well as her husband, catechized the eloquent Apollos and the great Apostle found no fault with her.
10. It will therefore be very proper for our ladies to spend part of their time in this retirement, in adorning their minds with useful knowledge.

Since Astell's *Proposal* is considered a feminist classic, it is interesting to note how she appears to reinforce the idea of women as weak sensualists, daughters of Eve, tending toward sin. Astell tells "the ladies" that their "confinement" will allow them to "be kept out of the road of sin," as if women can resist temptation only if they are removed from it (2). Further, she explicitly links all women to Eve, asserting that this "Happy retreat" will introduce them "into such a paradise as your mother Eve forfeited" (3). Astell's ladies will be able to reenter or recreate paradise not because they are any stronger or smarter than Eve, the epitome of feminine susceptibility, but because there will be "no serpents to deceive you" in Astell's "Happy retreat" (4).

In addition, the inducements Astell offers "the ladies" are themselves sensual, as if she can tempt them into a second paradise only by promising pleasure—in fact, the same pleasure for which women originally were ejected: in the garden of Eden, it was of course the forbidden fruit from the tree of knowledge that Eve could not resist; in Astell's retreat, women will get to enjoy such fruit once more, being able to "*feast* on pleasures" more durable than those of the world, avoiding "*the fruitless* search after new delights," entertaining themselves in these "*delicious* gardens" of learning (3). Astell seems here to be reinforcing the stereotype that women are controlled by their appetites: to entice them to learn, she discusses knowledge as if it were food—a "delicious" and fruitful "feast." Astell further seems to accept the conventional sexism of depicting women as aesthetic objects, concluding that it is proper for women to be "adorning their minds with useful knowledge" (10)—as if knowledge were valuable as an adornment, an intellectual sort of ribbon or bow to make women more attractive. In consecutive sentences, Astell promises ladies that the retreat will "entertain" (4), providing "entertaining employment" (5), as if women seek only diversion, avoiding diligence.

This reading of Astell's *Proposal* deals admittedly with only a portion of her text, but it could be extended easily, and it illustrates sufficiently, I think, one activity of feminist criticism: exposing stereotypes of women. Although this exposure is often at the expense of male authors, we should not be surprised to find such sexism in Astell's text, despite her place as an early feminist: how could she entirely evade the assumptions of her time? As Janet Todd puts it:

> If 'feminism,' in a 1970s sense, claims absolute equality of the sexes and complex identification of roles, then no women in eighteenth-century England advocated it; if it implies equal opportunity, then probably only Mary Wollstonecraft, who hinted at female politicians while extolling motherhood, might qualify. But if a feminist is one who is aware of female problems and is angry or irritated at the female predicament, then almost every woman writer and many men could claim the title. (qtd. in Ruthven 17)

We are all products of our culture, our language, our myths, and our history; therefore, attempting to identify the negative or stereotypical images in Astell's work does not constitute an attack on her. The vision in *A Proposal to the Ladies* of educated women *is* extraordinary.

In addition to this negative strategy of unmasking prejudices, feminist criticism also undertakes the positive business of reading women's writings with a particular attentiveness to their difference either from male texts or from the dominant discourse, supposed to be controlled by men, and therefore "patriarchal." Such a recuperative reading of these passages from Astell's *Proposal*, rather than targeting the depiction of women, might look more closely at what Astell was attempting to do with these images. How does Astell's own gender affect her discourse and its aim? As a woman, writing in the late seventeenth century, proposing a kind of "monastery" to educate women, Astell addresses her text "A Serious Proposal *to the Ladies,*" but any reflection at all must acknowledge that her audience had to include men. It would have been impossible, after all, in her day, to create the sort of institution Astell proposes without the approval and even the active support of men. Astell depicts herself as speaking to "the ladies," but she intends to be overheard by those holding the power. How does this dual audience affect her writing?

The most obvious critical strategy would be to look for contradictions, or for assertions that can be taken two ways, or for two different phrasings of the same assertion, as Astell speaks different things to different audiences with the same text. In fact, it seems reasonable to assume that Astell's position is hardly unique, that other women writers confronted a divided audience. Indeed, for Gilbert and Gubar, a strategy of both conforming to and undermining patriarchal cultural conventions has distinguished women's writing since Jane Austen. Although Astell's work appeared over a century before Austen's, much the same (if not worse) conditions applied.

What examples of a double-voiced discourse do you find in Astell's passages? For a start, we might notice that Astell first says her proposal is to "erect a monastery" for single women, but she quickly alters "monastery" to "religious retirement" (1). Astell says she makes this change to avoid the prejudice against the term "monastery," which would have linked her project to Catholic monks, who had a reputation in Astell's day, among some anti-Papists anyway, for dabbling in the supernatural ("superstitious practices," as Astell says). But Astell might have used "nunnery" or "priory" instead of "monastery"; so why did she first offer the term associated with monks, then withdraw it? Because, I would argue, "monastery" makes clear to one part of her audience that she is offering them a chance to move into a domain heretofore jealously controlled by men. By saying she wants "to *erect* a monastery," Astell subtly underscores the masculine privilege she wants to usurp. Lest some male readers be threatened by women assuming such erections, Astell immediately portrays her project as a "retreat," a "confinement," a withdrawal into a feminine space, not a masculine intrusion. But the empowering potential of the retreat's "delicious gardens" has already been indicated to Astell's discerning reader.

Having glimpsed this potential power, the ladies, Astell says in the second passage, will "have no reason to dislike this proposal." But, she continues, "I know not how the men will resent it to have their enclosure broke down, and women invited to taste of that tree of knowledge they have so long unjustly monopolized" (7). Earlier,

Astell has taken pains to make sure her proposal is not seen as an invasion, but rather a retirement. And in the body of her proposal, Astell has repeatedly limited the ambition of her idea, making it less threatening to men: she does not believe a woman needs to study "languages" as diligently as men, but only as "are necessary to acquaint her with useful authors"; she does not desire "that women should teach in the church, or usurp authority where it is not allowed them," but only that they be allowed "to understand our duty, and not be forced to take it upon trust for others" (116). But this subsequent image reverses the earlier one of "retreat": instead of the women confining themselves, they will be *breaking down* the "enclosure" of the men. If this proposal describes a retreat, it is a retreat into the intellectual space already occupied by men.

Likewise, although Astell has repeatedly alluded to Eve's weakness, confirming the patriarchal myth of mankind's fall, and thus reassuring part of her readers that she understands the dangerous and sinful nature of women, her concluding reference to the Genesis story also reverses the implications of the earlier allusions. Somehow Eve's disastrous deed, tasting the fruit from the forbidden tree of knowledge, has become precisely the activity that men have "so long unjustly monopolized" (7). Although Astell has appeared to reinforce the male-oriented view of the fall of "man," this version of the story now becomes problematic: men have been zealously indulging in the same activity for which Eve has been unceasingly castigated. How can "tasting" of the tree of knowledge be considered evil? Isn't knowledge good? Why have men monopolized it?

Astell thus shrewdly intimates that men—with Godlike presumption—have built their own paradise or "enclosure," eating from the tree of knowledge themselves, while forbidding women to partake. Despite her earlier concessions to the limited ambition of women's learning, Astell's position in the later passage is much bolder, asserting that women are "as capable of learning as men are, and that it becomes them as well" (8). This radical position is balanced, but not obscured, by Astell's more modest stances earlier. But even these earlier references to the weakness of women can be played two ways.

For instance, when Astell points out to the ladies that her "Happy retreat" will be "introducing you into such a paradise as your mother Eve forfeited" (3), she appears to be acknowledging woman's sinful nature and offering a chance to undo the Fall. But there is a dramatic difference between the first and the second paradise: no Adam will inhabit Astell's, for it will include single women only. This lack of men does not appear in the least to be a deterrent to the ladies' happiness; on the contrary, Astell's retreat will allow women to avoid "that brutish passion, which pretends to ape" true love (5). Instead of the love of men, which Astell suggests is animalistic, simian even, she holds out the promise of the ladies' "great and dear affection to each other" (6). The positive significance of this male absence is rather subtly conveyed by what must be seen as the most appealing aspect of this second paradise: "Here are no serpents to deceive you, whilst you entertain your selves in these delicious gardens." A single serpent ruined the first paradise for Eve (and the rest of us); but in pointing to this crucial difference, Astell uses the plural "serpents." Given the phallic symbolism of serpents, we can easily conclude that Astell is talking about bipedal serpents— the same ones who have now enclosed the tree of knowledge (which women had the courage to eat from!), keeping women out.

In this case, as I have read these passages, the negative view of women that emerges in one sort of feminist criticism (woman as written) becomes part of a positive strategy in the other kind (woman as writer).

THE WRITING PROCESS: A SAMPLE ESSAY

Let's see what opportunities a feminist approach affords a reader of the following poem, written by Samuel Johnson in 1746, about fifty years after Astell's proposal. Although he was struggling to make his reputation in 1746, Johnson would go on to become arguably the eighteenth century's greatest and most versatile writer, the second-most quoted author in our language (behind only Shakespeare).

Before you read the poem, it may be helpful to know (if you don't already) that "Stella" was often used in eighteenth-century poetry as a kind of generic name for a beautiful, youthful, charming woman. Likewise, "nymph" in this period also usually refers to such a woman, although the word literally means, in Greek and Roman mythology, a female spirit that inhabits and somehow embodies a feature of nature. (For instance, there might be a nymph of the Ohio River, who would be the spirit of the river, standing for it and living somehow "in" it.) So a nymph or a Stella would be a beautiful woman that one could imagine being part of a lovely rural setting. "Stella" and "nymph" in this poem refer, it seems clear, to the "Miss_____" of the title. And this person seems, at some point anyway, to have been a real person: when the poem first appeared, its title was "To the Honble [short for "Honorable"] Miss

Carpenter," who was Alicia Maria Carpenter, daughter of Lord Carpenter. A manuscript has the same title. But Anna Williams reprinted the poem in her *Miscellanies* with the current title; and since Johnson presumably assisted Williams with her collection of poems (Williams was a blind poet, given lodging and support by Johnson), it is likely he made or approved of the change.

Now read the poem several times, noting your reactions and questions on paper.

To Miss _____ On Her Playing upon the Harpsichord In a Room Hung with Some Flower-pieces of Her Own Painting

Samuel Johnson

When Stella strikes the tuneful string
In scenes of imitated spring,
Where beauty lavishes her pow'rs
On beds of never-fading flow'rs,
And pleasure propagates around   5
Each charm of modulated sound,
Ah! think not, in the dang'rous hour,
The nymph fictitious, as the flow'r,
But shun, rash youth, the gay alcove,
Nor tempt the snares of wily love.   10
    When charms thus press on ev'ry sense,
What thought of flight, or of defence?
Deceitful Hope, and vain Desire,
For ever flutter o'er her lyre,
Delighting, as the youth draws nigh,   15
To point the glances of her eye,
And forming, with unerring art,
New chains to hold the captive heart.
    But on these regions of delight,
Might Truth intrude with daring flight,   20
Could Stella, sprightly, fair and young,
One moment hear the moral song,
Instruction with her flow'rs might spring,
And wisdom warble from her string.
    Mark, when from the thousand
       mingled dyes   25
Thou see'st one pleasing form arise,
How active light, and thoughtful shade,
In greater scenes each other aid;
Mark, when the diff'rent notes agree

In friendly contrariety,   30
How passion's well-accorded strife
Gives all the harmony of life.
Thy pictures shall thy conduct frame,
Consistent still, though not the same;
Thy musick teach the nobler art   35
To tune the regulated heart.

(1746)

Preparing to Respond

After you've invested some effort in the poem, becoming familiar with it, compare the results of your reading to my own, printed below. The numbers in my notes refer to the line numbers of the poem.

Reading Notes on "To Miss _____"

Line 1: "strikes the tuneful string"? I suppose this means her playing upon the harpsichord.

Line 2: "In scenes of imitated spring"? What does this mean? It must refer to her paintings of "some flower-pieces," which would be an "imitated" spring.

Line 4: "never-fading flow'rs"—because they're painted, not real.

Lines 7–8: The warning here seems odd: "think not . . . / The nymph fictitious, as the flow'r," as if someone couldn't tell the difference between a girl playing the harpsichord and a painting! There must be something else going on here.

And why is this hour dangerous? Because of "the snares of wily love" (10). The speaker is afraid he will fall for the nymph if he doesn't watch out. Or, rather, he's afraid the "rash youth" (9) will fall. Is he the rash youth?

Lines 11–18: This section makes clear that the speaker fears the effect of Stella upon the youth. Her artistry will capture him if he is not careful, creating "New chains to hold the captive heart."

Lines 19–24: In this section the speaker points out that the tremendous power Stella has to take prisoners might also be used for good: "Instruction" might come from her painting (23); "wisdom" might come from her music (24). To get these benefits, "Truth" will have to "intrude with daring flight" (20) into "these regions of delight" (19). What does this mean? That her art and music will have to do more than just give pleasure or seduce the affections of rash youths. Stella herself will have to "hear the moral song" (22) if her charms are to have some useful purpose.

Lines 25–34: We're told to "mark," or take note of, the way painting works, and then the way music works. Specifically, we're told to notice how all the different "mingled" colors come together to make "one pleasing form," and how all the "diff'rent notes" come together in "friendly contrariety."

Lines 35–36: I think these lines make clear why we are instructed to "mark" how conflicting dyes and notes come together in harmony. The speaker is most concerned earlier in the poem by the charms of Stella's music and painting, which could make a "captive" of the "rash youth." These charms could be the forces for good, however, as the third section asserts. This fourth section then explains how harmony comes from contrariety. So what is the "contrariety" here? The speaker wants Stella's pleasure to be opposed, or complemented, or completed by instruction. The sensual indulgence of her art will serve some higher purpose if her painting could "thy conduct frame" (33) and her music could "tune the regulated heart" (36).

Who is "thy" in these closing lines? Stella? The youth? The speaker? The reader? My guess would be all of the above. Stella is being addressed—the poem is "To" her after all, which might mean "in honor of" or "to be sent to." But other readers clearly are meant to overhear, or "oversee," the advice, especially the rash youth, perhaps Johnson himself.

Now we want to evolve a feminist reading of the poem.

Johnson is not, I think it's safe to say, a neglected woman writer, and so the feminist approach that seems most promising here would focus on the following questions:

- What role does sex or gender play in this work?
- What image of women is conveyed by the poem?
- How is the relationship between men and women depicted?

Some material toward answering these questions is already beginning to appear, I think, in my notes above: the speaker of the poem clearly sees Stella, or her charms, or the charms of her music and painting, as "dang'rous" (7); and Stella is encouraged to add "Truth" (20) and "Instruction" (23) to the pleasures of her charming arts. The next step will be to identify materials that will allow me to address the questions above and then to think about the audience I'm trying to reach and what I'm trying to accomplish. Feminist criticism characteristically tries to intervene in the ongoing traditional discussion. How can a feminist perspective on this poem affect our thinking?

To Miss _____ On Her Playing upon the Harpsichord In a
Room Hung with Some Flower-pieces of Her Own Painting

Art,
Charm,

When Stella strikes the tuneful string

In scenes of imitated spring,　—— *Not real* *Seduction*

Where beauty lavishes her pow'rs *Excessive,*

Pleasure
is OK,
but shd.
it be so
promiscuous?

On beds of never-fading flow'rs, *unnatural*

And pleasure propagates around

Each charm of modulated sound, *Charm*
The danger?
Ah! think not, in the dang'rous hour, *falling in love*
or lust.
The nymph fictitious, as the flow'r, *Stay in the*
open.
But shun, rash youth, the gay alcove, *As if she is*
going to trap
Nor tempt the snares of wily love. *him like*
an animal
When charms thus press on ev'ry sense, *overwhelming*

What thought of flight, or of defence?

Deceitful Hope, and vain Desire,

Eve For ever flutter o'er her lyre,

Delighting, as the youth draws nigh,

To point the glances of her eye, *Art vs. Nature*
(Art—bad)
And forming, with unerring art,

New chains to hold the captive heart. *Love = Prison*

Like a
decadent
red-light
district?

But on these regions of delight, *Truth = Nature*
Moral
Might Truth intrude with daring flight,

Could Stella, sprightly, fair and young,

Her lust song
vs. moral song
One moment hear the moral song,

Instruction with her flow'rs might spring,

And wisdom warble from her string.

Mark, when from the thousand mingled dyes *Not real*

Thou see'st one pleasing form arise,

How active light, and thoughtful shade,

In greater scenes each other aid;   *Mix art with nature. Dangerous unstable balance?*

Mark, when the diff'rent notes agree

In friendly contrariety,

How passion's well-accorded strife

Gives all the harmony of life.

Thy pictures shall thy conduct frame,

Consistent still, though not the same;

Tune = art. Art to tame art?   Thy musick teach the nobler art
To tune the regulated heart.   *Impose order on her unfettered, dangerous art*

Before you look at my annotations here, I encourage you to look at the poem again yourself, then compare my notes to your own.

Shaping

My first impression had been that the poem celebrated Stella's (or Alicia Carpenter's) artistic and musical talents and encouraged her to add instruction and virtue to those charms. Focusing on a feminist stance altered my own view, and what emerged here for me was the speaker's unrelenting vision of Stella as a threat. As I continued to reread the poem, I was surprised by the intensity of the speaker's fear: what is so threatening about a young lady playing a harpsichord in a room with some of her paintings? The declared danger is her effect on the youth—love, or infatuation, or lust, which becomes some sort of loss of independence and autonomy. Everything I saw as I annotated seemed aimed at one thing: neutralizing, controlling, managing somehow the tremendous feminine power that Stella's charms represent—the power to enchain the heart of any rash youth, which certainly must include the speaker, who (I can't help suspecting) may be Johnson himself.

My goal at this point is beginning to emerge, as I realize that I want my audience to see that Johnson's overt morality may be something more oppressive: the poem aims to control "Stella" or get her to control herself, and the reason for this effort is precisely that the speaker fears he cannot control himself. It is not imperative to bring Adam and Eve into the discussion, but the poem does seem to replay that enduring story: woman as temptation, who causes man to fall. In other words, the poem seems to demonstrate once more Simone de Beauvoir's thesis that women tend to be presented as Eve or Mary, evil temptress or virginal saint. I imagined an audience that might think I'm making too much out of this—seeing something sinister when it's just a poem about self-control; so I planned to try to anticipate this reaction and provide careful, balanced support.

I jotted down my supporting ideas and played around with them until some logical progression began to emerge. Here is the order I came up with (the items may make more sense when you see them in my draft essay):

1. Erasing Miss _____'s name: the title
2. Thesis: Johnson aims to blank out women's sensuality and danger
3. Johnson's audience: Miss _____ ostensibly, but really a warning to the youth; to the reader; ultimately to Johnson himself
4. Surface message to "Stella": include instruction/wisdom
5. Restrictive actions become clearer in the end: to tune and to frame
6. Stella as danger: sensual enslavement ("Chains")
7. Sensual disorientation—what is real?
8. Promiscuity (woman as potentially uncontrollable desire):
   painting "lavishes" on "beds"
   music "propagates"
9. Stella is not real—a fiction: the speaker as confused as the youth
10. "Truth" called in: regulate Stella's art
11. Add instruction to pleasure
12. Morality for the youth's benefit, not hers
13. Identity: Limit hers to save his

Drafting

The next step was to transform my individual ideas and annotated poem into a rough draft, which I could then revise and polish.

I also did a little more research on the poem, reading the notes to the poem in the standard *Yale Edition of the Works of Samuel Johnson*. This step, as always, takes some time and patience; but if you're sufficiently prepared and you have adequate time, it has its substantial satisfactions. You may want to sketch out your own essay before you look at mine.

Beware of Women with Harpsichords and Paintings: On Samuel Johnson's Misogyny

Introduces the poem and the problem: the erasure of "Miss Carpenter."

The title to one of Samuel Johnson's occasional poems is perhaps most revealing in what it leaves out: "To Miss _____ On Her Playing upon the Harpsichord In a Room Hung with Some Flower-pieces of Her Own Painting." Why has the woman's name become a blank, especially since "Stella" appears in the first line, and since the poem was originally addressed "To the Honble Miss Carpenter" (the "honourable" Alicia Maria Carpenter, daughter of the second Lord Carpenter)? Why has Johnson erased Miss Carpenter and ignored "Stella," presumably his pseudonym for her? (The poem appeared first in Dodsley's *Museum* in November of 1746; it was reprinted with the altered title in a collection "edited" by Johnson's friend Anna Williams, who was blind, and who relied heavily on Johnson's assistance. I am assuming Johnson is responsible for the title change.)

Thesis: the poem is about the threat of women (women as Eve).

This paper argues that Johnson has removed Miss Carpenter's name because the poem really is about the threat that women pose and the need to blank them out, erase them, neutralize them, render them less dangerous. Although the poem is addressed "To Miss _____," its more urgent message is directed at another audience, the unnamed "rash youth" in the poem, who stands for anyone like the speaker, like Johnson, who is foolish enough to go near a woman with a harpsichord and some paintings—or any other props for that matter.

The surface reading: set-up for what follows.

The poem, to be sure, may appear on a superficial reading to be nothing more than advice to a young artist and musician, encouraging her to include instruction in her performances, adding morality, virtue, "Truth," to the pleasures of her forms and harmonies. The poem's conclusion summarizes this surface message:

> Thy pictures shall thy conduct
> frame,
> Consistent still, though not the
> same;
> Thy musick teach the nobler art
> To tune the regulated heart.
> (33–36)

The frame as containment.

But why, we must ask, does Johnson (or the speaker) believe that Stella's "conduct" needs a "frame"? Why does her heart need to be tuned and "regulated"? Although framing and tuning are laudable when applied to music or art, Stella is not a painting or a song, and Johnson's conclusion makes her an object and expresses a criticism: Stella needs to be closed in, limited, set apart (framed); she needs to be standardized, fixed, corrected (tuned). And the reason for this discipline and confinement is, quite simply, she is "dang'rous" (7).

Sexuality is dangerous.

The danger, specifically, is that Stella threatens to enslave any "rash youth" with her art, both aural and visual, forming "New chains to hold the captive heart" (18). Her "unerring" art, Johnson says, is so powerful that the poor youth is totally disoriented in the poem's first section, unable to tell what is real and what isn't: the flowers, Johnson feels compelled to tell the youth, are not real; the woman is. The point seems absurd (imagine telling someone this) until we realize exactly what the threat of "the dang'rous hour" is: it is sexuality, sensuousness, passion, "wily love"; and these entities are so powerful that they make truth and fiction run together.

Imagination is dangerous.

But the distinction between the woman and her art is crucial. Her art is promiscuous and enduring: her painting "lavishes her pow'rs / On beds of never-fading flow'rs"; "pleasure propagates around" with her music, indiscriminately pleasing all. But the youth should not confuse the painted beds or melodious propagation with real beds, real propagation: the woman is not a fiction or a fantasy, receptive to his "Hope" or "Desire" (13)—his "Deceitful Hope, and vain Desire." But the speaker, like the rash youth, is having trouble seeing what is real: "Stella," after all, is not the woman's name. She is the speaker's creation. The reality is that her "charms," which "press on ev'ry sense" at the moment, cannot be totally framed or regulated because the speaker and the youth participate in their creation. And because Stella, the "real" Stella, cannot be possessed, the overwhelming hope and desire that she stirs up become dangerous, threatening to engulf the identity of the youth, who will become simply the one who hopes and desires, the victim of his own imagination.

Conclusion: Miss Carpenter must be contained and blanked out by the poem; women are dangerous.

Rather than give in to the illusory "regions of delight," Johnson calls in the pleasure police—"Truth," who will supposedly rein in "Stella, sprightly, fair, and young" by exposing the artificiality of her charms. Sensual indulgence, Johnson asserts, should be neutralized by "friendly contrariety," as reason cancels out passion. The act of removing "Miss Carpenter" from the poem, then, leaving an empty space, is simply the logical extension of Johnson's effort to frame, regulate, abstract, and oppose the passion of women. Since the youth cannot control his imagination and desire, losing his ability to tell truth from art, then Stella must restrain her art. To save his identity, the poem takes away hers.

Revision: Gay and Lesbian Criticism

Earlier I referred to Jonathan Culler's assertion that "feminist criticism" is "the name that should be applied to all criticism alert to the critical ramifications of sexual oppression" (56). Certainly the forms of "sexual oppression" and gender expression in our society are more varied than this chapter has acknowledged so far, and we might expand our consideration here to include gay and lesbian studies and queer theory, which have made impressive contributions to the study of literature in the past few decades.

If we consider my own draft above, it seems clear that I have made a revealing and unwarranted assumption: the "rash youth," I have taken for granted, is a male. Specifically, I have assumed that the youth is a heterosexual male enamored of the presumably heterosexual Stella. But the sex of the youth, as you may have noticed, is actually nowhere indicated in the poem. If it is sexist to use "he" to refer to men *and* women (and it clearly is), then it's similarly heterosexist to assume that undesignated romantic or sexual relationships always refer to heterosexual couples, isn't it? Johnson doesn't make the sex of the rash youth clear, and he therefore opens up various other readings. Consider for a moment how the possibility that the youth is female might alter or further expand our reading of the poem.

For instance: the poem's caution against "pleasure" might immediately take on a different hue, for the "dang'rous hour" might be the one in which the youth is tempted to fall in love with another woman. And the odd injunction, "think not . . . / The nymph fictitious, as the flow'r" makes considerable sense, as the speaker warns the youth not to imagine that the nymph would be receptive to a lesbian encounter; or (alternatively) the speaker warns the youth not to imagine that the nymph is actually a man. The nymph is not "fictitious"; she is only what she appears to be, and falling in love with her would be disastrous for the female "youth," lesbian or not. Even though "charms thus press on ev'ry sense," the youth is being advised to resist these "New chains."

More specific is the warning to "shun, rash youth, the gay alcove, / Nor tempt the snares of wily love." An alcove is "a small, recessed section of a room, a nook" (*Webster's*)—or in other words, a closet. If "gay" had meant "homosexual" in Johnson's day (it apparently did not), then avoid "the gay alcove" would mean shun "the gay closet"—avoid being a hidden homosexual. For modern readers, "gay alcove" does suggest such a meaning, which it is difficult (for some readers anyway) to erase from the poem. Further, it would be difficult to say with certainty that "gay alcove" could not possibly have suggested to Johnson, extremely sensitive to connotations, the great lexicographer, something of its future meaning. Douglas Atkins in fact provides such an anachronistic reading of "gay" in Alexander Pope's poetry (see Atkins 124). This kind of emphasis upon the reader's response, rather than the author's assumed or even stated intention, enables gay and lesbian critics to construct illuminating and controversial readings. Barbara Smith, for instance, has argued in a pioneering essay that Toni Morrison's *Sula* (1973) champions the same-sex relationship between Nel and Sula and denigrates heterosexual marriage—a reading that Morrison herself has rejected. By its very name, queer theory strives to upset the sexual status quo, with critics such as Judith Butler, Alan Sinfield, and Eve Kosofsky Sedgwick challenging the simple division of human beings into homosexual and heterosexual, and thereby promoting a multi-faceted attack on homophobia.

Returning to Johnson's poem, such an anti-homophobic stance might suggest that "wily love" covertly refers to the danger of the "snares" of lesbianism, since "wily" has the same root word, *wigle* (Old English), as "witch." At least, we can now see better the point of the poem's conclusion, advocating "diff'rent notes," "friendly contrariety," and "well-accorded strife": Johnson's heterosexism urges us to endorse "difference" in love, attacking (in rather cloaked terms) same-sex love, which belongs in a closet we shouldn't enter.

The reading I have sketched here is obviously only one possibility—a rather daring one, in fact. I can also see an entirely different reading in which the youth is a gay man, and "shun the gay alcove" means "stay out of the closet; accept your sexuality."

Feminist, post-feminist, and queer theory approaches have much in common, as I have suggested. Their shared aim is to expose stereotypes and fight prejudice, dismantling oppressive ideas of two natural sexes or genders, uniformly opposed and attracted. The question whether homosexuality represents a choice or a destiny, a matter of preference or biology, becomes finally irrelevant to the more fundamental question of freedom and tolerance.

PRACTICING FEMINIST, POST-FEMINIST, AND QUEER THEORY CRITICISM

I hope at this point you have some idea of the way these approaches can make writing about literature more interesting and revealing. More important, I hope you can see how doing this kind of criticism involves you in an important exploration of our culture and your own principles. After this political criticism, it is especially difficult to say that the study of literature has no real relation to our lives. Literature is a particularly revealing and influential part of the myriad culture that surrounds and shapes (with or without our compliance or resistance) you and me. Literary criticism can help us see that and perhaps do something about it.

As I've suggested above, feminist criticism can be applied (at least in theory) to any work—including not just "great" novels or poems or plays, but also television shows, movies, detective stories, science fiction, advertisements, greeting card verse, bumper stickers, whatever. To get you started, I've provided below two well-known poems and an intriguing short story by a modern master. All respond richly, I think, to these perspectives, and I offer some questions after each one that I hope will stimulate your thinking.

Shall I Compare Thee to a Summer's Day?
William Shakespeare

Shall I compare thee to a summer's day?
Thou art more lovely and more temperate.
Rough winds do shake the darling buds of May,
And summer's lease hath all too short a date.
Sometimes too hot the eye of heaven shines,   5
And often is his gold complexion dimmed;
And every fair from fair sometimes declines,
By chance, or nature's changing course, untrimmed.
But thy eternal summer shall not fade,
Nor lose possession of that fair thou ow'st;   10
Nor shall death brag thou wand'rest in his shade,
When in eternal lines to time thou grow'st.
    So long as men can breathe or eyes can see,
    So long lives this, and this gives life to thee.

(1609)

QUESTIONS

1. The poem aims to be flattering, it seems clear, but what is the basis of its flattery? That is, what does the speaker value?

2. It is usually assumed that this poem is addressed to a woman. Is there any support for this supposition in the poem itself? What is the sex of the speaker of the poem? Do

these questions alter your perception of the poem or open up alternative readings?

3. If the loved one is a woman, how does this poem reinforce conventional ideas about aging and beauty? How is a person not like a summer's day?

4. How comforting would the final couplet be to the person addressed? What is the source of the loved one's immortality? Who has the power? How does the poem reinforce this power?

My Life had stood—a Loaded Gun
Emily Dickinson

My Life had stood—a Loaded Gun—
In Corners—till a Day
The Owner passed—identified—
And carried Me away—

And now We roam in Sovreign Woods—   5
And now We hunt the Doe—
And every time I speak for Him—
The Mountains straight reply—
And do I smile, such cordial light
Upon the Valley glow—   10
It is as a Vesuvian face
Had let its pleasure through—

And when at Night—Our good Day done—
I guard My Master's Head—
'Tis better than the Eider-Duck's   15
Deep Pillow—to have shared—

To foe of His—I'm deadly foe—
None stir the second time—
On whom I lay a Yellow Eye—
Or an emphatic Thumb—   20

Though I than He—may longer live
He longer must—than I—
For I have had the power to kill,
Without—the power to die—

(1863?)

QUESTIONS

1. What is "Vesuvian"? (You'll find a dictionary helpful.) What is an "Eider-Duck"? What is the "Yellow Eye"? What do you think the "emphatic Thumb" might be?

2. Assuming the speaker is female, what is the significance of comparing her life to a loaded gun? How does she view herself? Does the speaker have any autonomy or independence?

3. What is implied about the relationship of men to women? Who has the power? What kind of power?

4. What is the source of the speaker's pleasure, do you think?

5. How would the poem change if the speaker were assumed to be male? How would the central metaphor, for instance, be affected?

6. How does the final stanza reinforce conventional or archaic ideas about women and their relationship to men?

7. Does the speaker have any autonomy or independence?

Say Yes

Tobias Wolff

They were doing the dishes, his wife washing while he dried. He'd washed the night before. Unlike most men he knew, he really pitched in on the housework. A few months earlier he'd overheard a friend of his wife's congratulate her on having such a considerate husband, and he thought, *I try.* Helping out with the dishes was a way he had of showing how considerate he was.

They talked about different things and somehow got on the subject of whether white people should marry black people. He said that all things considered, he thought it was a bad idea.

"Why?" she asked.

Sometimes his wife got this look where she pinched her brows together and bit her lower lip and stared down at something. When he saw her like this he knew he should keep his mouth shut, but he never did. Actually it made him talk more. She had that look now.

"Why?" she asked again, and stood there with her hand inside a bowl, not washing it but just holding it above the water.

"Listen," he said, "I went to school with blacks, and I've worked with blacks and lived on the same street with blacks, and we've always gotten along just fine. I don't need you coming along now and implying that I'm a racist."

"I didn't imply anything," she said, and began washing the bowl again, turning it around in her hand as though she were shaping it. "I just don't see what's wrong with a white person marrying a black person, that's all."

"They don't come from the same culture as we do. Listen to them sometime—they even have their own language. That's okay with me, I *like* hearing them talk"—he did; for some reason it always made him feel happy—"but it's different. A person from their culture and a person from our culture could never really *know* each other."

"Like you know me?" his wife asked.

"Yes. Like I know you."

"But if they love each other," she said. She was washing faster now, not looking at him.

Oh boy, he thought. He said, "Don't take my word for it. Look at the statistics. Most of those marriages break up."

"Statistics." She was piling dishes on the drainboard at a terrific rate, just swiping at them with the cloth. Many of them were greasy, and there were flecks of food between the times of the forks. "All right," she said, "what about foreigners? I suppose you think the same thing about two foreigners getting married."

"Yes," he said, "as a matter of fact I do. How can you understand someone who comes from a completely different background?"

"Different," said his wife. "Not the same, like us."

"Yes, different," he snapped, angry with her for resorting to this trick of repeating his words so that they sounded crass, or hypocritical. "These are dirty," he said, and dumped all the silverware back into the sink.

The water had gone flat and gray. She stared down at it, her lips pressed tight together, then plunged her hands under the surface. "Oh!" she cried, and jumped back. She took her right hand by the wrist and held it up. Her thumb was bleeding.

"Ann, don't move," he said. "Stay right there." He ran upstairs to the bathroom and rummaged in the medicine chest for alcohol, cotton, and a Band-Aid. When he came back down she was leaning against the refrigerator with her eyes closed, still holding her hand. He took the hand and dabbed at her thumb with the cotton. The bleeding had stopped. He squeezed it to see how deep the wound was and a single drop of blood welled up, trembling and bright, and fell to the floor. Over the thumb she stared at him accusingly. "It's shallow," he said. "Tomorrow you won't even know it's there." He hoped that she appreciated how quickly he had come to her aid. He'd acted out of concern for her, with no thought of getting anything in return, but now the thought occurred to him that it would be a nice gesture on her part not to start up that conversation again, as he was tired of it. "I'll finish up here," he said. "You go and relax."

"That's okay," she said. "I'll dry."

He began to wash the silverware again, giving a lot of attention to the forks.

"So," she said, "you wouldn't have married me if I'd been black."

"For Christ's sake, Ann!"

"Well, that's what you said, didn't you?"

"No, I did not. The whole question is ridiculous. If you had been black we probably wouldn't even have met. You would have had your friends and I would have had mine. The only black girl I ever really knew was my partner in the debating club, and I was already going out with you by then."

"But if we had met, and I'd been black?"

"Then you probably would have been going out with a black guy." He picked up the rinsing nozzle and sprayed the silverware. The water was so hot that the metal darkened to pale blue, then turned silver again.

"Let's say I wasn't," she said. "Let's say I am black and unattached and we meet and fall in love."

He glanced over at her. She was watching him and her eyes were bright. "Look," he said, taking a reasonable tone, "this is stupid. If you were black you wouldn't be you." As he said this he realized it was absolutely true. There was no possible way of arguing with the fact that she would not be herself if she were black. So he said it again: "If you were black you wouldn't be you."

"I know," she said, "but let's just say."

He took a deep breath. He had won the argument but he still felt cornered. "Say what?" he asked.

"That I'm black, but still me, and we fall in love. Will you marry me?"

He thought about it.

"Well?" she said, and stepped close to him. Her eyes were even brighter. "Will you marry me?"

"I'm thinking," he said.

"You won't, I can tell. You're going to say no."

"Let's not move too fast on this," he said. "There are lots of things to consider. We don't want to do something we would regret for the rest of our lives."

"No more considering. Yes or no."

"Since you put it that way—"

"Yes or no."

"Jesus, Ann. All right. No."

She said, "Thank you," and walked from the kitchen into the living room. A moment later he heard her turning the pages of a magazine. He knew that she was too angry to be actually reading it, but she didn't snap through the pages the way he would have done. She turned them slowly, as if she were studying every word. She was demonstrating her indifference to him, and it had the effect he knew she wanted it to have. It hurt him.

He had no choice but to demonstrate his indifference to her. Quietly, thoroughly, he washed the rest of the dishes. Then he dried them and put them away. He wiped the counters and the stove and scoured the linoleum where the drop of blood had fallen. While he was at it, he decided, he might as well mop the whole floor. When he was done the kitchen looked new, the way it looked when they were first shown the house, before they had ever lived here.

He picked up the garbage pail and went outside. The night was clear and he could see a few stars to the west, where the lights of the town didn't blur them out. On El Camino the traffic was steady and light, peaceful as a river. He felt ashamed that he had let his wife get him into a fight. In another thirty years or so they would both be dead. What would all that stuff matter then? He thought of the years they had spent together, and how close they were, and how well they knew each other, and his throat tightened so that he could hardly breathe. His face and neck began to tingle. Warmth flooded his chest. He stood there for a while, enjoying these sensations, then picked up the pail and went out the back gate.

The two mutts from down the street had pulled over the garbage can again. One of them was rolling around on his back and the other had something in her mouth. Growling, she tossed it into the air, leaped up and caught it, growled again and whipped her head from side to side. When they saw him coming they trotted away with short, mincing steps. Normally he would heave rocks at them, but this time he let them go.

The house was dark when he came back inside. She was in the bathroom. He stood outside the door and called her name. He heard bottles clinking, but she didn't answer him. "Ann, I'm really sorry," he said. "I'll make it up to you, I promise."

"How?" she asked.

He wasn't expecting this. But from a sound in her voice, a level and definite note that was strange to him, he knew that he had to come up with the right answer. He leaned against the door. "I'll marry you," he whispered.

"We'll see," she said. "Go on to bed. I'll be out in a minute."

He undressed and got under the covers. Finally he heard the bathroom door open and close.

"Turn off the light," she said from the hallway.

"What?"

"Turn off the light."

He reached over and pulled the chain on the bedside lamp. The room went dark. "All right," he said. He lay there, but nothing happened. "All right," he said again. Then he heard a movement across the room. He sat up, but he couldn't see a thing. The room was silent. His heart pounded the way it had on their first night together, the way it still did when he woke at a noise in the darkness and waited to hear it again—the sound of someone moving through the house, a stranger.

[1985]

QUESTIONS

1. Explain the story's last sentence. Why does it end with the word "stranger"?

2. Why does Ann pursue this question? Did the husband come up with the right answer? Explain. Why does Ann ask her husband to turn off the light?

3. Is the husband a sexist? A racist? How would you describe him? How does Wolff want us to see him? How might this story affect a reader opposed to interracial marriage?

4. How do the small details of washing the dishes contribute to the story? Consider, for instance, the still-greasy dishes, the color of the washing water, the injury to Ann. Consider especially the husband's decision to mop, and the way he describes the floor.

Useful Terms for Political Criticism

Canon: The canon is that group of works that are usually reprinted, read, assigned, written about, and taken most seriously. Feminist criticism has been particularly effective in arguing that some works are included and others ignored on largely political grounds. Historically, women as a rule have had few opportunities to write; and when they have somehow managed to produce works of merit, these often have not been appreciated or understood (some women writers have adopted male pseudonyms in order to get a fair reading). Critics have similarly pressed to open the canon to African American, American Indian, and other neglected writers.

Constructed: This term is particularly powerful because it reminds us that any representation of a particular ethnic or racial or sexual group is something that is made up. It is not inevitable, nor does it fully (or even partially) depict reality. Our notions, in other words, of women, or African Americans, or American Indians, or gay men, or any other segment of society are just that: our notions.

Double-voiced: A member of an oppressed group, attempting to speak to and through the dominant culture, faces a tricky situation: how to speak one's mind without being silenced? One strategy is to write with two voices, saying what can be taken on the surface in a nonthreatening way, and on a deeper level in a subversive or challenging way. Because the various strands of political criticism often look at the way an oppressed group represents itself in a text, teasing out a text's double-voicing has been a recurrent critical activity.

Exclusion: What we value as great literature depends on what values we bring to our reading. Since white European males have dominated the worlds of publishing and criticism, it is not surprising that white European males have dominated the canon of literature. Some works may have been excluded from study because of the status of their authors; others may have been excluded because their virtues are not appreciated by established literary values.

Gender: "Gender" refers to the cultural aspects of sexuality. In other words, gender includes not just biological factors, but also psychological and social factors as well. We are still trying to discover just how much of "maleness" and "femaleness" can be attributed to biology, and how much to other factors. It seems clear that gender is not entirely constructed by cultural influences, that there are some differences between the sexes (surprise!). But the wide range of variation within "male" and "female" makes it difficult to say definitively what those differences always are, and thus how "gender" (the construction of male and female) relates to "sex" (the biological status).

Marxist: Because Marx considered issues of economy and class to be fundamental, shaping everything, literary criticism that focuses on economy and class is often termed "Marxist," even when the critic does not embrace the same principles as Karl Marx. This way of reading, attaching primary importance to the material sources of a work in class and money, is also sometimes called "materialist," especially when the physical conditions and circumstances are the focus.

Materialist: See *Marxist.*

Patriarchy: Literally, "father-ruled," the term points to the superior status of men within a culture. The opposite term, "matriarchy," refers to a culture in which women are superior.

Sex: See *Gender.*

Sexist: Assuming that someone has certain characteristics because of his or her sex is sexist. Usually, the term is used to describe pejorative characterizations of women as a group, or of individual women as representative types of that group.

Works Cited: Feminist Criticism, Post-Feminism, and Queer Theory

Astell, Mary. *A Serious Proposal to the Ladies.* London, 1692. Excerpt (with omissions) rpt. in *The Norton Anthology of Literature by Women.* Ed. Sandra Gilbert and Susan Gubar. New York: Norton, 1985. 113–17.

Atkins, Douglas. *Reading Deconstruction, Deconstructive Reading.* Lexington: UP of Kentucky, 1983.

Brooks, Ann. *Post-feminisms: Feminism, Cultural Theory, and Cultural Forms.* London: Routledge, 1997.

Butler, Judith. *Bodies That Matter: On the Discursive Limits of Sex.* London: Routledge, 1993.

———. *Gender Trouble.* London: Routledge, 1990.

Culler, Jonathan. "Reading as a Woman." In *On Deconstruction: Theory and Criticism after Structuralism.* Ithaca, NY: Cornell UP, 1982. 43–64.

Davis, Robert Con. "The Sexual Dialectic." In *Contemporary Literary Criticism.* Ed. Robert Con Davis. New York: Longman, 1986. 161–65.

de Beauvoir, Simone. *The Second Sex*. Trans. H. M. Parshley. New York: Vintage, 1974. Trans. of *Le deuxieme sexe*. 2 vols. Paris: Gallimard, 1949.

Ellman, Mary. *Thinking About Women*. New York: Harcourt, 1968.

Gilbert, Sandra, and Susan Gubar. *The Madwoman in the Attic*. New Haven, CT: Yale UP, 1979.

Hitchens, Christopher. *Unacknowledged Legislators*. London: Verso, 2000.

Johnson, Barbara. *A World of Difference*. Baltimore: Johns Hopkins UP, 1987.

Laquer, Thomas. *Making Sex: Body and Gender from the Greeks to Freud*. Cambridge: Harvard UP, 1992.

Ruthven, K. K. *Feminist Literary Studies: An Introduction*. Cambridge: Cambridge UP, 1984.

Sedgwick, Eve Kosofsky. *Tendencies*. Durham: Duke UP, 1993.

Showalter, Elaine. *A Literature of Their Own: British Women Novelists from Bronte to Lessing*. Princeton: Princeton UP, 1977.

Sinfield, Alan. *Cultural Politics—Queer Reading*. Philadelphia: U of Pennsylvania P, 1994.

Smith, Barbara. *Toward a Black Feminist Criticism*. New York: Out and Out Press, 1977.

Torsney, Cheryl. "The Critical Quilt: Alternative Authority in Feminist Criticism." In *Contemporary Literary Theory*. Ed. G. Douglas Atkins and Laura Morrow. Amherst: U of Massachusetts P, 1989. 180–99.

Woolf, Virginia. *A Room of One's Own*. 1929; New York: Harcourt, 1981.

Recommended Further Reading:
Feminist Criticism, Post-Feminism, and Queer Theory

Crewe, Louie, and Rictor Norton. "The Homophobic Imagination: An Editorial." *College English* 36 (1974): 272–90. A pioneering essay, helping to open the door for gay and lesbian studies.

Donadey, Alice, with Françoise Lionnet. "Feminisms, Genders, Sexualities." In *Introduction to Scholarship in Modern Languages and Literatures*. Ed. Joseph Gibaldi. 3rd ed. New York: Modern Language Association, 2007. 225–44. A standard introduction.

Eagleton, Mary, ed. *Feminist Literary Criticism*. London: Longman, 1991. An appealing collection for further study because essays offering opposing views are paired.

Gamble, Sarah. *The Routledge Companion to Feminism and Postfeminism*. London: Routledge, 2001. Fifteen authoritative essays by various experts on everything from "Second Wave Feminism" to "Feminism and Film."

Gilbert, Sandra, and Susan Gubar. *No Man's Land: The Place of the Woman Writer in The Twentieth Century*. New Haven: Yale UP, 1988. By the authors of the landmark *Madwoman in the Attic*. Includes an important chapter on gay criticism.

Jehlen, Myra. "Gender." *Critical Terms for Literary Study.* Ed. Frank
    Lentricchia and Thomas McLaughlin. Chicago: Chicago UP, 1990.
    An excellent far-ranging essay, unfolding usefully the relationships
    between "gender" and "sex."
Phoca, Sophia, and Rebecca Wright. *Introducing Postfeminism.* New York:
    Totem Books, 1999. An entertaining and engaging illustrated intro-
    duction.
Queertheory.com. Ed. Danne Polk. 2003. Erraticimpact.com. July 30, 2007
    <http://www.queertheory.com/. A plethora of resources, with pages
    and many links devoted to literary topics.
Sedgwick, Eve Kosovsky. *Epistemology of the Closet.* London: Harvester,
    1991. An engaging book, important in establishing gay and lesbian
    criticism.
Smith, Barbara. "Toward Black Feminist Criticism." In *New Feminist
    Criticism.* Ed. Elaine Showalter. New York: Pantheon, 1985. An impor-
    tant perspective, lucidly presented.
Woods, Gregory. *A History of Gay Literature: The Male Tradition.* New
    Haven: Yale, 1999. A fascinating history.

CHAPTER

Investigating the Work

Research and Documentation

> But the whole thing, after all, may
> be put very simply. I believe that
> it is better to tell the truth than to
> lie. I believe that it is better to be
> free than to be a slave. And I
> believe that it is better to know
> than to be ignorant.
>
> —H. L. Mencken

THE PURPOSE OF RESEARCH

You are free to gather information and opinion from all over the planet. You are free to enter—virtually or actually—thousands of libraries, seeking the truth about whatever you wish, dispelling the mists and fogs of ignorance. In the history of civilization, at no time or place have so many people had such a freedom and privilege. By the same token, however, it has probably never been easier to acquire so much misinformation and deception. How should you identify reliable sources of information? And how should you use them to enrich and support your own writing?

This chapter offers some guidance on what to do whenever you're asked (or allowed) to use secondary sources in writing about literature. Oftentimes teachers in writing-about-literature classes want students to apply only their own insight and creativity or to use only resources that the teacher has provided. Learning

267

how to think about and engage with a literary text on your own, without guidance or influence, stretches your mind and imagination. And with some critical orientations (such as New Criticism, deconstruction, reader response), secondary sources are likely to be less important; but with other stances (new historicism, feminist criticism, African-American criticism), resources beyond the text itself are more likely to be crucial, and may themselves become part of your focus as secondary and primary sources tend to merge. So, when you're given a writing assignment, you need to determine what role research is supposed to play: Is it required, encouraged, allowed, discouraged, or prohibited? If research is involved, how are you supposed to use it? Are you going to argue against someone else's reading, adjusting it slightly or rejecting it? Pushing back against another reading is a good way to explore a literary text and brainstorm your own reading. For example, if readers have assumed that John Milton would have intended in *Paradise Lost* to make Satan unattractive, but just didn't quite pull it off, what if you argued the opposite—that Satan is supposed to be attractive, beguiling, tempting, and that's how he fooled Adam and Eve, just as he fools us in Milton's poem? That's the simple and stunning move that Stanley Fish makes in *Surprised by Sin*, a landmark work of literary criticism, showing us how readers repeat the fall of Adam and Eve.

Besides simply testing the established positions and assumptions of other readers, what else can you do with the materials you find? That depends, of course, on what you've been asked to do, and the kinds of materials you uncover. You might relate some readings to others, giving your reader a sense of how literary criticism has dealt with a work or group of works. You might take another reader's interpretation one step further, adding some insight of your own, or simply confirm another person's interpretation, showing why this reading and not that one works best. You might do research on an author's life, or time, or other works, or works by other authors, and say something helpful or appreciative or corrective or negative. You might use the interpretations of previous critics to argue for some bias or blindness in the readers of a particular text. What you can do with your resources in other words is limited only by your assignment and your imagination, and I hope you can see in the preceding chapters how an awareness of different theoretical stances might be valuable. But it certainly can be pretty intimidating to be told that you are supposed to be creative, to use your resources to do "original" interpretive work.

Is it really reasonable to expect students at an introductory level to make sense of professional scholarship, in literary criticism and other fields, and to say something new about great literary works?

You may not be able to produce publishable criticism—although some undergraduates have, and an increasing number of journals are devoted in fact to publishing undergraduate research (for opportunities, see the Council on Undergraduate Research's website, at www.cur.org). You certainly can come to your own original insights and conclusions, with or without scholarly resources, simply because you are a singular individual. And you can make more sense out of the scholarship of various fields than you might imagine—and your comprehension will only get better as you swim in the academic ocean longer.

Academic scholarship is often described not as swimming, however, but as a conversation, which sounds friendly and inviting, but as a student in an introductory course, you may quite reasonably find that this conversation is very difficult to comprehend, let alone enter. As Jeanne Martinet's best-selling book *The Art of Mingling* suggests, making conversation in real life is tough enough. In this case, you're arriving at a party that has been going on for a long time, and people seem to be talking about things that have been their passions for years, and they've even evolved shorthand ways of talking and protocols of etiquette that you know little or nothing about. It's not necessarily a comfortable feeling, and we ought to acknowledge that.

But don't leave! To be sure you may not understand everything in some scholarly works, and in others you may not understand much of anything. But I want to suggest first that you may well be surprised to see how much you do understand in many publications, and the sheer pleasure of learning new things is one important purpose of doing research. Here for instance is the opening of an essay from a very prestigious journal, the leading scholarly journal in its field, *Eighteenth-Century Studies;* the essay is entitled "'A Conviction of the Reality of Things': Material Culture, North American Indians, and Empire in Eighteenth-Century Britain":

> In 1762 a Cherokee embassy arrived in London to solidify a shaky peace with Britain following nearly three years of brutal, costly, and mostly fruitless war. Indian visits were not new, but the public response to these Cherokee visitors was noticeably different. As in earlier instances, Londoners flocked to catch a glimpse of the foreigners, and printers flooded the market with newspaper articles, portraits, and chapbooks, but the

> tone of the public response was remarkably more focused on the "reality of things" than it had been during the last popularly celebrated Indian embassy, the 1710 Iroquois visit. (29)

These sentences, written by Troy Bickham, published in 2005, are not hard to follow (if you are able to follow this one), and the subject matter is intriguing: Did you know that Cherokee Indians were in London in 1762, and this wasn't the first time either that Native Americans had crossed the Atlantic? The essay is relatively easy to comprehend throughout and contains lots of information about how the Indians and their possessions were depicted and perceived, and how that representation influenced the English notion of "empire." This essay, you may be thinking, sounds like an example of postcolonial criticism, and this tentative framework will also help you to know what to expect and how to make sense of the essay.

You might have been led to this essay because you are working on the representation of American Indians in early American literature, or perhaps you are thinking about how African Americans were viewed in the eighteenth century, and you're wondering if the treatment of Native Americans is similar or different or somehow instructive. In fact, in a moment we'll talk about how to find research relevant to your chosen topic, but let's look at another essay, the next article in this same journal, "Queer Gardens: Mary Delany's Flowers and Friendships" by Lisa L. Moore, which begins with these sentences:

> Mary Granville Pendarves Delany, born in 1700 to an aristocratic family with court connections, is perhaps best known as a friend of Jonathan Swift's; Johnson called her "Dean Swift's Mrs. Delany." She is much more interesting than this nickname suggests. As an aristocratic lady of leisure nonetheless possessed of a punishing work ethic and a truly fearsome ambition, Delany left behind an impressive corpus of literary and visual art. (49)

Again, these sentences are not convoluted or mysterious, although the beginning of this essay may cause problems if you're unfamiliar with Jonathan Swift and Samuel Johnson, eighteenth-century British authors. So one piece of research may require you to consult other resources, but such reference volumes are easy to access (see the discussion of reference works below). It should be fairly obvious what Moore appears to be up to here: she is recovering the undeservedly neglected works of an eighteenth-century woman writer, an endeavor in the best tradition of early feminist scholarship. You might use Moore's discussion to see how Delany's work compares to more canonical figures, or you might want to offer your own interpretation of these works that have not been thoroughly worked over by generations of critics.

One more quick example: The first article in this scholarly journal is Carolyn Steedman's "Poetical Maids and Cooks Who Write," which begins with these sentences:

> The verse of two eighteenth-century plebian women—maidservants both of them—draws attention to recent developments in the linguistic, social, and economic theory by which modern historians interpret the lives and circumstances of people like them, living through England's transition to industrial capitalism, between about 1750 and 1820. Eighteenth-century scholars first compiled the histories of language and produced the linguistic theory that held sway until very recently. For the main part they understood writing—in the words of a twentieth-century inheritor of their work—as "a technology that restructures thought."

Steedman's first sentence is a bit long, but it's not hard to understand (although you might need to look up "plebian"), and it's packed with information. If you didn't know when England made the transition to industrial capitalism, now you do, at least according to her: it's 1750 to 1820, and that's the period that the essay will focus upon. Steedman, we see, is going to use the poetry of two ordinary women (the maids and cooks in her title, we presume) to highlight in some way our understanding of this period. Specifically, this sentence reveals that she is going to "draw attention" to "recent developments" in three kinds of theories—"linguistic, social, and economic." In other words, if you want know how our approaches to language, society, and economy in this period have changed, then this is the article for you. Steedman, you may notice, appears likely to be laying the groundwork for a feminist recovery of forgotten writing by women, and she is also clearly doing historical work on England and literary criticism.

Although the openings of these scholarly essays constitute a tiny sample, my point here will hold for the vast majority of what is published in established scholarly journals and in books by academic presses: you can understand and participate in the conversation. Some people won't make any sense at all, and for others the effort to understand may hardly seem worth it—but any conversation might suffer from those flaws. The purpose of research, then, is to allow you to engage more fully in the intellectual life. That includes, of course, completing successfully any writing assignments that call for research.

HOW TO DO RESEARCH

The Topic and the Task

The researcher, like the detective, may have only a vague idea of what he or she is looking for at the outset; indeed, figuring out what you're looking for is often at least as important and difficult as finding it. If you're responsible for inventing your own topic, then the usual textbook advice says to begin by choosing a broad topic that interests you and then narrowing it down. That advice sounds quite reasonable. But where does one find a list of broad topics from which to select an interesting one, and what if none of the broad topics that you can scare up seem stimulating?

From nothing you get nothing, as the old saying goes, and you may have to do some reading, thinking, talking, brainstorming, writing in order to generate a list of potential topics. Let's say you're trying to come up with some possible topics for a research paper in a Shakespeare course. You might go to the library and browse through some recent articles or books on Shakespeare; even an encyclopedia entry would probably give you some ideas. You might think about the class discussions and what you've found intriguing or puzzling. You might ask someone who's an expert for some suggestions—or even ask someone who's not an expert, "What would you like to know?" You might free-associate or freewrite, letting your brain roam around for ten minutes or so. If you're willing to supply *something,* virtually *anything* can lead you to some potential topics.

Don't believe it? You need go no further than what you're likely to be sitting on right now to find some possible topics. Are there any chairs in Shakespeare? (Can't think of any, but there are lots of thrones.) What makes a chair into a throne? (The king, or maybe the queen, is sitting on it, I suppose.) How many thrones appear in *Hamlet?* (Two? One for Claudius and one for Gertrude?) What do they signify? (Power, to Claudius; a lost father, to Hamlet; what, for Gertrude?) What should they look like on stage? Who gets to sit on them? By this point, lots of broad topics have occurred to me from these specific questions: the idea of "the king" in Shakespeare, the politics of succession to the throne in Shakespeare's time; the importance of furniture or other stage properties in Shakespeare; the importance of setting in general in Shakespeare, or even perhaps the significance of *sitting* in Shakespeare (is there any?) and many more. The idea here is that there really aren't any rules for coming up with topics. You can just start anywhere asking questions, and just keep on thinking until you hit something potentially interesting. (Really, *anything* can be interesting if you're sufficiently curious and imaginative.)

Once you have some broad topics to consider, there are really only two ways to narrow them: you can limit them in space or limit them in time. The conventional wisdom says, for instance, that you shouldn't try to write on "Religion in Shakespeare's England," which is far too broad. Rather than all of Shakespeare's England, why not focus on "Religion in *Hamlet*"? That's still a pretty large topic, so perhaps you should restrict yourself to "Church Doctrine in *Hamlet*." The topic still seems large, so perhaps you could focus on one aspect of church doctrine that you connect to one aspect of Shakespeare's play—maybe "Church Doctrine and Hamlet's Ghost."

You should limit your topic, in other words, to a subject that might not take years to research and several books to cover, that you might realistically be able to get control of in the time and space available. There are, however, some things to consider regarding this commonsensical "narrow-down" advice. For one thing, the advice appears to doom students to think always on a small scale. Someone who finds the admittedly expansive idea of "Religion in Shakespeare's England" truly fascinating may think that "Church Doctrine and Hamlet's Ghost" is too esoteric and constricting to have much appeal. Certainly we all need to be encouraged to think about large things and small, about both the meaning of life and the cost of cabbages. And yet, on the other hand, what student can hope to cover "Religion in Shakespeare's England" satisfactorily in a single research paper? Just imagine all the religious books published in Shakespeare's day, all the different churches and personalities in England at that time, the whole history of religion beforehand and its influence on Shakespeare's England.

It is often possible, however, to think about particular aspects of a large topic, to focus your vision rather than giving it up. You might consider a paper, for example, summarizing and evaluating some of the recent scholarship on religion in Shakespeare's England: your paper then focuses on part of the scholarship about a subject rather than the subject itself. You get to think about religion in Shakespeare's England, but in a manageable framework. Or you might remind yourself (and your reader) of the potential connection between your narrowed topic and the larger one—how church doctrine regarding ghosts, as it influences Shakespeare's *Hamlet*, may well be an important clue to religious beliefs in Shakespeare's day, for instance. Guidance from your instructor, always worth seeking, is especially valuable in such ambitious research projects.

The "narrow-down" advice, however you decide to implement it, may seem to require you to restrict your focus before you've done any research: quite simply, you may well not know *how* to narrow a topic most intelligently until you've researched the topic. To many people, "Religion in Shakespeare's England" certainly sounds like a fascinating topic, something it would be interesting to pursue. But if you try to narrow the topic down before you've learned anything about it, you might end up with, say, "Presbyterianism in *Hamlet*" or "Religion in Shakespeare's London." The first would appear to be impossible to research; the second doesn't reduce your task much at all.

This might look like a catch-22 situation—where you can't do research until you've narrowed the topic, and you can't narrow your topic until you've done research. In truth, however, you probably just need to do some basic fly-by research first—by reading an encyclopedia entry, a general overview, a portion of some important work; or by talking with an expert or at least someone familiar with the subject.

Part of this preliminary research should include investigating yourself, exploring what you already know and feel about the topic. This self-research needn't be anything elaborate: just sit down for ten minutes and write out whatever your mind can generate on the topic—questions, suspicions, concerns, observations, whatever. You may find, to your surprise, that you know more about the topic, or have more interest in it, or in certain aspects of it, than you might have imagined at the outset. Or you might find that you have even less interest or knowledge than you thought. In any event, this self-inventory likely will help to reveal what you need to do in order to make the topic your own—to get yourself intellectually engaged in the subject and to get the project to the launch pad.

If writing a research paper is like writing anything else, then it's usually messy, not proceeding in any simple linear fashion, but rather jumping all around from one task to another to three others all at once. You can't expect to go through a neat series of steps, choosing your topic, locating sources, collecting information, finding a thesis, making an outline, writing a draft, revising. You might actually start off with a fully formed thesis, before you've even done any research; or you might find, as you're making an outline, that you need more sources; or you might discover as you're revising that you're actually writing about the wrong topic; or whatever.

If you are given a specific assignment, as opposed to inventing your own project, then the process obviously begins with understanding what you're supposed to do. Imagine, for instance, that you've been given this assignment:

1. Using at least five different sources, provide information about Yeats's life around the time of "Sailing to Byzantium." Limit your paper to about eight pages, including documentation.

The topic here appears to be defined clearly enough: Yeats's life about the time of "Sailing." But is the researcher's *task* made clear? A topic designates an area for investigation, but the writer's task in a research paper involves more than just the topic: the writer needs to consider the audience, the materials, the *purpose* of the research.

Compare this assignment to the one above:

2. In a formal research paper addressing your classmates and other interested students, discuss how Yeats's life helps us to understand "Sailing to Byzantium." Use at least five different sources, including at least two biographies, one critical essay, and one other poem. Eight pages maximum.

In this assignment, the writer's task is delineated: the audience, the materials, and the purpose are laid out. Not only must the writer locate and organize and present relevant facts; this biographical information should be used to read the poem. The assignment also makes clear enough which critical stance the writer should think most immediately about adopting. The assignment doesn't say "perform an act of biographical criticism," but the student who understands the fundamentals of that critical approach should be sitting pretty.

Consider, by way of contrast, this assignment:

3. In a formal research paper addressing your classmates and other interested students, provide your own original close reading of Yeats's "Sailing to Byzantium." Compare/contrast your reading to at least three other interpretations. At least two of these other readings should be published in scholarly journals or books.

Or this one:

4. Identify two conflicting interpretations of Yeats's "Sailing to Byzantium" and attempt to provide biographical, historical, or textual support for both readings. Do not try to resolve the conflicts; instead, try to convince an audience of general readers that the two readings cannot be resolved.

Or this one:

5. Relying primarily on sources published in Yeats's lifetime, consider how Yeats's contemporaries might have responded to "Sailing to Byzantium." How might their responses differ from the response of a reader today?

As you can see, these last three assignments call for critical stances distinctively different from each other and from the previous assignments. To understand the task involved in an assignment, the researcher needs to understand the critical theory essentially involved: for number 3, for instance, the researcher needs to employ New Critical strategies; number 4 calls for a deconstructive attitude; number 5 invokes reader-response and historical approaches. Even if the assignment is one that you are giving to yourself (an open topic, in other words), it's very useful for you to consider the nature of the critical approach involved in the task. Otherwise, you won't know what to do with the materials you've so patiently captured.

Finding and Using Resources

Getting some idea what has already been said about a literary work does two good things. Ideas of your own may be sparked, and you can place your ideas within the context of what others have said.

The reader will be interested in knowing, for example, if your interpretation of a poem is totally different from what anyone has said, or if it is similar to the mainstream reading, or if it falls into one of several camps. By situating your insights in the context of other voices, you'll also be convincing your readers that you are informed and worth listening to.

So how do you find secondary sources to skim, sift, or devour? Let's talk about the different kinds available.

Background Sources: Encyclopedias, readers' guides, biographical dictionaries, and other such general references are available online and in a modern college library. There are many reasons to get out of your chair and actually move your body into a library (in addition to getting some exercise and perhaps meeting a friend). For instance:

- Reference librarians inhabit libraries, and they can be enormously helpful.
- Most materials in a library have been published by someone. While anyone (with basic skills and internet access) can put up a website, anyone cannot walk into a library and deposit materials for other people to consult. Not everything that is published and placed in a library is entirely trustworthy, but a reference volume published by Oxford University Press is likely to be more authoritative than "Mrs. Bondalay's 7th-Grade Guide to W. B. Yeats."
- Libraries are organized in a fairly logical way. If you find one book of interest, look on the shelf around it: there may be other useful volumes sitting there.
- Libraries have subscriptions to services and databases that are stunningly powerful, allowing you to locate all the essays published on W. B. Yeats in the major scholarly journals for the last, say, twenty-five years; or see all the articles in the *New York Times* that mention Yeats since 1935. If your library has a subscription to *Eighteenth-Century Collections Online,* to take one example, you can search for the appearance of a word, phrase, name, or idea in 150,000 printed works and editions from the eighteenth-century.

Most of us, however, are more comfortable in our chairs clicking a mouse. It's especially important to evaluate the reliability and quality of any Internet resources you locate. Fortunately, in most cases, that's easy enough. Obviously, the F. Scott Fitzgerald website at the University of South Carolina's Thomas Cooper Library is much more likely to have reliable information than Amelia Hooper's "I Love Scottie" webpage, produced for her eleventh-grade English class. The key question is this: does the person or group responsible for the website appear to have the necessary credentials and expertise?

Many libraries allow you to access some of their materials online, and some of the same services and databases that are available within the library may be available externally to students. The most reliable works on the Internet are those works that have in-print counter-parts. For instance, the *New Encyclopedia Britannica* is available online and on the shelf, and it offers authoritative background information and can guide you to other sources. Many other encyclopedias offer more specialized coverages, such as the *Encyclopedia of Asian History* or *The New Princeton Encyclopedia of Poetry and Poetics*. For literary research, *The Reader's Encyclopedia* is especially worth noting, since it covers characters, authors, books, and terms.

These encyclopedic works may include biographical entries, but there are also volumes devoted only to biography. The two most famous biographical references in English are the *Dictionary of National Biography* for Great Britain and the *Dictionary of American Biography* for the United States. The *Dictionary of Literary Biography*, or *DLB* as it's affectionately known, has numerous volumes devoted to particular biographical interests. Volume 67, for example, edited by Gregory Jay, has extended entries for twenty-seven *Modern American Critics Since 1955*. Volume 57, edited by William Thesing, covers *Victorian Prose Writers After 1867*. If there is a *DLB* volume rele-vant to your topic, which is likely, you'll most probably find a wealth of information; it's certainly worth checking. *The Atlantic Brief Lives* is a wonderful compendium of biographies of writers, artists, com-posers, written by a leading authority on each figure. Many rather specialized biographical sources exist—*Chicano Scholars and Writers*, for example. Again, a reference librarian can direct you.

Literary handbooks and literary histories can also provide valu-able background information. The standards: *The Oxford History of English Literature* (13 volumes), and Spillers's *Literary History of the United States* (2 volumes); Holman and Harmon's *Handbook to Literature*, or Roger Fowler's *Dictionary of Modern Critical Terms*, or *The Johns Hopkins Guide to Literary Theory and Criticism*. The *Oxford Companion* series features expert overviews on a wide range of subjects: *The Oxford Companion to English Literature*, *The Oxford*

Companion to American Literature, The Oxford Companion to Medicine (2 volumes), *The Oxford Companion to the Mind, The Oxford Companion to Philosophy*, and many more.

You don't want to cite such general sources in your paper usually: they're just part of your preliminary research, providing you with whatever is common knowledge. And as a rule, "common knowledge" does not require documentation, even if it's news to you, unless you use the words or phrasing of the original. If you do use the words, ideas, phrasing, structure of *any* source in your paper, then you must cite the source. When in doubt, of course, ask your teacher—or go ahead and provide the citation.

Bibliographies, Indexes, Catalogs: When you want to move beyond general background sources, bibliographies and indexes can tell you where to look. The *MLA Bibliography,* which is updated annually, is arguably the most important guide to literary scholarship, and the place I usually look first. In most university libraries, the *MLA Bibliography of Books and Articles* is available electronically, allowing you to search quickly and thoroughly for a particular author, work, subject, or combinations thereof. The *Reader's Guide to Periodical Literature* is another extremely useful resource, similar in scope to the MLA guide. By beginning with the most current year, and working backwards in these indexes, you can get a wealth of materials to consult. Usually you'll be able to tell from the title whether the citation will be relevant to your topic. You should also know that *The Essay and General Literature Index* has the particular virtue of including references to essays published in collections.

Reviews of books are often particularly useful, providing not only a brief summary of a book's contents, but also paths to other resources. To find book reviews, consult the *Index to Book Reviews in the Humanities,* the *Book Review Digest,* or the *Book Review Index.*

For references to criticism on poems or short fiction, consult *Poetry Explication: A Checklist of Interpretation since 1925 of British and American Poems Past and Present* and *Twentieth-Century Short Story Explication: Interpretations 1900–1975.* There are also bibliographies on particular subjects (science fiction, the medieval romance, prose fiction in seventeenth-century magazines). There is even (my favorite) a bibliography of bibliographies, edited by my colleague Trevor Howard-Hill. The publication dates of such bibliographies should be noted, since some will of course be more current than others.

Such guides and bibliographies are often convenient and thorough, but to find books on a particular subject, of course, you simply need access to your library's card catalogue and a good grasp of the alphabet. But if the library's holdings are listed online, then you can create your own starting bibliography simply by searching for an author, a text, or a subject. The Library of Congress has an incredibly useful (and busy) website, consulted by scholars and researchers around the world, in industry and academia. My own institution, the University of South Carolina, has a website that allows you to jump to the catalogue of the library's holdings, for instance; or you can go to the English department's home page and get information on the faculty's various research interests.

You can also consult specialized bibliographies. For a major author, it's likely that someone has published a bibliography devoted to that author and related matters. For Samuel Johnson, for instance, you could consult Clifford and Greene's *Samuel Johnson: A Survey and Bibliography of Critical Studies,* which has an opening essay discussing all the scholarship on Johnson up to 1970 and then lists hundreds and hundreds of books and articles under various headings, such as "General Comment on Johnson," "Johnson's Views and Attitudes on Various Subjects," and "Johnson's Prose Style." For scholarship on Johnson after 1970, you'd want to see Greene and Vance's *Bibliography of Johnsonian Studies, 1970–85.* These two volumes, the Clifford-Greene and the Greene-Vance bibliographies, would show up in a search of almost any library catalogue. For the years after 1985, no Johnsonian bibliography has yet been published—in the traditional sense of "published," anyway. But Professor Jack Lynch has created an online bibliography listing some 1600 items from 1986–1997 and allowing for one-word searches. Not all Internet resources for literary research will turn out to be as useful and authoritative as Lynch's Johnson site; but so long as you evaluate your sources critically, it's certainly worth the time and effort to see what is available.

Any proper library has a catalog of its holdings. If the library has an online catalog, it almost certainly also has a card catalog, and the physical catalog may contain some items that for one reason or another don't appear on the online catalog. In addition to books, organized by subject, a research library will have periodicals (journals, magazines), microforms (rolls or sheets of film with photographs of documents), newspapers, manuscripts (these will be in special collections or a rare books room), and even some audio and video resources.

Online Sources, Ethics, Plagiarism: If your library has access to a search service called EBSCO, to take one example, you can identify relevant articles in over 3100 periodicals (articles in about 1500 of these can be downloaded or e-mailed to you). Of course you know about search engines, like Google, which may turn up valuable sources, but are more likely to unearth questionable things. Google does have a Google Scholar engine, which can be very handy; and the Google corporation is engaged in digitizing whole libraries, which will make many more books available and searchable. In addition to search engines that are freely available, there are searches and databases available only by subscription, such as DIA-LOG, Nexis/Lexis, or eTC. For literary criticism, databases such as JSTOR and Project MUSE have gathered a wealth of searchable scholarly essays. Thousands of websites, mounted by libraries, organizations, and individuals, provide access to diverse materials. The website for the library at the University of California at Berkeley, for instance, contains over 300,000 references to critical and industry articles on films. There are also interest groups, newsgroups, websites, electronic mailing lists, chat rooms, and more—all of which may have interesting and useful information, but the risk of misinformation increases as you move down the intellectual food chain from scholarly books and journals to personal websites: a university-press book is probably more reliable than a privately printed one; a scholarly journal article probably has more clout than a piece in a newspaper or popular magazine, and so forth.

You won't need to consult all or even most of the background sources or indexes mentioned or alluded to here, of course. When you locate just one good source, it will likely cite other good sources, which will all cite more useful sources, and so forth. Most research projects seem to start slowly but pick up momentum rather quickly. With only a little effort, you'll have no trouble finding more material than you can use for almost any topic. And more references than you can use, in this case, is usually the right amount you need, because some sources may not be available (checked out, lost, otherwise unavailable); others may be redundant, incomprehensible, or off-target. Thus, it's absolutely crucial if you're doing research that you get into the library as soon as possible. Some students put off going to the library because they're afraid they'll get lost or won't know how to find things. But that's the whole point: of course you'll get lost, and of course you don't know how to find everything. I've spent many hours prowling the stacks of many libraries, and I've yet to see the bleached bones of a lost student. You will get lost, but you'll find your way around eventually, and you'll run into who-knows-what adventures in the meantime; you won't know where things are, but you'll find them, if they can be found.

As you find resources, you must record some essential information: the author, the title, publisher, place of publication, date, and the page numbers (if appropriate). You'll need this information later if you cite the work, thereby allowing other people to check your research for themselves and also to pursue their own research.

Jay, Gregory.

America the Scrivener. Ithaca, NY: Cornell UP, 1990.

For a journal article, list the author, title, name of the journal, date of publication, volume number and page numbers. Like this:

Thesing, William.

"The Inevitable Demise of Victorian Scholarship." *Victorian Studies* 87 (May 1997): 43–813.

For an Internet source, you should provide the editor or author of the site (if it's given); the title(s) of the site, project, database, and/or text; the date of the material on the site; the organization sponsoring the site (if given); the date you visited the site; and the address of the site.

Lynch, Jack. "A Bibliography of Johnsonian Studies, 1986–1997."
9 March 2005.
http://www.english.upenn.edu/~jlynch/Johnson/sjbib.html

It's important that you record this information accurately: you'll not only use it to find the resource but also to make your list of "Works Cited," the bibliography for your project.

As you begin to gather resources and make connections, it will be crucial to keep in mind that your research paper is not simply a string of quotations and paraphrases: it is an argument. It's easy enough for students, as their secondary resources pile up, to forget about their own essential role in writing the research paper. You've got all these interesting quotations and ideas, and it may come to seem that your job is simply to introduce them and bring them on stage. But for most research projects, you're more than the master of ceremonies: the critics and documents that you bring on stage are there to support and illuminate *your* discussion. In other words, for most projects, you need to evolve a thesis—an assertion, an idea, that can be stated as a sentence. It should be an original idea, not a mere echo of someone else's thinking (although you certainly may rely on others' ideas). A thesis should also be arguable—meaning that you are *able* to support it, or argue for it, with evidence, and also that you *need* to support it, or argue for it, because not everyone will immediately agree with your idea, without seeing your argument, that is. A thesis should also unify your materials, as the driving force behind your project. Once you have this thesis—an original and arguable assertion that pulls your material together—then you're ready to start drafting in earnest.

This point leads to some crucial questions: How does a research project become your property, your intellectual off-spring? And how do you make sure that your use of other sources is legal and ethical?

Let's start with the most brain-dead option. It is, as almost everyone knows, very easy to find websites that will sell you a research paper on virtually any topic. Students who procrastinate, or who fear they can't succeed on their own, might be tempted by these evil sirens, but it's an incredibly foolish thing to do. Not only are such students cheating themselves out of an education, they are also quite likely to be caught cheating, and the penalties will range from flunking the course to dismissal from school. Anyone considering submitting someone else's work as his or her own should know that 1) teachers can tell when the prose style isn't consistent with a student's other work; 2) it's often ridiculously easy to track where a plagiarized paper has come from, even without the subscription software dedicated to identifying plagiarism; and 3) although websites may promise to deliver a unique paper, they don't always do that—and who'd want to trust his or her future to people who are aiding and abetting intellectual thievery? You should vehemently discourage anyone you know who might consider "borrowing" someone else's work.

Since you're doing research to see what other people say, it might seem possible to borrow too much inadvertently. It's your responsibility to make sure that doesn't happen. Using the words or ideas of someone else without clearly acknowledging the source is plagiarism. Unintentional plagiarism is often hard to distinguish from the more deliberate brand: if the security guard finds a sirloin roast in your coat pocket, you may have difficulty proving that you didn't mean to steal it, that you put it there by accident, that it was just an innocent mistake. If you have someone else's words or ideas in your paper, then you've got the academic equivalent of a sirloin in your coat in the checkout line. Notice that you can't just put someone else's ideas into your own words, and call them your own. Let's focus for a moment on this issue and make sure that it's absolutely clear where the line is that you don't want to cross.

It's essential to keep in mind, as you're drafting, that your reader should be able to see instantly and unambiguously which ideas are yours and which ideas have some other source. Your reader, as we noted, is ultimately interested *in what you have to say*, not in how many quotations and references you can cut and paste together. So make sure that you give yourself appropriate credit. But also make sure that you give your supporting cast appropriate credit. Since the principles of documentation are fairly simple and straightforward, it's easy enough to avoid any potential problems. You do *not* need to identify a source for common knowledge— information that any informed person already knows or that is available in a number of sources. You also don't have to give anyone else credit for your own ideas and findings. So what does that leave that does require citation?

1. Direct quotations, where you use someone else's words. Put his or her words inside quotation marks, and make sure the page number and the source of the quotation are clear.

2. Ideas, insights, illustrations, lines of argument—*anything* that you take from someone else. You may summarize without quotation marks if the wording is your own, but be sure to identify what you're summarizing; you may not rely on anyone else's thinking without attribution.

3. Assistance from other people, including friends, teachers, experts. If you're talking about your paper and a friend offers an idea you can use, be sure to recognize the friend's contribution.

Occasionally, you may be unsure whether some information is common knowledge, or whether some insight is your own, or something you might have read late at night as you were dozing off. If you're in doubt, err on the side of giving credit. It's even possible to have a note like this one, which appears somewhere in the published works of Morse Peckham: "I regret to say that I am unable to identify the source of this information, but I believe that it was reputable."

To illustrate more specifically how to reference sources appropriately, let's look at some examples. First, imagine that you notice and copy a passage from pages 171–72 of a secondary source, Albert Ketcheman's *William Butler Yeats*. Here's the passage:

> And the poems, even the most crucial one, "Sailing to Byzantium," are clear enough. The reader's only real problem in that poem is to see why Byzantium itself was so attractive to Yeats.

And here's what your note might look like:

Clarity, attractiveness of Byzantium
    Ketcheman 171–72:
    "And the poems, even the most crucial one, 'Sailing to Byzantium,' are clear enough. The reader's only real problem in that poem is to see why Byzantium itself was so attractive to Yeats."

You also copy down another passage, this one from page 199 of Clark's *Yeats*, as your note indicates:

Clarity, beginning lament
    Clark 199:
    "The movement of 'Sailing to Byzantium' is quite clear, and so are its essential terms. The poem begins with the familiar lament for lost bodily vigor and sexuality, a regret not overcome by the compensating sense of increased wisdom, a Yeatsian obsession which, in the earlier fragment, is exceedingly blunt."

Now, imagine that you write the following sentence in a draft:

1. Some critics might think that "Sailing to Byzantium" is quite clear, but at least three terms in the poem are ambiguous.

The critical context is vaguely presented in your sentence: do critics actually think that, and who are they? It's also not entirely clear if the assertion of ambiguity is your own idea or a contradictory supplement to some critics' thinking. The reference isn't very fair or helpful.

So you revise the sentence, coming up with this more explicit statement:

2. Albert Ketcheman says "Sailing to Byzantium" is "clear enough" (171), and Justin Clark says its "movement" and "essential terms" are "quite clear" (199), but at least three terms in the poem are ambiguous.

This version is definitely better, but the significance of your assertion is still not directly stated. It's not really clear who says that three terms are ambiguous.

Here's another revision:

3. Typical opinions are offered by Ketcheman, who says "Sailing to Byzantium" is "clear enough" (171), and by Clark, who says its "movement" and "essential terms" are "quite clear" (199). I find, however, at least three terms that these critics explain in contradictory terms and which remain ambiguous and puzzling.

Now this is starting to sound good. In this version, both the critical context and your place within that context are made clear. There's no question who's saying what, and there's no question that you've got something interesting to add to the critical discussion.

In a writing-about-literature course, the format for documenting your research sources will most likely be the new Modern Language Association (or MLA) style, although *The Chicago Manual of Style* is also a popular guide. The *MLA Handbook for Writers of Research Papers* (6th edition, 2003), which should be available in any reference area and just about any bookstore, provides a clear and extremely thorough explanation of how to use the MLA style—including guidance on how to document Internet sources. But you'll need to check with your teacher—other styles of documentation are also available, each with its own advantages and admirers. The goal for all documentation styles is the same: to identify clearly the writer's sources. You can learn a great deal about documentation just by paying attention to how it is handled in your sources: notice how authors are quoted, how ideas are attributed, how works and writers are named and cited.

THE WRITING PROCESS: A SAMPLE RESEARCH PAPER

I think it would be useful now to trace in brief the process of writing a sample research paper. Here is the assignment:

In a research format, writing for your classmates and other interested readers, briefly discuss at least two different interpretations of Yeats's "Sailing to Byzantium" and compare these readings to your own.

And here is how one hypothetical student, Anna Olivia Williams, proceeded.

Getting Ideas

Anna immediately charges into the library and starts browsing through various sources, identified by looking in the *MLA Bibliography,* which happens to be online in her school's library. Skimming through the first four articles that look promising, Anna notices that Cleanth Brooks's study of this poem is often mentioned. So she locates *The Well-Wrought Urn* and makes a "Works Cited" entry for it in a computer file or on a notecard.

Brooks, Cleanth.

The Well-Wrought Urn. New York: Holt, 1947.

She then reads through the essay, making the following notes:

Brooks 178–91

The tension for Brooks:

nature vs art

becoming vs being

sensual vs intellectual

here vs Byzantium

aging vs timelessness

Anna doesn't put any quotation marks here because this set of oppositions is her own interpretation of Brooks's argument. She has noticed that he repeatedly identifies oppositions in the poem and so she lists them. Can you see these oppositions? In the first stanza, for instance, Yeats discusses the world of nature ("fish, flesh, or fowl," "sensual music"), and he concludes that those in the world of nature neglect art ("monuments of unaging intellect").

Anna puts the page numbers where this discussion occurs at the top of the card. This is a good idea because she might forget to put down the page number after she's made the note. Then she'd have to hunt around to find the material.

Brooks 188–89: "artifice" and unity
    "The word 'artifice' fits the prayer at one level after another; the fact that he is to be taken out of nature; that his body is to be an artifice hammered out of gold; that it will not age but will have the finality of a work of art."
    Brooks thus believes Yeats favors the latter items in the list of elements in tension.

You'll notice that Anna uses quotation marks for part of the note: these are Brooks's words. It's crucial to keep straight what is your summary of the criticism and what is quoted. Otherwise, you might mistakenly use the critic's phrasing, thinking it's your own. Anna has also put a tag word at the top to suggest what the note is about. As her notecards pile up, these tags will allow her to sort them and move them around more easily. As she understands how her paper is going to develop, she may add to or alter these tags.

Brooks 189: "artifice" and irony
    "But 'artifice' unquestionably carries an ironic qualification too. The prayer, for all its passion, is a modest one. He does not ask that he be gathered into the 'artifice of eternity.' The qualification does not turn the prayer into mockery, but it is all-important: it limits as well as defines the power of the sages to whom the poet appeals."

Brooks's focus on irony here should suggest that his stance is indeed New Critical.

Brooks 186–87: thesis
    "To which world is Yeats committed? Which does he choose?
    The question is idle—as idle as / the question which the earnest schoolmarm puts to the little girl reading for the first time 'L'Allegro—Il Penseroso': which does Milton really prefer, mirth or melancholy? . . .
    Yeats chooses both and neither."

On this card Anna has a slash after "as" to let her know where the page break comes in Brooks's essay. If she needs to quote only a part of this passage, she'll know which page(s) to cite. She has also left out material, indicated by the ellipsis.

Brooks's point here suggests the complexity of Yeats's poem, refusing easy categorization into one thing or the other.

> Brooks 189–90: irony of the golden bird—both natural and supernatural
> "The irony [of the poem] is directed, it seems to me, not at our yearning to transcend the world of nature, but at the human situation itself in which supernatural and natural are intermixed—the human situation which is inevitably caught between the claims of both natural and supernatural. The golden bird whose bodily form the speaker will take in Byzantium will be withdrawn from the flux of the world of becoming. But so withdrawn, it will sing of the world of becoming—'Of what is past, or passing, or to come.'"

Brooks's New Critical stance is clear here, as he finds irony, unity, complexity. Thus, using her notecards, Anna sketches out what she might say about Brooks:

Operating as a New Critic, Cleanth Brooks identifies a number of tensions in Yeats's poem—between nature and art, becoming and being, the sensual and intellectual, "here" and Byzantium, aging and timelessness (178–91). How Yeats manages to unify these tensions is epitomized for Brooks by the word "artifice" in the third stanza. The word suggests that Yeats's speaker will be taken out of nature (188–89), but it occurs in a phrase that ironically qualifies this suggestion: the speaker will become an "artifice of eternity," rather than genuinely a part of eternity (189). Thus, Brooks says, of the oppositions set up by the poem, Yeats "chooses both and neither" (187). The poem is unified by the idea that the golden bird, like "the human situation," is "inevitably caught between the claims of both natural and supernatural" (189–90).

You'll notice that Anna names the source, Brooks, and simply puts the page reference where the quotation or reference ends. She is following here the new MLA style of documentation. The Works Cited page, at the end of her essay, will give the reader the bibliographical information needed to track the source down.

Second Source   In the card catalogue, Anna comes across a work by Brenda Webster, *Yeats: A Psychoanalytic Study*—obviously a distinctive approach. Here are the notes she makes while reading Webster, which turns out to be a difficult work to understand:

Webster, Brenda.
    Yeats: A Psychoanalytic Study. New York: MacMillan, 1973.

Here are some of the few sentences Anna thinks she understands:

Webster 213–14: bird as defense
    "The bird functions as a defense against anxieties unconsciously raised by the poem—not just the fear of aging and thwarted sexuality . . . , but the overarching fear of a loss of integrity."

    Webster 214: Yeats's operation
    "Sailing" was written before Yeats had a "Steinach operation, which increased his sense of sexual vitality."

Anna makes a note to see what a Steinach operation is.

Webster 214: union with the mother
    "The old man's frustrated sexual desire is the visible strand of what we shall see is a submerged theme or fantasy of union with the mother." A few sentences later: "in the works by Yeats that embody incestuous fantasies, the hero is often symbolically castrated or mutilated by the mother figure before he can be loved. In 'Sailing' Yeats endows the aging process itself with the threatening qualities of a cruel mother. Now it is age that sexually frustrates the old man and threatens him with disintegration and loss of self."

Then she sketches out what she might say about Webster:

According to Brenda Webster, Yeats's speaker wants to become a golden bird as "a defense against anxieties unconsciously raised by the poem" (113). Yeats's fears included, Webster says, aging and thwarted sexuality; soon after the poem, Yeats would have a Steinach operation, increasing his sexual vitality (Webster 214). But the most important anxiety, Webster believes, was Yeats's fear of "a loss of integrity" (214). Yeats dreams of becoming a golden bird so that he might have an ageless body. But this desire is part of a deeper one: he wants to reunite with his mother, and removing his manhood by becoming a golden bird is, so Webster says, part of that process.

But I don't see how a golden bird can join with the mother any more easily than a grown man, or a wooden pig, or a crystal do-do bird.

Third Source   Anna's teacher has mentioned one source in class, "The Practice of Theory" by Lawrence Lipking. Anna gets this essay and finds (as we have seen above) that Lipking examines Yeats's poem from a deconstructive perspective in order to show what is wrong with deconstruction. For the essay itself she makes a card:

Lipking, Lawrence.
   "The Practice of Theory." In Literary Theories in Praxis. Ed. Shirley Staton. Philadelphia: U of Pennsylvania P, 1987. 426–40. Rpt. from Profession 83 (1983): 21–28.

Then for each point that she thinks she might use, Anna also makes a card:

Lipking 431: Singing—pro or con?
   Lipking asks why should soul "louder sing/ For every tatter in its mortal dress"? He sees two possibilities. (1) The soul is singing to distract itself from the tatters of its mortal dress (for example, sore throats, hemorrhoids, arthritis). (2) The soul is singing in celebration of its body falling apart because the tatters bring the soul closer to eternity and separation from the body. Lipking concludes there is no way to tell which of these meanings is right, and therefore "the line does not make sense" if by "sense" we mean that a statement cannot mean one thing and the opposite thing at the same time.

Lipking 431: singing school—yes or no?
   Lipking asks if there is a singing school. If "Nor is there singing school" means there isn't one, then how come the speaker wants some singing masters in the next verse? The lines are contradictory: the poem doesn't make sense.

> Lipking 432: Status of eternity?
> Lipking asks if the artifice of eternity is "something permanent (an eternal artifice) or something evanescent (an illusion without any substance)." He says he can't decide based on the poem.

> Lipking 432: "That"
> Lipking points to the uncertainty of the opening "That." Yeats himself, Lipking points out, said it "was the worst syntax he ever wrote."

> Lipking 432–33: the bird–obvious contradiction
> Lipking finds one contradiction in the poem "so important and obvious that it is noticed by a great many students, and even some critics." Namely, the speaker cannot claim he will "never take / My bodily form from any natural thing" because, Lipking says, "every bodily form must be taken from nature, whether the form of a bird or simply the golden form embodied by an artist."

At this point, Anna tries to write a quick summary of what she has learned. This step is useful but too often passed over; it allows you to work with your materials, to evolve your own ideas before you actually start trying to write the paper itself. Here is what Anna writes:

> In "The Practice of Theory" Lawrence Lipking simply says what nearly every student who has read Yeats's poem carefully thinks: the poem does not make sense. The reference of the opening "That" is never made clear, as Lipking says (432). Nor can the reader tell if there is a singing school or not: as Lipking notes, "Nor is there singing school" seems to say there is no singing school, but then the speaker immediately desires to have singing masters in the next verse (431). The lines are thus contradictory.
>
> Lipking also points to the uncertainty involved in the assertion that the soul should "louder sing / For every tatter in its mortal dress." Does this statement mean that the soul should sing to distract itself from the decay of the body, its "mortal dress"? Or does it mean that the soul should sing in celebration of its body falling apart, since such disintegration brings the soul closer to eternity and separation from the body? Lipking concludes there is no way to tell which of these meanings is right, and therefore "the line does not make sense" if by "sense" we mean that a statement cannot mean one thing and the opposite thing at the same

time (431). Likewise, Lipking notes that the speaker cannot carry out his declaration to "never take / My bodily form from any natural thing" because "every bodily form must be taken from nature, whether the form of a bird or simply the golden form embodied by an artist" (432–33).

In pointing out these problems in the poem, Lipking's point is not that Yeats's poem is a poor one. The problem, Lipking says, is that when we adopt a deconstructive stance, we are inevitably committed to seeing how a work fails to make sense. Language always, if we read closely enough, fails to make sense.

Organizing

At this point Anna determines she's got plenty of secondary sources to satisfy the assignment. Now she needs to work on her own reading. Her first reaction to "Sailing" was quite different from any of the critics she has read. She did not find the speaker of the poem to be appealing. Yeats, or his spokesman, strikes Anna as self-absorbed, fretful, whining, and even a bit pompous. She wonders about the implied attitude toward women in the poem. She decides that her view is so different that it should be interesting to her readers, and she determines after looking over the poem again that her reading can be supported. So she writes the following shaping draft of her reading:

1. I'd like to see what a feminist critic would do with this poem. Women appear only as the imaginary "ladies of Byzantium" who no doubt drop grapes and cherries into the mouths of the lords of Byzantium. Women are conspicuous by their absence. Yeats doesn't even consider whether "That" country, whatever it is, is a place for old women or even old people. It's just no country for old men. An "aged man" is "a paltry thing," but an aged woman apparently isn't worth considering.

2. Why is Yeats so self-absorbed and depressed that he desires the ridiculous transformation into a singing golden bird? (Is this the best paradise he can come up with?) Given three wishes, he wants to be a bird? And not even a real bird?

   Yeats frets because he is obsessed with aging. But what aspect of aging? Sex appeal, it seems. He focuses on "The young / In one another's arms," and the other images relate to sexuality: salmon struggling upstream to reproduce and die; mackerel crowded together to mate. The "birds in the trees" are linked in our culture to romance. The reference to "dying generations" compresses the problem: he is dying while generations continue to be produced.

3. When an older man today perceives his sexual appeal is waning, he might buy a Porsche, take Viagra, and chase younger women. Yeats's solution is even more desperate and absurd. He aims to do away with the physical altogether. Yeats changes sex into music: the transition is the reference to "sensual music." So he wants to leave the world of the sensual, passing from sensual music to music alone. As a golden bird, his sensual music will be outside nature. He will avoid the male horror of aging. Why can't our culture be more comfortable with life's natural processes?

Drafting

At this point Anna is ready to put it all together. With this much preparation, she simply needs to introduce the critical statements, refine them, and link them together. How can these statements be related?

She could simply describe how they relate to one another and contrast them to her own position. A more ambitious approach would be to present the other positions in some sort of sequence leading up to her ideas. What kind of sequence could there be? Brooks's New Critical reading sees some oppositions, and he argues that they are unified by the ironic status of the golden bird, both within and without nature. Lipking's deconstructive reading, however, refuses to allow such a resolution, identifying logical problems that cannot be explained away. And Webster's psychological study suggests why Yeats's logic should fail: he is attempting to deal with an impossible desire, the Oedipal impulse to rejoin his mother. Anna's point is a variation of Webster's position: the poem's problems do stem from Yeats's psychological distress, but that distress is not so weird as an Oedipal obsession. It is simply the fear of growing old and sexually unattractive.

After a draft or two and a close revision, the following paper emerges:

Anna Olivia Williams
Professor Callie Taylor
March 24, 2005

Five Views of Yeats's "Sailing to Byzantium"

W. B. Yeats's "Sailing to Byzantium," one of the most-read poems in the English language, is also one of the most challenging. Yeats scholars keep insisting that the poem is clear, yet various interpretations keep appearing.[1] The syntax of the poem can be difficult. Yeats, in fact, said the opening line was "the worst syntax he ever wrote" (qtd. Lipking 432). But even after the reader has determined what the lines mean, certain difficulties remain. Perhaps the most crucial question is how the poem resolves the opposing forces it sets up. Every reader perceives that nature and art, youth and age, and a number of other elements are opposed. But how does Yeats's desire to become a golden bird, an "artifice of eternity," resolve the poem's tensions?

A persuasive discussion of how the poem's oppositions are resolved occurs in Cleanth Brooks's New Critical reading. Brooks argues that they are unified by the ironic status of the golden bird. He means that the bird is, as Yeats puts it, an "artifice," and it is therefore outside of nature. His body will not age but will have "the finality of a work of art" (189). Brooks reveals here his adherence to the New Critical idea that the work of art has a stable presence and permanence. But "artifice," as Brooks recognizes, is qualified by Yeats, who wants to become an "artifice of eternity." About this qualification, Brooks says the following:

> The qualification does not turn the prayer into mockery, but it is all-important: it limits as well as defines the power of the sages to whom the poet appeals. (189)

---

[1] See for instance Ketcheman, who says "Sailing to Byzantium" is "clear enough" (171), and Clark, who says its "movement" and "essential terms" are "quite clear" (199). They disagree, however, on several points.

Thus Brooks believes the poem is unified by this balancing of its various oppositions.

But Brenda Webster strives to discover why such a complex process of unifying opposites would appeal to Yeats, and her Freudian reading finds the answer in, of course, the Oedipus complex. For Webster, the golden bird is not an ironically unifying device; it is rather "a defense against anxieties unconsciously raised by the poem—not just the fear of aging and thwarted sexuality . . . , but the overarching fear of a loss of integrity" (213–14). Yeats overcomes this fear of self-loss, Webster argues, by desiring a union with his mother, a kind of return to the womb. The symbol of the golden bird is part of this desire, Webster says, because in Yeats's other works involving "incestuous fantasies, the hero is often symbolically castrated or mutilated by the mother figure before he can be loved" (214). But, Webster tells us:

> In "Sailing" Yeats endows the aging process itself with the threatening qualities of a cruel mother. Now it is age that sexually frustrates the old man and threatens him with disintegration and loss of self. (214)

For Lawrence Lipking, and I must confess for me, such psychoanalytical explanations are not satisfying. Lipking simply admits that crucial lines in the poem do not make sense (431). Lipking sees two possible answers to the question of why the soul should "louder sing / For every tatter in its mortal dress." On the one hand, perhaps the soul is singing to distract itself from the tatters of its mortal dress. On the other hand, perhaps the soul is singing in celebration of its body falling apart because the tatters bring the soul closer to eternity and separation from the body. Lipking concludes there is no way to tell which of these meanings is right, and therefore "the line does not make sense" if by "sense" we mean that a statement cannot mean one thing and the opposite thing at the same time (431).

Lipking likewise considers whether there is a singing school in the poem. The line "Nor is there singing school" seems to say there is no such school, but the speaker desires some singing masters in the next verse. Rather than attempting some ingenious explanation, Lipking simply acknowledges that the lines are contradictory and the poem at every point deconstructs itself. Brooks's unification of the poem, Lipking would say, simply overlooks the evidence, engaging in wishful thinking. The golden bird, rather than being the key to the poem's unity, involves it in an obvious contradiction, "so important and obvious that it is noticed by a great many students, and even some critics" (432). Namely, the speaker cannot claim he will "never take / My bodily form from any natural thing" because, Lipking says, "every bodily form must be taken from nature, whether the form of a bird or simply the golden form embodied by an artist" (433).

I agree with Webster and Lipking that this much-honored poem contains hopeless contradictions, but I think the explanation is less hidden than an Oedipus complex and less shocking than the deconstructive idea that all language is contradictory. Instead, Yeats is undergoing the sort of crisis many older men undergo when they perceive themselves to be aging and growing unattractive. He wants to become a golden bird because he wants to be beautiful, but he does not want to engage in sexual competition for women.

This retreat from sexuality is prepared for in the first stanza, where Yeats focuses on "The young / In one another's arms." Other images also relate to sexuality: salmon struggling upstream to reproduce and die; mackerel crowded together to mate. Also "birds in the trees" are linked in our culture to romance. The problem Yeats faces is compressed into the reference to "dying generations": he is dying while generations continue to be produced.

Yeats is so intent on escaping the sexual that he cannot even consider whether "That" country, whichever it is, is a place for old women or even old people. All he can consider is that it is no country for old men—really, for one old man in particular. An "aged man" is "a paltry thing," but an aged woman apparently is not worth considering. Thus, Yeats aims to do away with the physical altogether. He combines sex and music in the "sensual music," and in becoming the golden bird he will make the transformation complete, turning his sexual being into music alone. As a golden bird, his sensual

music will be outside nature, and he will avoid the horror—
which is for him, strictly masculine, strictly his own—of aging.

Works Cited

Brooks, Cleanth. <u>The Well-Wrought Urn.</u> New York: Holt, 1947.

Clark, Donald. <u>Yeats.</u> New York: Basic Books, 1962.

Ketcheman, Albert. <u>William Butler Yeats: A Life.</u> New York: Harper, 1958.

Lipking, Lawrence. "The Practice of Theory." <u>Profession 83</u> (1983): 21–28.

Webster, Brenda. <u>Yeats: A Psychoanalytic Study.</u> New York: MacMillan, 1973.

Works Cited: Writing Research Papers

Booth, Wayne, Gregory Colomb, and Joseph Williams. *The Craft of Research*. Chicago: U of Chicago P, 1995.

Gibaldi, Joseph. *MLA Handbook for Writers of Research Papers*. 6th ed. New York: Modern Language Association, 2003.

———. *MLA Style Manual and Guide to Scholarly Publishing*. 2nd ed. New York: MLA, 1998.

Recommended Further Reading: Writing Research Papers

Cook, Claire Kehrwald. *Line by Line: How to Edit Your Own Writing*. Boston: Houghton, 1985. Clear and helpful.

Elbow, Peter. *Writing with Power: Techniques for Mastering the Writing Process*. New York: Oxford UP, 1981. Inspiring advice.

Faigley, Lester. *The Longman Guide to the Web*. New York: Longman, 2000. Useful on finding and evaluating web resources.

Hairston, Maxine, John Ruskiewicz, and Christy Friend. *The Scott, Foresman Handbook for Writers*. New York: Longman, 1998. Excellent advice on much more than just grammatical issues.

Appendix

John Donne
(1572–1631)

The Canonization

For God's sake hold your tongue, and let me love,
Or chide my palsy, or my gout,
My five gray hairs, or ruined fortune, flout,
With wealth your state, your mind with arts improve,
Take you a course, get you a place,   5
Observe His Honor, or His Grace,
Or the king's real, or his stampèd face
Contèmplate; what you will, approve,
So you will let me love.

Alas, alas, who's injured by my love?   10
What merchant's ships have my sighs drowned?
Who says my tears have overflowed his ground?
When did my colds a forward spring remove?
When did the heats which my veins fill
Add one more to the plaguy bill?   15
Soldiers find wars, and lawyers find out still
Litigious men, which quarrels move,
Though she and I do love.

Call us what you will, we're made such by love
Call her one, me another fly,   20

We're tapers too, and at our own cost die,
And we in us find th' eagle and the dove.
The phoenix riddle hath more wit
by us: we two being one, are it.
So, to one neutral thing both sexes fit,   25
We die and rise the same, and prove
Mysterious by this love.

We can die by it, if not live by love,
And if unfit for tomb and hearse
Our legend be, it will be fit for verse;   30
And if no piece of chronicle we prove,
We'll build in sonnets pretty rooms;
As well a well-wrought urn becomes
The greatest ashes, as half–acre tombs;
And by these hymns all shall approve   35
Us canonized for love:

And thus invoke us: "You whom reverend love
Made one another's hermitage;
You, to whom love was peace, that now is rage;
Who did the whole world's soul contract, and drove   40
Into the glasses of your eyes
(So made such mirrors, and such spies,
That they did all to you epitomize)
Countries, towns, courts: Beg from above
A pattern of your love!"   45

(1633)

Credits

Chapter Two

Excerpt from pages 16–17 from *Here at "The New Yorker"* by Brendan Gill. Copyright © 1975 by Brendan Gill. Used by permission of Random House, Inc.

Chapter Three

"Ars Poetica" from COLLECTED POEMS 1917–1982 by Archibald MacLeish. Copyright © 1985 by The Estate of Archibald MacLeish. Reprinted by permission of Houghton Mifflin Company.

Atkinson, Michael, "Deadpan Walking Welcome to the droll house: American geekhood finds a new icon in a clueless Idaho teen" from *The Village Voice,* June 7th, 2004. Reprinted by permission of Michael Atkinson.

Reprinted By Consent of Brooks Permissions.

Copyright © 1980 by Lucille Clifton. Now appears in GOOD WOMAN. Published by Boa Editions, Ltd. Reprinted by permission of Curtis Brown, Ltd.

Copyright © 1969 by the Antioch Review, Inc. First appeared in the *Antioch Review,* Vol. 39, No. 3. Reprinted by permission of the Editors.

Chapter Four

From MY WICKED WICKED WAYS. Copyright © 1987 by Sandra Cisneros. Published by Third Woman Press and in hardcover by Alfred A. Knopf. Reprinted by permission of Third Woman Press and Susan Bergholz Literary Services, New York, all rights reserved.

Reprinted with the permission of Scribner, an imprint of Simon & Schuster Adult Publishing Group, from IN OUR TIME by Ernest

Chapter Five

Chapter Six

Chapter Seven

Chapter Eight

Index